MW01488138

Overcoming Bipolar Disorder & Other Mental Difficulties

A Christian Perspective

Joseph Beckham

Copyright © 2016 by Joseph W Beckham

All rights reserved. This book or any portion thereof may not be reproduced or used in any manner whatsoever without the express written permission of the publisher except for the use of brief quotations in a book review or scholarly journal.

First Printing: 2016

ISBN 978-1-365-04568-4

Birmingham, AL 35236

www.TheBlogInTheFog.com

Ordering Information:

Special discounts are available on quantity purchases by corporations, associations, educators, and others. For details, contact the publisher at the above listed address.

U.S. trade bookstores and wholesalers: Please contact Joseph Beckham

email josephwbeckham@gmail.com

Preface

What you're about to read is a very different book about healing mental disorders, specifically bipolar disorder.

The author's goal in writing this manual is to help those struggling with bipolar disorder – or other brain disorders and difficulties – find hope that there is something available to them other than taking lifelong medication. As a medical doctor and a Christian, I certainly realize the wonderful ways that God uses medicine to help people. Each of us must decide what is best and whether God may have another plan for healing our minds from whatever afflicts us. I have practiced medicine for more than 40 years, and I realize the need for proper medication and advice, based on professional experience and education. However, God is the Great Physician who made the brain and the body, but life, beginning in the womb, has many pitfalls that can affect the way we think and view life.

There is great trauma from the womb to the tomb that impacts us. Unless God miraculously intervenes to provide instantaneous healing of brain chemistry difficulties—and He can and does—the journey to healing can be long and sometimes quite a challenge! The question is, what if you don't take steps toward your healing? You would remain at a standstill, seeking no remedy that God could provide. You would remain in the dark as far as what you could do to assist yourself in finding greater peace and more healthy and happy living.

As a Christian, I know that life is all about being changed into Christ's image (Romans 8:29). It is a lifelong journey from whenever we call upon the Name of the Lord to save us. The word salvation is the Greek word, "Sozo," which means to heal, deliver, protect and save. Obviously, this involves our brains and our minds that need "sozoing." I believe Joseph Beckham has pieced together the chapters in this book that will bring great meaning to this word, sozo, as it relates to the transformation and healing of the mind. It is imperative that anyone seeking healing for their mental difficulties give heed to the "recipe" in this book. Each chapter is designed to bring insights into what God has shared with Joseph and from the many wonderful writers, psychiatrists, counselors, scientists and physicians whose work is cited herein. There is no magic bullet outside of divine and instantaneous healing, but there is a journey toward wholeness as truth in this book is received and applied. May God bless you and heal you, according to your own persistence and the grace He offers to you!

Joe Blankson, MD

Foreword

Three percent of the U.S. population suffers from some aspect of bipolar disorder! This percentage translates to just under 9.5 million people in the U.S. alone who are could be suffering needlessly from the disorder or its associative difficulties. Most of us at some time or another, have known and been affected by someone who suffers with bipolar disorder. Whether it is our personal struggle or that of a family member, friend or coworker, at some level we have probably experienced the pain and havoc of this highly misunderstood disorder. Left untreated, the ravages of bipolar disorder upon those involved may be extreme. Not only are suicides much more common among people with bipolar disorder, but marriages are often destroyed, job opportunities lost and at the very least, everyday life becomes a battlefield of unpleasant and uncontainable upheavals.

Medical science has produced some relatively good medicines that help manage the symptoms and manifestations of bipolar disorder, but unfortunately the disorder itself often lends itself to the sufferer's mismanagement of those medications. This mismanagement may range from neglecting prescribed medicines, to abusing and overmedicating, sometimes episodically, sometimes chronically. Such misuse only exacerbates problems associated with the disorder. While proper use of medications may help people cope with symptoms, they generally only mask underlying problems and do not resolve root issues. Since God created science, we cannot rule out the scientific methods of treatment for physiological symptoms, (such as the chemical imbalances as seen in bipolar disorder) nor resulting psychological dysfunctions (such as depression). However, if we stop at the scientific level, we have addressed only one facet of what may be understood as a three-fold problem.

Our behaviors are a result of the how the mind, will and emotions (our "souls") are triggered by various physiological brain activities. In addition, we also consider our "spirit-man," (human spirit) designed to live in a spiritual bond or relationship with God, whereby our inner spirit connects with the Holy Spirit of God and is transformed according to God's design. If we accept the fact that our very being is comprised of spirit, soul and body, it makes sense that our wholeness is dependent upon those three facets of our being coming healthily and cohesively together into oneness with God and the character of God. It also stands to reason that God, who created us, has the ability to heal every kind of ailment or wound in any of the three facets of our being.

He heals the brokenhearted and binds up their wounds (Psalm 147:3).

Scriptures reveal that Jesus came to provide us with a whole, full and abundant life, so that we would not live in a downtrodden or oppressed state, as brought on by the sins of man and a fallen world, but instead that we would be set free from every oppressive thing.

The thief comes only to steal and kill and destroy; I have come that they may have life, and have it to the full (John 10:10, NIV).

[18]The Spirit of the Lord [is]upon Me, because He has anointed Me [the Anointed One, the Messiah] to preach the good news (the Gospel) to the poor; He has sent Me to announce release to the captives and recovery of sight to the blind, to send forth as delivered those who are oppressed [who are downtrodden, bruised, crushed, and broken down by calamity], [19] to proclaim the accepted and acceptable year of the Lord [the day when salvation and the free favors of God profusely abound] (Luke 4:18-19, Amplified).

From there he went all over Galilee…. He also healed people of their diseases and of the bad effects of their bad lives. Word got around the entire Roman province of Syria. People brought anybody with an ailment, whether mental, emotional, or physical. Jesus healed them, one and all (Matthew 4:23 The Message).

For the last 15 years, in practicing a Biblical counseling and healing ministry, I have found that neglecting or eliminating any one of the three facets of our being will negatively affect our behavioral system and produce less than lasting and satisfying results in achieving health, peace and wholeness. Our transformation, as guided by the Holy Spirit, is hindered by unresolved emotional wounds and negative or false beliefs and mindsets. However, when all three facets of our being are touched by the truth and provision of God, as fulfilled through Jesus Christ and empowered by the Holy Spirit, our needs are met, our wounds are healed, the ravages of sin are overcome, and we find lasting victory.

So if the Son sets you free, you will be free indeed (John 8:36).

In this handbook, Joe Beckham seeks not to diagnose bipolar disorder, nor to refute the achievements and discoveries of medical science in this area. Instead, he provides insight into *how* and *why* the brain reacts negatively to certain painful or deceptive aspects of life and to the series of events that affect us from the time we are formed and fashioned in the womb until the day we die. He provides Biblical truths that supply answers and solutions for overcoming those negative responses that can forever change the course and direction of our lives to one of victorious freedom. Moreover, he shares these discoveries out of the reality of his own personal journey to healing and victory over bipolar disorder.

The methods and principles described in this handbook have been used and proven true for many years and have provided lasting results and peace to those who faithfully apply them. When the truth of God's mercy and grace, as demonstrated in the Gospel of Jesus Christ, is instilled deeply into the wounded heart by the power of the Holy Spirit, healing occurs, the mind is renewed, transformation occurs, and the results are manifested not only in our thinking, but in our physiological responses and ultimately our actions.

Overcoming Bipolar disorder and Other Mental Difficulties: A Christian Perspective shows us how to embrace and put into practice the Biblical principles for a life of greater peace, wholeness and freedom!

Rev. Sherrlyn Frost

LifeWater Biblical Counseling Ministry

From the Author

It's recommended this manual be read in its entirety. Some may choose certain chapters that seem to pertain more to the problem of bipolar disorder or other mental disorders. However, each chapter is intended to build upon another. The key to getting healed of bipolar or other disorders is transformation of the mind and healing of the spirit, and that's why I have included many chapters that are geared to address this. The journey toward wholeness could be long or shortened by how serious the reader is about following what is essential to change. It's likely the bipolar disorder you, your loved one or friend is facing was the direct result of wounds that were received very early in life, perhaps even prenatal, but most likely these wounds were compounded by many painful experiences during their lifetime. Therefore healing for the one needing it may require a great deal of active participation in the process. As God told Joshua before he entered with Israel in the Promise Land:

Have I not commanded you? Be strong and courageous! Do not be terrified or dismayed (intimidated), for the Lord your God is with you wherever you go." (Josh 1:9 Amplified).

Joe Beckham

February 2016

Table of Contents

CHAPTER 1

Bipolar disorder: What is it?

According to the Center for Disease Control (CDC), bipolar disorder (formerly known as "manic-depressive disorder") is a major mood disorder in which the individual most commonly experiences episodes of depression and episodes of mania. Mania is characterized by clearly elevated, unrestrained, or irritable mood, which may manifest in an exaggerated assessment of self-importance or grandiosity, sleeplessness, racing thoughts, pressured speech, and the tendency to engage in activities which appear pleasurable, but have a high potential for adverse consequences. Depression is characterized by depressed or sad mood, diminished interest in activities, which used to be pleasurable, weight gain or loss, psychomotor agitation or retardation, fatigue, inappropriate guilt, difficulties concentrating, as well as recurrent thoughts of death. But depression is more than a "bad day"; diagnostic criteria established by the American Psychiatric Association dictate that five or more of the above symptoms must be present for a continuous period of at least two weeks. As an illness, depression falls within the spectrum of affective disorders.

In simple terms, bipolar disorder is a chemical imbalance in the brain that causes a person to go through mood swings. A person will have very high highs with grandiose thoughts (thinking he or she can do the impossible), rapid speech, rapid thoughts, sometimes going without sleep for days yet still having boundless energy. A person will also have low lows. They may be depressed, lethargic, with no desire to get out of bed and tired despite adequate sleep. They may lack motivation and interest in activities and hobbies, etc.

A person with bipolar disorder can also be normal at times, too, obviously, and there are times when there are mixed states (both manic and depressive symptoms) or rapid cycling (very quickly between the two extremes; usually, bipolar disorder symptoms will last a couple of weeks. In this case, the person is switching maybe every few hours, every few days, etc.). Depending on the type of bipolar disorder the person has, auditory and visual hallucinations may accompany episodes of either type, and the person may lose touch with reality or may stay lucid enough to realize it's not real.

During periods of depression there may be crying, poor eye contact with others and a negative outlook on life. The risk of suicide among those with the disorder is high at greater than 6 percent over 20 years, while self-harm occurs in 30–40 percent. Other mental health issues such as anxiety disorder and drug misuse are commonly associated.

The causes of bipolar disorder are not certain, although there are many possibilities. For example, a person may have experienced child abuse or prolonged stress. Other factors such as environment and culture all also may contribute. Bipolar disorder rates are higher in the U.S. than in other countries.

Chemical Imbalances

Here's a simple explanation of what may happen in the brain of a person affected by bipolar disorder:

Neurotransmitters (baseball)

The brain uses neurotransmitters, which are molecules that are used to communicate messages from a transmitting nerve cell to a receiving nerve cell. This is kind of like a baseball game. The pitcher is the transmitting nerve cell, the catcher is the receiving nerve cell, and the baseball is the neurotransmitter molecule. When the ball is thrown and caught, a little message is transmitted. The catcher's mitt is called a "receptor." After the catcher has caught the ball, he or she throws it back to the pitcher to the pitcher so it can be thrown again.

Problems (shortages)

If the receptor is clogged, we will have trouble communicating. If the baseball is missing, one will have trouble communicating. If the leather that was used to make the ball is missing, then the ball will be missing, and one will have trouble communicating. If the train that transports the leather to the ball factory breaks, one will have trouble communicating. If the train that transports the ball from the ball factory to the baseball field breaks, one will have trouble communicating. Easy. You get the picture.

Different Kinds of Neurotransmitters (baseballs)

There are several different neurotransmitters (baseballs). The main ones are called Noradrenaline (NA), which is sometimes referred to as "norepinephrine," Dopamine (DA), Serotonin (5HT), and GABA.

The brain communicates with itself by sending out chemical information from one neuron, or nerve cell to another. Brain chemistry is the sum of all the chemical messaging that takes place in the brain, which allows it to carry out its daily functions, such as generating movement, speaking, thinking, listening, regulating the systems of the body, and countless others.

A Cascade of Chemicals

Reuptake inhibitors (pitcher glove clogger)

There is a class of drugs called a reuptake inhibitor, which clogs the pitcher's glove (or makes it smaller) and makes it hard for him to catch the ball when the catcher throws it back to him. When this happens, the ball hits a wall behind the pitcher, and it bounces back to the catcher. It is not exactly known what happens here, yet it is known this has an affect on the amount of communication between the pitcher and catcher using that type of ball (neurotransmitter).

Serotonin Reuptake Inhibitor Drugs

Drugs that clog (or shrink) the serotonin pitcher's glove are called serotonin reuptake inhibitors (SSRI). Popular SSRIs are Prozac, Luvox, Paxil, Zoloft, and Celexa. Other ways to boost serotonin are to take the over the counter supplements, L-Triptophan or 5-HTP. SSRIs are famous for relieving depression, which also means that low levels of serotonin or clogged serotonin receptors can cause depression. Heavy metals and proteins from genes are examples of things that can clog a receptor. There are also some serotonin receptors, which are inhibitory, which means that stimulating inhibits feelings (e.g. the serotonin 5-HT1A receptor inhibits worrying). Therefore, it is possible for drugs that increase serotonin can increase (not decrease) depression. Also, if a serotonin receptor is clogged, then increasing the level of serotonin may not help, and one may need a Serotonin Agonist instead to unclog it.

Noradrenaline Reuptake Inhibitor Drugs

Drugs that inhibit noradrenaline reuptake are referred to as noradrenaline reuptake inhibitors (NARI). A popular NARI drug is called Wellbutrin SR (Buproprion).

All this suffices to say people's brains can get out of balance because of these chemicals. Besides the causes listed here we can deep a little deeper into a person's negative experiences that can trigger these outcomes.

It's not important that you understand all of the above. The main thing is to know you or someone you know and/or love is struggling with these mood swings – like "Billy."

Out of Balance: Billy's Story

Now a tenth-grader, Billy had been experiencing severe depression since he was in seventh grade. Everyone feels down or depressed every now and then, but Billy felt this way most of the time. He had a hard time making friends, he was not interested in his schoolwork, and he spent most of his time hanging out in his room alone. He had even thought about suicide. At first, his parents believed that this was just a phase he was going through, but then they became really concerned.

What was happening to their son, who had been generally upbeat and friendly until a few years earlier? At the insistence of his parents and teachers, Billy started seeing a psychiatrist, who tried to help him talk about what he was feeling. Based on her meetings with Billy, she decided to prescribe a type of medication known as an antidepressant. This medication increases the amount of a brain neurotransmitter called serotonin (ser-ah-TO-nin), which is associated with feelings of well-being and control. The medicine, a selective serotonin reuptake inhibitor (SSRI), works by preventing (inhibiting) neurons from reabsorbing (reuptaking) the chemical messenger serotonin once it is released into the brain. As a result, there is more serotonin available, and this sometimes helps alleviate the symptoms of depression. If Billy's depression were being caused by too little serotonin, the medication likely would help him.

Sure enough, it did. Billy continued to see his psychiatrist while taking the medication. After about 6 months, his doctor decided to try taking Billy off the SSRI. Billy was afraid that his terrible feelings would return, but they did not. He found that talking through any problems with his doctor was enough to keep him on track.

Understanding the Roots of Bipolar disorder

God made the brain. It wasn't formed by evolution and happenstance. The fact is things happen in life that cause all of us to experience fear, especially in the form of trauma, that can induce chemical changes in the brain that may be lifelong—unless Jesus Christ is allowed to intervene.

Dr. MKStrydom, who has extensive knowledge of psychosomatic diseases including bipolar disorder, says antidepressants and lithium (the drug of choice used to treat or prevent mania) are not long-term answers to bipolar disorder because they do not deal with the underlying problem. These drugs are just a form of a form of disease management, which often complicates the problem with their Pandora's box of side effects.

Apart from unpleasant side effects such as nausea, anorexia, diarrhea, excessive urination, fatigue, hair loss, swelling of the feet, skin eruptions and weight gain, lithium can have more serious problems such as kidney failure, hypothyroidism, and can have a toxic effect on nerves causing tremors, in-coordination, interference with concentration and memory (Note: Not everybody experiences all these side effects). Total healing of bipolar disorder is only going to come through dealing with the root issues and toxic mindsets behind it. You also need to deal with the fear that has come in through relationship breakdowns. Dr. Henry Wright says disease occurs when there is a breakdown in our relationship with God, others and ourselves. Healing then, involves restoration of all three.

Further, Dr. Strydom says, *Bipolar disorder is characterized by episodes of unpredictable swings in mood from one extreme of depression to the other extreme of mania. A deficiency of serotonin causes depression. This is a result of a low self-esteem and guilt in a person's thought life. An excess of serotonin causes mania, which is the opposite of depression and the other half bipolar disorder. Thus in bipolar disorder (which means two opposite poles) there is a deficiency and then an excess of serotonin, which causes the mood swings. The diagnostic criteria for a manic episode is defined in the box below:*

Criteria Used to Diagnose a Manic Episode

(Taken from the Diagnostic and Statistical Manual of Mental Disorders, 4th Edition)

1. An abnormally and persistently elevated or irritable mood lasting at least one week (or any duration if hospitalization is necessary).

2. During the period of mood disturbance, three or more of the following symptoms have been present to a significant degree:

Inflated self-esteem or grandiosity occur because the serotonin levels are abnormally high. Remember serotonin is the chemical that makes you feel good about yourself, so when the levels are increased, you have an elevated feeling (like being on a high) where you feel great about yourself – it is as if you can take on the world).

Decreased need for sleep (for example, you feel rested after only 3 hours of sleep).

Increased goal-directed activity (i.e. you become hyperactive) either at work, socially, sexually or you are not able to sit still - somebody would describe you as having "ants in your pants" (the medical term for this is psychomotor agitation).

More talkative than usual or pressure to keep talking.

Flight of ideas – the feeling that your thoughts are racing.

Easily distracted.

During a manic episode the person tends to become involved in pleasurable activities that have a high potential for painful consequences, for example, going on an unrestrained shopping spree and getting severely into debt.

- *Sexual indiscretions.*

- *Foolish business investments.*

3. The mood disturbance is sufficiently severe to cause significant impairment in occupational functioning or in relationships with others. There are two types bipolar disorder: In bipolar disorder type 1 the manic episodes are more severe and can require hospitalization to prevent harm to self or others. A person with bipolar disorder type 1 can also experience psychotic features such as hallucinations (for example, hearing or seeing something that is not really there) or delusions (a false belief that cannot be corrected by reasoning – for example, the person may believe that a chip in his tooth controls world events). A person with bipolar disorder type 2 has less severe manic episodes that do not require hospitalization and does not have psychotic features such as hallucinations or delusions.

4. The symptoms are not due to the direct physical effects of a substance, for example, drug abuse or a side effect of a medication or another medical condition such as hyperthyroidism. **The serotonin excess in mania is a result of fear and anxiety** *(author's emphasis bolded).*

Dr. Strydom says, "I spent several months working in a psychiatric hospital where I treated many patients with bipolar disorder. What I personally noticed is that most, if not all of them, came from dysfunctional families. There is often abuse involved, whether it is verbal abuse, emotional abuse, physical abuse or sexual abuse. There is always an atmosphere of strife, victimization, fear and not feeling safe. 1 John 4:18 says that he who fears is not made perfect in love. If the home is filled with a lack of love, fear comes in the door. That fear puts the person into stage 2 and 3 of stress, and there is an overproduction of certain hormones in the body, including the overproduction of serotonin in the brain which caused the symptoms of mania."

A More Excellent Way...

In this manual we will examine the means for not only controlling bipolar disorder, but also how to allow Jesus Christ to manifest His perfect love (agape) in those afflicted with this, as Dr. Strydom pointed out. Also you will read of instantaneous, miraculous healing of bipolar disorder. Thank God when this happens! However, you may recall the story of Jesus and the 10 lepers, which also provides a different kind of hope—they were healed ON THE WAY!

Now on his way to Jerusalem, Jesus traveled along the border between Samaria and Galilee. As he was going into a village, ten men who had leprosy[a] met him. They stood at a distance and called out in a loud voice, "Jesus, Master, have pity on us!" When he saw them, he said, "Go, show yourselves to the priests." **And as they went, they were cleansed. One of them, when he saw he was healed, came back, praising God in a loud voice. He threw himself at Jesus' feet and thanked him**—*and he was a Samaritan. Jesus asked, "Were not all ten cleansed? Where are the other nine? Has no one returned to give praise to God except this foreigner?" Then he said to him, "Rise and go; your faith has made you well" (Luke 17:11-19 NIV).*

Are you or your loved one afflicted with brain chemistry disorders? I believe there's healing for you, and I pray for a miraculous healing, but like the 10 lepers you may be healed "along the way."

CHAPTER 2

People and Their Stories

Bipolar disorder touches many lives, and the impact can range from mild to horrendous. The following stories are real, very real; only the identities have been changed or omitted. You're going to read about a wife and mother whose experience was dreadful to say the least. You'll hear from a young woman whom Jesus healed of this, a brother and a son, a sister's experience with her father and sister, and a mother who lost her daughter to this horrible condition. Last you will read of amazing testimonies in which Jesus Christ miraculously healed people of this seemingly unconquerable disorder! It happens, and I know we all desire to see many more healed this way, but this manual is about progressive healing for the most part, as I have written here.

Author's note: The following testimonies were written by the people themselves.

A Brother, a Son and a Husband

Sophia Donskaya is a small plumpish doctor of psychiatry educated in Russia. She speaks with a heavy accent and is, to put it mildly, blunt. "Howz it goik? Drink with zee medicine, and it won woik!! I landed in her office about a decade ago. A GP diagnosed me as "depressive" eons ago. Depressive is your run of the mill complaint. Aren't we all depressed now and then? But that isn't clinical depression. So I'm asking: "Why don't I look people in the eye?" "Why did I do that?" "How come I'm yelling at traffic" (there are 5 million people in Houston so I'm out of breath).

How come, as the saying goes, "I'm feeling mighty low?" Or why am I "luxuriating in delusions of grandeur"? When, not if, I win the lottery I'm getting a Bentley convertible, and I'm going to drive to the Texans' games even though I have no ticket. Why am I charging $1,000 on my credit card when my bank account is barren? Dr. Donskaya asked me about a dozen questions. "You're bipolar," she said. Then she prescribed four or five meds. This is not like taking aspirin for a headache. Turning points take time and often changing medicines and doses. Where's this entire business coming from? In most cases the cure starts with a doctor who asks the right questions.

The question is how does mental illness affect someone day to day? The 1948 film, "The Snake Pit," exposed the wretched conditions in asylums, more or less housing people like so many animals and using bogus treatments. "A Beautiful Mind" is about the late John Nash (recently killed in an auto accident) and his rise as among the world's renowned mathematicians as a paranoid schizophrenic. "Silver Lining Playbook" is a good one because all the players are psychotic. They sit around and compare meds. "Say, Tiffany, did Seroquel work for you?"

There is a series, *Homeland* that realistically depicts how Bipolar disorder affects the life of a CIA agent, Carrie Madison, played by Claire Danes. It's covered in-depth in an article in *Psychology Today* by Dr. Jeffry Lieberman https://www.linkedin.com/pulse/20141117035028-125117017-homeland-a-true-portrayal-of-mental-illness "Homeland: A True Portrayal of Mental Illness." Every aspect of her behavior is illustrative and consistent with the symptoms, psychological characteristics and emotional nuances of people with bipolar disorder. Even the medications that she takes (clozapine, lithium, nortriptyline, clonazepam), prescribed by her psychiatrist sister, are appropriate and realistic.

In a perverse way, mental illness is coming to the fore every time someone engages in some deadly or even strange behavior. The media's first reaction usually is the person "has a history of mental illness" or is bipolar, schizophrenic or sociopathic. No question the links between violent acts and mental illness are there, but cause and effect without mitigating circumstances doesn't hold up.

Large population studies suggest that mental illness alone does not increase the likelihood of violence," says psychiatrist Michael Peterson, MD, PhD, an assistant professor in the department of psychiatry at the University of Wisconsin School of Medicine and Public Health in Madison. The missing piece is virtually all of these people are out of treatment, failing to take their medication and affected by drug and alcohol abuse.

Commentary about mental illness often revolves around "control." Are people in command of their actions? Do they know right from wrong? Well, yes and no. People like me sometimes do things that seem like a good choice at the time, without regard to consequences. This explains why I am at the bottom of the heap managing money. Bipolar disorder people create conflict, which is why I did poorly working in large corporations, except when I was an executive assistant to the CEO. They left me alone!

You've all heard of "writers block," during which you stare at the computer screen with nothing doing. Writing is hard work. Consider this interview with Earnest Hemmingway:

Interviewer:

How much rewriting do you do?

Hemingway: It depends. I rewrote the ending of Farewell to Arms, the last page of it, thirty-nine times before I was satisfied.

Interviewer: Was there some technical problem there? What was it that had stumped you?

Hemingway: Getting the words right.

There's more. There are times when I simply don't do much at all, and when I do it's a waste of time. I wrote a book about my experience with prostate cancer eight years ago and never finished it. I edited it to death and lost interest. Winston Churchill was bipolar and called those episodes of depression his "black dog." He also was one of the most celebrated leaders, perhaps ever, and when manic, a prolific writer. Since I was diagnosed in my 60s and surely had this "black dog" all my life, were there any signs? Any tips of what was to come? Sure and here are some of them:

Cognitive dissonance. Cognition is the set of all mental abilities and processes related to knowledge: attention, memory and working memory, judgment and evaluation, reasoning and so on. Here's a sure sign. In grammar school I took a class called "shop." We made stuff. In Introduction to Carpentry I made this candleholder out of wood that looked like the leaning tower of Pisa. It was in my mother's house for years. There are other manifestations of the deficit. I am puzzled by puzzles. Crosswords? Forget it. Fix things around the house? You must be kidding. I am not handy! Playing cards? Unlikely. I'm the guy who flags a graduate entrance exam and ends up making all A's. How did I get in? The Almighty intervened.

I hate math. My math grades in high school were abysmal. My sophomore year I landed in a geometry class. It was like dyslexia. I learned the word congruent. I kept asking how on earth this would do me any good after my education? You've heard this one: the system is to blame. Yes, it was. Any error in a problem meant caput. So let's say there are five problems, and I made two errors on two of them and I fail. Worse, when I did a crappy job, the teacher sent me down to Coach Tucker who busted my butt with a paddle with a hole in it. I scraped by with a D, and even then I had to make an A on the final. Don't ask.

Mania. It's periods of hyperactivity and thinking. It's something like ADHD. I found a report card from the 2nd grade – (written on papyrus). Guess what? I got a P or poor in conduct. We had a class called "Library." The teacher would say, "This above all to thine own self be true." I once ended up under her desk while she was there! Good grief! That was pretty much standard including high school. The system was based on demerits. If you accumulate 40, you're out of there. I got 30 more than once. This was Phillips High in Birmingham, AL, where my mother graduated. She made me do it whatever it was.

In the Marines I had a few discipline flare-ups of the "what was of the thinking variety." I am a musician so I sang in the Parris Island base choir. A singer among killers! It was freedom from tyrannical Drill Instructors and lots of cokes. In the Corps, Cokes and are called "Pogey Bait." Who knows? So I didn't go to practice—why I have no idea—and the chaplain sent for me. The DIs thought I had written home to mama complaining about abuse. So they put me through a grinder—some you wouldn't believe—all the time yelling, "Do you want to go home in a pine box"?

I've always had trouble with a sense of direction. So in the field my shooting an azimuth would put the company in the hands of the enemy. I was "captured" during Infantry training. They asked, "Where is your unit?" I said, "You are surrounded." The answer wasn't well received. The sergeant whatever hit me over the head with my helmet. This is why I ended up bipolar. Or as happens now and again I get lost driving my car, even with a GPS. My stepson is paranoid schizophrenic, so he has more problems with cognition than I. We plan to create a comedy routine called the Cognitive Deficit Duo. The audience will fall in the aisles laughing while watching the two of us try to wrap a Christmas package.

A few years ago something happened and the person said, "I hurt Jim's feelings." My ex-wife said, "Jim has no feelings." Exactly right. Almost catatonic at times. My golf buddy said, "You are on the Isle of Catatonia. How does it look?" I said, "Pastel." I forget birthdays and holidays. For years I couldn't sit to read a book. Couldn't focus.

Abusing alcohol, chasing women in and out of marriage, and making lousy economic choices are hallmarks of bipolar disorder. Carrie Madison engages in what's called "risky behavior." When you get down to it, folks, mental illness causes people to make poor decisions.

Then what about treatment? There are two answers from the psychiatric perspective. First, the organization that helps mentally ill people the most is NAMI. National Alliance on Mental Illness. There are forums for families and persons about mental illnesses. What's the cause? The symptoms? Treatments including medications. And, what does a family do when one of them breaks down or drifts into a mental fog? NAMI is also about removing the stigma of mental illness. There's still a way ago: Here's a quote from best-selling author and mental health advocate, Pete Early. "Sometimes I feel the only way I can get a major publisher interested in mental illness is if I find a character who has bipolar disorder and is also a love-sick vampire attending an English school called Hogwarts. But I'm not giving up."

A word about treatment. Among my pet peeves, in addition to the dolts who leave buggies or whatever you want to call them in parking lots are people who think taking medicine is some sort of heroic act. "I have a headache." Take an aspirin. "I don't take pills." Then shut up and suffer. I saw a study about post-heart attack patients who were given medication, and half of them didn't take it at all. Let me put it this way: A mentally ill person cannot survive without medication. Sure, in some cases therapy does some good. But the bedrock of managing an illness and performing in the world is medication, in my opinion. Schizophrenics, for example, have no insight so they don't believe they're sick. Without medication they often lapse into a sort of coma of confusion and suffering.

Medication works for me. It really does. My illness is there, but it's managed more or less successfully—thanks to that plump Russian woman who talks funny and knows whereof she speaks.

…A Wife

I will share as a mother of someone diagnosed with bipolar disorder and a former wife of someone with bipolar disorder. I was six when my baby brother was born with Down's syndrome. I grew up to be a Special Ed teacher working with children with Down's syndrome. I started volunteer work with the Youth Association of Retarded Citizens in the 10th grade. At a National ARC convention in Miami I met my future husband. He was an officer in the group and was smart and witty, and I was smitten. I pictured us working with these kids forever as a team and a ministry. He had an adult uncle with mental retardation, and they lived in Hattiesburg, MS. My future husband and I corresponded for a year, and he took me to the senior prom at my school. We were engaged my senior year. His letters were wonderful. I met his family and started college at the University of Southern Mississippi in Hattiesburg. He had 18 hours until he graduated in Special Ed. In the summer at the end of my second term, instead of my coming home or going out for rush in a sorority, we eloped.

My grandmother and great grandmother had eloped as young people as well. I became pregnant and had a baby the next year. But my husband was more of a baby than my sweet little girl. He would have breakdown crying jags in the middle of the night, and his parents would rush over. What was the matter with him? He changed his major to criminal justice. Huh? He changed jobs ...a lot...He started developing pictures in the hospital where our baby girl was born and worked his way up to personnel manager... Then he quit...He became a jailer... It seems he and his younger sis were adopted when he was five, and he had been abused. He never wrote about this in any letters. He isolated me...didn't want me to go to school or work. He didn't like my friends or family to visit from home. He didn't like me to visit anyone. I taught Sunday school. After Sunday school I would visit his granny. If I were 15 minutes late, he accused me of seeing someone else. Huh? He was Very jealous. He said he didn't believe our baby girl was his. Does anyone see a pattern here?

After five years of this madness, he became a NARC and brought home pictures of children shot dead in drug raids. He said he became a policeman because his biological mom had been a prostitute, and he wanted to search out her police records. He never wrote about that to me. So I left and gave him everything as long as I could have my baby girl. I moved home tail tucked between my legs, humiliated as a divorcee with my child conceived in love born out of rebellion... (Yes, eloping was rebellion because my mother was a good provider but an argumentative hell-raiser, and my sweet dad could have her...I wasn't going back there, I told myself ...We didn't ask permission, just eloped).

So back home I got my degree and masters in Special Ed and met my next husband. We met in church, dated a year and have been married 36 years. We had two more daughters over the years. My ex-husband went on to marry three more times and finally became a Methodist minister. I always said I could work with the mentally retarded, but I said the mentally ill had no excuse—they were lazy and got over on society, blah, blah, blabbing angrily. I was very judgmental of mental illness and unforgiving of ex-husband. My new husband and I paid for our daughter's college and fully supported her. My ex gave $100 a month child support. That was it.

…Same Person as a Mother of a Child Who was Bipolar

My first-born was reading at age three and gifted. She graduated in accounting and got a job at Protective Life. She went on to work for Thomson Consumer Electronics (RCA) and had territories to cover. She'd travel and loved it. She got promoted and moved to Indianapolis, and they paid for her to get her MBA. She was so smart and beautiful. She got promoted from there and moved on to Boston. Now because of teleconferences her territory was even larger, which included Massachusetts, New York, and Connecticut.

Seven years later she cashes in her stocks in the company and her retirement and moves to Australia to go to University of Sydney to get a diploma in Life Coaching and lived in a house on the beach for a year. She goes $50,000 in debt. She comes home, and her life coaching falls through, a few romances fail, and about 10 major stressors like these hit, and she had the first breakdown. Her doc told us she probably used to pull herself out of valleys, but with hormonal changes at age 36, she couldn't pull herself out this time. She was gone. She was suicidal. She cut her hair off with scissors. She had racing thoughts and thought someone poisoned her so she then goes into complete food and drink refusal. She didn't sleep but paced all night.

We got her to go to the ER and on to a rehab hospital. She still had rights and continued to refuse any meds or to eat or drink. She became catatonic and vegetative and was about to die. We can't even send her anywhere else for a second opinion, as she was too medically fragile. Oh, dear God. She only wanted a Bible in the psyche ward. She confessed to me in the ER that she had two abortions since college. What???? I was in shock and grief and loss far beyond any pain I had ever known. She was double minded about her faith and very much into the New Age movement. I was given no treatment plan. I got some diagnosis called bipolar disorder. WHAT IS THAT???? I wondered. I called her dad, and he said he got the same diagnosis three years before. So I had a child who was mentally ill and must now have ECT shock treatments to revive her from her death spiral ...Oh my God. I was agog. I had no language for my anguish. I had been so judgmental of "those folks," and now it was my baby girl.

She slowly came back. I found a Save-A-Life counselor, and we attended sessions together, and she continued in a Bible study, specifically for abortion focus. I attended a service for my grand babies in heaven. She repented and received forgiveness, named her babies, and we gave them to God. Seven years she continued healing and working out her issues and did med maintenance but got back in the New Age stuff. She was double-minded indeed! She met her future husband one year into her healing. They married and had two children and all was okay. When the second baby was eight months old, my baby girl had her second breakdown.

She had taken such good care of her babies that she neglected herself. She went into a hospital psychiatric ward, and her husband saw this episode. He had been told she was bipolar, and I explained to him how serious it was, but he had to see it to believe it. He told me he wasn't pagan but was "spiritual" but not a Christian or praying man. I told him he needed to pray! She recovered and had a competency hearing, and he stood by her. One and one-half years later she broke down again.

She wrote suicide notes to her husband and children. She was in a hospital, and she got close to God. She was totally different this time.

After her release, she attended a Bible Study, and we also attended the first part of an inner healing Bible study for 12 weeks. She started taking her the children to church. She told me that when her dad was stable he stayed close to the Lord. That bore witness to her.

I have repented of judging others who are mentally ill. I now go to the crisis center support group to be a blessing and not a judge. My daughter has fought hard, and the devil has attacked her and her children, and it has taken its toll on her husband. He is now divorcing her. Recently, she rededicated herself to Christ. Her dad came to our church and baptized her two children. I declare she is saved, healed and delivered, and I'm praying her marriage will be restored, according to God's will, in Jesus' name!

My other two daughters call what they experienced "riding the bipolar train." This is really a trip, I tell you. Staying prayed up and strong in Christ is our hope. This is what it was like for me. It is like packing for a trip to some wonderful dreamy place like Hawaii, but you end up shipwrecked in Africa! You don't know the language or culture. You crawl to shore for help, and people give you books to read and some direction around the island. You get along and regroup and rally and set sail, but the fierce winds pick up again and blow you back to that dreaded place. This time you remember and go back, retracing your steps and finding familiar friends who helped you before. You start again with stronger sails and a compass, and you pray and pray and pray and your friends pray. Now two more are on your boat so you must use your map and compass carefully for you have precious cargo. You may never get to Hawaii, but you are out of Africa!

One ship sails East the other West,

With selfsame winds that blow,

'Tis the set of the sails and not the gales,

That determine which way you go."

A Mother Who Lost Her Child

As a shy, quiet little girl growing up, she manifested no particular problems until her teen years. At that time her father began to drink to excess, and as with all alcoholic-centered families, she became the target of his verbal abuse. She shared with me once that she couldn't bear to be in the same room with him. As a result, she did not have the benefit of a stable male relationship. She became depressed and was monitored by a psychiatrist who had her placed as an inpatient for three weeks at a local healthcare She was medicated with Prozac, which exacerbated her depression. She described her condition as "trying to hold onto a rope, but continuing to slip."

She was not particularly happy in high school, but graduated and attended community college for two years, earning a lucrative salary in an artistic area, which allowed her to be easily employable. A few years later she fell in love, married, and had two beautiful children; however, her marriage was fraught with episodes of discord and brief separations. She medicated with alcohol. At one point, she was an inpatient at an out-of-state facility, but it made no appreciable impact on her depressed state. She seemed to be in a downward spiral, so I implored her to seek the help of a psychiatrist once again. She complied, had a meeting with the doctor and was diagnosed as bipolar. She was placed on Lithium and another drug and was scheduled to return to the doctor in a week. The next day she was tragically killed in an automobile accident. She was my youngest daughter.

Bipolar Disorder and No Meds

Some who experience episodes often fail to take medicine or do so sporadically. A father and his daughter share a sad story about two people who refused to either take medicine or show little change in behavior from taking it.

Once when he was having an 'episode' (because he quit taking his medication) he hardly knew who he was, and since he was so in love with the Lord, he kept asking me if he was saved, and did Jesus still love him...he was very confused and not sure of anything.

Another with No Meds ...

Betty has told me several times when he (John) has gotten off his meds that he acts like a totally different person...she has named that person "Steve!" Kind of funny, really. Every time he had an episode, (per Betty) he turns into another person entirely pretty much, but I have only experienced it firsthand the one time. She says he will go outside and wave his hands, and I really can't remember what all she has told me. I just know he acts nuts! Also, the one time he got off his meds, and I went up there to see if I could help, he was angry, and I had to be quite careful about what I said to him. I tried to focus on Jesus' love for him and how Jesus wanted to set him free from the way he was feeling.

Another...

Sally acted pretty arrogantly, and her opinion was the only one that really mattered. Her father was bipolar as well but always refused medicine after a friend of his was misdiagnosed and ultimately committed suicide. The two of them would argue incessantly when they got together.

Miraculous Healings

I was diagnosed with bipolar disorder at 19 years old. I remember when I was around 4 years old I would lock myself in the bathroom and break the mirrors, screaming how I hated myself because I was so ugly. Those depressive and theatrical tantrums continued throughout my life. Around age five they tried giving me Ritalin. I barely slept and the word "hyper" just didn't cover it. Mood swings and depression ruled me until two years ago. I turned 39 in April. When I was 13 I began cutting and self-mutilating. I would do crazy things to get my mind off of the emotional pain. When I was happy people would tell me how animated I seemed. My emotions were so extreme, and I had no control of them.

I was constantly embarrassing myself. I once cried to a shrink that I didn't want to scare children and old people anymore.

Of course there are many factors that played a part in this rollercoaster ride. I was the baby of the family with five older brothers, so I was the only girl. So naturally I was spoiled and allowed to wear the pants in my house. With no direction and no one to teach or discipline me, I had absolutely no clue what self-control was. At 19 I began using drugs to ease the emotional down swing. I attempted suicide on many many occasions.

I have been on virtually every antipsychotic drug ever invented. They would work for a while, but mostly I just gained an extreme amount of weight and quit taking the meds. During manic episodes I have done dangerous and impulsive things. I hitchhiked to California once. I was never able to hold a job longer than six months at a time. I tried to go back to college countless times but was unable to stay stable long enough to piece any sort of a life together. I usually never had a boyfriend longer than three months. No one could handle my mood swings.

Finally, I met JESUS. I began to get better little by little. For the first two years as a Christian I remained medicated. I prayed for deliverance. A lot of meditation went into my prayer life. I decided if I was gonna be emotional, then it was going to be JESUS who had to deal with my emotions. When I was depressed, I would hit my knees and squall to the Lord. But strangely when I would finish and stand up, it would be gone. Pouring out the sadness at the altar seemed to empty me enough to be filled with Him. When I got manic and overly excited about something I would run to pray. I would squeal and tell the Lord all about whatever had me so happy. Over the course of about a year slowly came what I had been searching for—BALANCE!!!!!

No More Meds

As I poured the medications into my hand every morning and every night, and there were a lot, I heard the sweetest voice say, "You don't need those anymore." For two weeks day and night He simply repeated this to me. Finally I said, 'Well, JESUS how do you suppose I come off of all these pills? The doctor is not about to let me do that!" He told me to do exactly as He said. So He began telling me which ones to break in half and for how long. One by one he winged me off every pill. I never had one side effect or withdrawal. It took three months.

Then the Lord told me He wanted me to walk by faith for a while. He had really been loving on me through this process. He said it was time to break my addiction to my feelings. WHAT? I didn't even know that was possible. Today, I am free. I've been med free for over a year and a half. I have worked at an office job for almost a year now. I decide how I react; I decide to have character. I am not a slave to my emotions anymore. Although ice cream makes me happy, Jesus gives me true sustaining joy. I'm not depressed, and I walk through hard times and fire clinging to the hope of Jesus!! I am not a slave. I'm free in Christ! I am only a slave to his righteousness!!!

Miracle Healings as Recorded at Bethel Church, Redding, CA

Editor's Note: Bethel Church sees many miracles of various types. The following testimonies concern bipolar disorder. I'm certain there are other healings across the country, but as I write this, I'm unaware of those.

I have been married for almost 39 years to a wonderful man. However, he had a problem with severe mood swings—from rage to depression and thoughts of suicide. Doctors diagnosed him with clinical depression and prescribed antidepressants—but the side effects only made things worse. Because he was called to the ministry as a pastor only made things even worse. He was not able to hold a position for more than a few years. He ultimately and reluctantly resigned from his pastorate. Shortly afterward, he was pacing and very agitated. I interceded for him, asking God what we were dealing with. "Bipolar disorder," the Lord said. I did research and found that that is what we had been dealing with for years.

Two days later, I was impressed to take with me on my job (I was on the road that day) the CDs of Pastor Bill's (Johnson) conference that he did in January 2008, in Kansas City. The 2nd session opened with a testimony of a woman from Louisville, whom God healed of bipolar disorder and then taught on the testimony of the Lord. I felt impressed to receive that for my husband and spoke that word all day. When I returned home, he was sitting in his recliner with a smile on his face saying he'd had a great day! Today, he is walking free of that and beginning to move toward the calling of God on his life—that of teaching the word and equipping the saints. Thank you, Pastor Bill, for being obedient and coming to our hometown. God healed my husband of this torture and freed him to be what God has called him to be!!!!

Word of Knowledge – "Two White Polar Bears"

On May 10, 2008, during a wave of healing in the 10:45 Bethel Church morning service, the nursery alarm accidentally went off. Just before that, a man had a word of knowledge of two big white polar bears. He asked the Lord what it meant, and he understood it meant bi (meaning two) polar-the healing of bipolar disorder. After hearing that word, Pastor Bill said, "If there is anyone here with bipolar, we want to pray for you. This is the time. We command this to come into order right now—every imbalance, every bit of disorder, we forbid in the name of Jesus. In the name of Jesus, let healing come." Pastor Bill then asked how many people had previously been healed of bipolar, and seven or eight people raised their hands. He continued, "We declare over you the testimony of Jesus, that Jesus alone puts things right. I declare over you that God is healing minds right now in Jesus' name.

Healing in the Presence of the Lord

Only about one of the 18 cases of bipolar healing that Pastor Bill Johnson knows of occurred after a prayer for healing. All the rest happened when they heard the testimony, or the anointing just came into the room, and suddenly everything was in order. The healings started because of the presence of the Lord. Pastor Bill said, "When you host the presence of the Lord, more happens through you accidentally than ever did on purpose. The great privilege of life is to carry His presence. What happens is people end up getting healed." In June of 2006, a girl came to a meeting and said, "The voices stopped." Her grandfather met Bill in another city two or three days later with tears in his eyes and said, "I've got my granddaughter back." About two weeks later, her father came to the church and said, "I've got my daughter back." When Pastor Bill shared that testimony at church, two men that had had bipolar for over 20 years were instantly healed the moment the testimony came out of his mouth!

Blood Test Confirms Man Healed of Bipolar disorder

In March 2007, a woman recounted Pastor Bill's word about bipolar disorder healing on her dad's answering machine with the message: "I release healing in Jesus' name." He immediately stopped taking his medicine for bipolar disorder. A week later, he had a blood test, and his doctor pronounced him completely healed and told him he no longer needed his lithium. A few months earlier, he had tried stopping his medicine after receiving prayer but had had to start taking it again three days later when symptoms returned. Now, after 21 years, he is completely healed!

Healed and Off My Medicine

In April 2010, someone sent in this testimony: "I am a college student from Arkansas and have been connected to ibethel through friends I met at my church. I was running on a treadmill when I heard the testimony of multiple cases of bipolar being healed. I was diagnosed with the same condition three years ago, and it had gotten worse, but as soon as that testimony was released, I felt a warm tingling sensation run through my brain, so much so that I had to brace myself from falling to the ground. That was one month ago. I am now off medication and totally healed!! Thank You Jesus!!

CHAPTER 3

God and the Brain

**(Information was taken from The Brain
and the Bible, CreationScience.com.)**

When God created Adam and Eve, He gave them characteristics that made them different from the animals. These characteristics reside within the unique "spirit of man" that dwells within each and every one of us. Hence, the Biblical revelation is that these characteristics are NOT physical. That is, they originate from something spiritual—from the "spirit in man."

Science with its tremendous insight and continuous unfolding of the once inexplicable, by its very nature, deals with the physical. That's why modern day science often refuses to acknowledge the supernatural. It will try to find a purely physical explanation to everything. All it knows is what can be tested and evaluated and analyzed by instruments and experimentation. God, needless to say, can't be put into a test tube!

So, with this in mind, let's examine some of the "unsolved mysteries of the human brain" as outlined in the Discover magazine article, "10 Unsolved Mysteries of The Brain."

1. Take, for instance, the mystery of how information is "coded." Scientists can SEE the human brain, can MEASURE electrical pulses traveling within the brain, etc., but how can this explain our thoughts? Another scientific article goes on to draw this comparison: *"The challenge is something like popping the cover off a computer, measuring a few transistors chattering between high and low voltage, and trying to guess the content of the Web page being surfed."* Science will never find this out because the origin of our thoughts is not physical; they are from the spirit within us. And spiritual things can't be put into a test tube. Much of the article was

written as if the human brain is a complex computer. However, this is only an analogy. **The human mind is much more complex than any man-made computer and operates on a different level – a spiritual level.**

The brain has a "baseline" level of activity. That is, **a brain at rest still has activity even without any outside stimulation.** According to the article, *"Most things we care about reminiscences, emotions, drives, plans, and so on, can occur with no external stimulus and no overt output that can be measured."* The article goes on to mention that: *"When your eyes are closed during dreaming, you still enjoy rich visual experience."* The reasons for dreams are unknown to science. Computers don't dream! The Bible tells us that dreams can serve as an avenue for fellowship with our Creator: *"...Your young men will see visions, and your old men will dream dreams"* (Joel 2:20 quoted by St. Peter in Acts 2:16-21). We see in various places in the Bible where God communicated with people in a dream (see Genesis 28:12, Daniel 2:1, Matthew 2:13, and many others). This is a function of the human spirit in communication with God.

What gives us the ability to plan out what we want to do before doing it? The Bible tells us that God has given this basic ability to us: *"**God ... has ... set eternity in the hearts of men; yet they cannot fathom what God has done from beginning to end"*** (Ecclesiastes 3:11). This very helpful God-given ability in the human spirit to think ahead (and in the past as well) is very essential to our existence as human beings. Yet, ultimately it has its limits.

What are emotions? A very basic question indeed. While emotions can be described, what are their origins? Computers don't have emotions. Ultimately, emotions stem from the very nature of God Himself who describes Himself in the Bible as having emotions. His creation reflects these same characteristics and human emotions mirror God's emotions.

What is intelligence? The Bible makes it clear from chapter 1 that man is distinct from the animals in terms of the human spirit. Furthermore, even our bodies were made directly from the dust of the earth, the same method God used for the animals (compare Genesis 2:7 and 2:19). Again, Zechariah 12:1 specifically tells us that the human spirit is unique. God created it. Man can't duplicate it.

How is time represented in the brain? In fact, what IS time? Nobody really knows. We measure "it," but we don't know what it is. Researchers have failed to find evidence for a single "time organ" in the brain. Again, Zechariah 12:1 and Eccles. 3:11 help us to see that "time" is something put within the heart or spirit of man by his Creator and thus has a supernatural origin.

"Why do brains sleep and dream?" the article in DISCOVER magazine asks. While there are plenty of ideas, the article states, "there is no universally agreed-upon answer...." Whatever it is, sleep isn't something that God needs: "…[God] who watches over Israel will neither slumber nor sleep" (Psalm 121:4). The Bible uses sleep as a type of the death of the body. Daniel 12:2, speaking of Christ's Second Coming, says: "Multitudes who sleep in the dust of the earth will awake: some to everlasting life, others to shame and everlasting contempt." Sleep by its very nature is a necessary form of rest for the body. Without it, we die. And, ultimately, our bodies enter what is commonly called eternal rest. Eternal in the sense of the time before Christ's return.

How do the specialized systems of the brain integrate with one another? Much research has gone into the different activities of the brain. Neuroscientists have a good idea of how the brain is divided into seemingly different compartments for hundreds of different tasks, but *"despite their disparate functions, these systems seem to work together seamlessly. There are almost no good ideas about how this occurs."* The human spirit works in conjunction with the physical brain. It ties things together we might say. The Bible reveals that the spirit can function separately without the human brain or body. St. Paul, for example, spoke of a time when he was taken into God's heaven, and he wasn't even sure whether it was just his spirit that went or his whole human body! *"…I will go on to visions and revelations from the Lord. I know a man in Christ who 14 years ago was caught up to* *the third heaven. Whether it was in the body or out of the body I do not know – God knows. [and then he repeats it for emphasis] And I know that this man—whether in the body or apart from the body I do not know, but God knows—was caught up to paradise. He heard inexpressible things, things that man is not permitted to tell"* (II Cori. 12:1-4). Jesus said that we should not fear those able to kill the body but unable to kill the soul/spirit (Matthew 10:28). At death, our bodies return to the dust and our spirits return to God in heaven (Eccles 12:7). The real you is the spirit within you. St. Paul likens it to living in a tent: *"Now we know that if the earthly tent we live in is destroyed, we have a building from God, an eternal house in heaven, not built by human hands…* [therefore, for this reason, St. Paul said that Christians should] *…prefer to be away from the body and at home with the Lord" (II Cor. 5:1 and 8).*

10. Scientists find it difficult to explain consciousness. **"An explanation of consciousness is one of the major unsolved problems of modern science."** "If I give you all the Tinkertoys in the world and tell you to hook them up so that they form a conscious machine, good luck. We don't have a theory yet of how to do this; we don't even know what the theory will look like." After God made Adam directly from the dust of the Earth (and before He created Eve out of Adam's rib), Adam not only had consciousness, but he was out naming the animals! Man, from the very beginning, because of the unique human spirit placed within him, had consciousness, intelligence, and all these "mysteries" of modern science! The answer is plain. Science is limited in scope. It can't see or measure the unseen spiritual world, be it our human spirit or the Spirit of God! Only when God reveals Himself to us, as He has in the Bible and in the life of Jesus Christ, can we even begin to understand those things, which will forever be a "mystery" to the one who rejects God in his knowledge. (The previous information was taken from The Brain and the Bible, CreationScience.com.)

God the Creator (Excerpt from an article by Dr. Caroline Leaf). This article was taken from Dr. Leaf 's online article (http://drleaf.com/about/scientific-philosophy/).

God is the Creator of the universe and is the author of science. Since God is the author of the Bible, the Bible is therefore the ultimate authority in any scientific matters. The study of science is therefore the study of God's handiwork and is a way of admiring His creation. God, the Creator, is the One to be worshipped, not the creation. The creation, however, reflects the glory of God and points to His divine attributes.

Spirit, Soul and Body

Man is a triune and is comprised of spirit, soul and body. The mind operates in the spirit and by extension the spiritual realm. The mind also operates in the body and therefore the physical realm. Since the physical realm was created out of the spiritual realm, the spiritual and therefore the spirit is higher in importance, power, scope and influence than the physical realm and hence, the body. The mind is intermediate in prominence between the spirit and the body. The spirit of man was created to control the mind. The mind is supposed to control the body and therefore the physical realm. Any aberration in the hierarchy of the spirit, soul and body of man is a reflection of a fallen state and is not the original intent of God.

The Mind

The brain is part of the physical body and therefore is controlled by the mind. The mind does not emerge from an accumulation of brain activity. Brain activity, rather, reflects mind activity. Even though the mind controls the brain, the brain feeds back to, and influences, the mind. The brain seats the mind, and therefore the mind influences the physical world through the brain.

Free Will

God has given man free will and therefore man has the ability to choose. Free will is not an illusion. Choice is an activity of the mind that is expressed by particular types of brain activity. The mind, through its capacity for free will, is able to assess influences from the spirit and the body (including the brain) and make rational choices.

Mind Controls Matter

Since the mind controls the body and by extension the physical realm, it can be said that mind controls matter. The mind is not what the brain does, rather, the brain does the bidding of the m*ind. Thinking, an activity of the mind, affects the brain in very specific ways and on many levels: systemic, structural, functional, chemical, electromagnetic, molecular and genetic and even quantum physics.*

Quantum Physics and the Mind

There is growing evidence that biological systems operate at the level of quantum physics. The quantum zeno effect has been described within the science of quantum physics. When applied to neuroscience, the quantum zeno effect implies that the brain becomes what you focus on. Focus is directed attention and is a function of the mind. Thus, quantum physics supports the notion of mind over matter.

Neuroplasticity

There is mounting recent evidence for neuroplasticity, that is, the ability of the brain to change according to experience. *The anatomy and physiology of the human brain is much more malleable and plastic than we once thought. This shows that the brain changes according to how we use it. The saying "Use it or lose it," which is usually applied to the musculo-skeletal system, can now be applied to the brain as well. Thinking, a mind activity, affects gene expression. Gene expression produces proteins. Proteins are fashioned into structural elements and enzymes (biological catalysts), which change brain anatomy (structure) and physiology (function). Therefore thinking changes brain structure and function.*

Neurogenesis

It was once thought that nerve cells do not regenerate and thus we lose them throughout our life span without any replacement. However, since the mid-1990s, it has been shown that new nerve cells are actually generated in the brain (neurogenesis), especially surrounding the ventricles and the hippocampus. It was even demonstrated that elderly terminally ill patients still produced new nerve cells. Interestingly, the new nerve cells born in the hippocampus, a structure essential for learning and memory, are only incorporated in the neural network if something new and challenging is learned—

Otherwise they die. This implies that mental activity, and therefore thinking, profoundly affects neurogenesis.

Epigenetics

The genome has been prominent in general scientific thinking; however, because of the recent discoveries in the growing field of epigenetics, the perceived pre-eminence of the gene is waning. The science of epigenetics describes how gene expression is controlled by mechanisms other than changes in DNA sequence. The mind thinks and produces thoughts. Thinking epigenetically affects DNA and gene expression. Thinking therefore lies within the sphere of epigenetics. Thinking affects gene expression in somatic cells of the brain and the rest of the body. This in turn affects the anatomy (structure) and physiology (function) and subsequently the health of the body. Therefore aberrant (toxic) thinking can adversely affect the normal functioning of the body, leading to particular psychological and somatic disorders and diseases. Epigenetic mechanisms have been demonstrated in germ cells (eggs and sperm) and can affect our progeny. **Therefore, thinking can affect our children. There is even epidemiological evidence of epigenetic effects in multiple generations.**

Thinking Affects Health

Thinking affects all the body systems. There is mounting scientific evidence demonstrating the intimate relationship between the brain, the rest of the nervous system, the endocrine system and the immune system shown by the emergence of the sciences of psychoneuroendocrinology and psychoneuroimmunology. These two fields of medical study and practice are basically shedding light on the how the relationships between thinking, stress, the brain, hormones and the body's immune defenses affect psychological and physical wellbeing.

Because mind controls matter, therefore, thinking is the pre-eminent influence on health. It has been shown from various sources that 75% to 98% of illnesses are a direct result of our thought life. The association between stress and disease is a colossal 85% (Dir. Brian Luke Seaward).

The International Agency for Research on Cancer and the World Health Organization has concluded that 80% of cancers are due to lifestyles and are not genetic, and

They say this is a conservative number (Cancer Statistics and Views of Causes Science News Vol.115, No 2 (Jan.13 1979, p.23). According to Director Bruce Lipton (The Biology of Belief, 2008), gene disorders like Huntington's chorea, beta thalassemia, cystic fibrosis, to name just a few, affect less than 2% of the population. This means that the vast majority of the world's population come into this world with genes that should enable the to live a happy and healthy life.

He says a staggering 98% of diseases are lifestyle choices and therefore, thinking. Interestingly Herbert Benson MD, the president of Harvard Medical School's Mind-Body Institute (http://www.massgeneral.org/bhi/research/), toxic thoughts lead to stress, which affects our body's natural healing capacities. Toxic thinking literally "wears down"' the brain and the rest of the body. According to Dir. H.F. Nijhout (Metaphors and the Role of Genes and Development, 1990) genes control biology and not the other way around. According to W.C. Willett (balancing lifestyle and genomics research for disease prevention Science (296) p 695-698, 2002) only 5% of cancer and cardiovascular patients can attribute their disease to hereditary factors. According to the American Institute of Stress it has been estimated that 75 – 90% of all visits to primary care physicians are for stress-related problems.

The Three Brains

The main coordinating center of the nervous system is the brain, which is located in the skull. However, there is a group of neurons in and around the heart, a "mini-brain" that controls the heart. In fact the heart can still operate, although not optimally, when it is not in communication with the rest of the nervous system. Similarly the enteric nervous system, located in the gut wall, is the 'brain' of the gastrointestinal system. The gut, like the heart, can function when it is cut off from the rest of the nervous system. Normally the skull brain, the heart mini-brain and the gut brain communicate with each other. The mind controls all three brains. However, the three brains feed back to, and therefore influence, the mind.

Wired for the Positive

Traditionally the fields of clinical psychology and psychiatry have operated in the medical or disease model. In the disease model the health practitioner looks for what is wrong in the patient, or what disease process is present. Once the disease is diagnosed it is corrected by a cognitive or pharmacological intervention. The focus is on the

Negative aspects of the mind and brain. However, recent research has shown that there is an "optimism bias" wired into our brains. We seem to be "wired for love"; in other words, we are wired to expect good things for ourselves; we are wired for the positive. It has been shown that this bias has a positive impact on our mental, physical and financial health. This discovery is at the core of the recently emerging fields of Positive Psychology and Positive Psychiatry.

In contrast to being wired for love, we have to be conditioned to fear, according to Pavlovian principles. In other words even though we are naturally wired for love, we have to learn fear. There is even a state called "Learned Helplessness" in which a person has to be forced into a type of depression.

In summary, therefore, the preponderance of evidence is pointing to the fact that we are wired for love (positivity) and we have to learn fear (negativity). This will have huge implications in the health care industry.

What Does All This Mean?

God made all of us, even those who think He didn't. The human brain is an amazing instrument. According to Discover Magazine, "In principle, our thoughts could race far more efficiently if all the axons in our brains were thick. But the human brain has at least a quarter of a million miles of wiring—more than enough to reach from earth to the moon—and is already packed tight. Sam Wang, a Princeton University neuroscientist, calculated how big our brain would be if it were built with thick axons. "Making an entire brain out of them would create heads so large that we couldn't fit through doorways," he concluded. Such a brain would also consume a tremendous amount of energy.

Given the constraints of biology and physics, our brains appear to have evolved to run very efficiently. For instance, neurons in the brain tend to be joined together into small networks, which are then linked to one another by relatively few long-range connections. This kind of network needs less wiring than other arrangements, and therefore shortens the distance signals need to travel."

God the Creator (Excerpt from an article by Dr. Caroline Leaf). This article was taken from Dr. Leaf 's online article (http://drleaf.com/about/scientific-philosophy/).

There is no question that something went desperately wrong in the brain. If we are "evolving," why does sin (and we have to contend with it on Planet Earth), keep bringing us into such conditions as bipolar? There has to be an explanation. The effect of sin on the brain certainly provides some answers.

CHAPTER 4

Sin and the Brain

Despite God's miraculous work of original creation (no evolution needed) of the perfect brain, something we call "The Fall" did great damage to the human psyche. When sin entered the human race through Adam and Eve's choice to eat off the Tree of the Knowledge of Good and Evil, their brains, human spirit and bodies took a nosedive along with relationships and the environment. The collateral damage of the fall caused great deception to occur in the mind/brain, placing separation between the first couple and their Creator, Father God. For the first time, man was "on his own." The prophet Isaiah described it this way:

We all, like sheep, have gone astray, each of us has turned to our own way; and the LORD *has laid on him the iniquity of us all (Isa. 53:6).*

The Apostle Paul wrote: *Now the mind of the flesh [which is sense and reason without the Holy Spirit] is death [death that comprises all the miseries arising from sin, both here and hereafter]. But the mind of the [Holy] Spirit is life and [soul] peace [both now and forever]. [That is] because the mind of the flesh [with its carnal thoughts and purposes] is hostile to God, for it does not submit itself to God's Law; indeed it cannot* (Romans 8:6-7 Amp).

Iniquity, as used in the Isaiah scripture, means to "warp or twist." It's essentially a heart for sin, and that heart for sin has made its way through thousands of generations since then. In some cases iniquity causes damages to the brain and emotions, setting the stage for what medical science terms "disorders," many of which have no known origin.

That's likely because although scientists and psychologists often can determine that a traumatic event caused the brain neurons to misfire, they usually can't fix it because it is a spiritual problem that can only be fixed by spiritual answers. The problems with the brain and emotions can produce sicknesses that are referred to as "psychosomatic" or soul-body sicknesses. Doctors say from 75-90 percent of all sicknesses fall into this category (see previous chapter's section by Dr. Caroline Leaf).

In the Bible God condensed most curses (more on this later) down to one source: idolatry. In Exodus 20:4-5 He said that the sin of idolatry (iniquity) would be passed from the originator of the sin to the third and fourth generations of people:

You shall not make yourself any graven image [to worship it] or any likeness of anything that is in the heavens above, or that is in the earth beneath, or that is in the water under the earth; [5] *You shall not bow down yourself to them or serve them; for I the Lord your God am a jealous God, visiting the iniquity of the fathers upon the children to the third and fourth generation of those who hate Me,*

We call this the sins of the fathers. If you go to the doctor for a checkup, and they ask you to fill out paperwork on your family line's health, what do they ask you? "What kinds of illnesses did your parents' have? Heart disease, cancer,"etc? It's the same thing with spiritual problems; go back to your ancestry to find some of the answers.

Idolatry: the Foundation of Iniquity and Curses

The violation of God's command in Ex. 20:4-5 is what constitutes idolatry, and idolatry brings curses. Idolatry is trusting in other things, bowing down and worshipping with our hearts things other than God. In other words, if our main focus in life is on things rather than God, we commit idolatry.

Included in idolatrous practices are secret societies that are nothing more than false religions such as freemasonry, cults, spiritualist churches, witchcraft, Satanism, psychics and the use of power other than that of God Himself to get things. Lesser things such as love of money, power, prestige, adoring rock stars and the environment are included, where these things are venerated above God. All this is iniquity. Iniquity involves lawlessness, wickedness, unrighteousness, transgression and perversion.

"The sins of the fathers"(SOTF), as we saw in Ex. 20:4-5, include mothers, grandparents, the entire family line. Here's a typical example of one found in the Bible in which the son walked in the sins of his father:

Ahaziah son of Ahab began his two-year reign over Israel in Samaria in the seventeenth year of Jehoshaphat king of Judah.52 He did evil in the sight of the Lord and walked in the ways of his father [Ahab] and of his mother [Jezebel] and of Jeroboam son of Nebat, who made Israel sin. 53 He served Baal and worshiped him and provoked the Lord, the God of Israel, to anger in all the ways his father had done (1 Kings 22:51-53).

Israel's Kings Walked in Their Fathers' Sins

Other examples:

1 Kings 14:9: *But (you Jeroboam) have done evil above all who were before you; for you have made yourself other gods, molten images, to provoke Me to anger and have cast Me behind your back—*

15-16 – 15: *The Lord will smite Israel, as a reed is shaken in the water; and He will root up Israel out of this good land which He gave to their fathers and will scatter them beyond the [Euphrates] River, because they have made their Asherim [idolatrous symbols of the goddess Asherah], provoking the Lord to anger. 16 He will give Israel up because of the sins of Jeroboam which he has sinned and made Israel to sin.*

1 Kings 15:25-26 25: *Nadab son of Jeroboam began to reign over Israel in the second year of Asa king of Judah, and reigned two years. 26 He did evil in the sight of the Lord and walked in the way of his father and in his sin, with which he made Israel sin.*

1 Kings 16:30-31 30: *And Ahab son of Omri did evil in the sight of the Lord above all before him.*

31 As if it had been a light thing for Ahab to walk in the sins of Jeroboam son of Nebat, he took for a wife Jezebel daughter of Ethbaal king of the Sidonians, and served Baal and worshiped him.

There are many more examples of these sins of the fathers found in the Bible.

We Are All Under Iniquity

Isaiah 64:6

6 For we have all become like one who is unclean [ceremonially, like a leper], and all our righteousness (our best deeds of rightness and justice) is like filthy rags or a polluted garment; we all fade like a leaf, and our iniquities, like the wind, take us away [far from God's favor, hurrying us toward destruction].

Iniquity is likened to standing against a gale. It pushes us to commit the same sins that our ancestors committed. Why does one fall into sinful practices and not another?

Example: Two 12-year-old boys secretly look at porn. One walks away essentially unscathed from the experience, while the other becomes hooked. Why? It's because of iniquity. Consider the epidemic of homosexuality. If one's ancestry practiced homosexuality, iniquity will push their descendants to commit the same sin. Hence, many would say, "I feel like God made me a homosexual" because of iniquity. Committing a homosexual act doesn't make one a homosexual!

Iniquity Involves:

- Lawlessness – "without or outside of" the law; not regulated or based on the law; not restrained or controlled by the law; unruly.

- Wickedness – morally bad, evil, fierce, vicious; causing or likely to cause harm or trouble.

- Unrighteousness – contrary to the right way or thing; unjust; lacks right standing with God.

- Transgression – crossing the line; moving outside the law of God; violating a command.

- Perversion – turning away from what is right or good; corrupt; contrary or opposing what is right; preventing the normal godly way.

II Timothy 3:1-5 NAS - *But realize this, that in the last days difficult times will come. For men will be lovers of self, lovers of money, boastful, arrogant, revilers, disobedient to parents, ungrateful, unholy, unloving, irreconcilable, malicious gossips, without self- control, brutal, haters of good, treacherous, reckless, conceited, lovers of pleasure rather than lovers of God; holding to a form of godliness, although they have denied its power; and avoid such men as these.*

Frequently occurring sins of the fathers

- Abandonment

- Abuse, verbal, physical, mental

- Parental inversion

- Physical infirmities

- Pride

- Rebellion

- Rejection, insecurity

- Religious bondage, Cults

- Sexual Sin & Perversion

- Unbelief

- Unworthiness, low self-esteem, inferiority

- Witchcraft, Occult, Satanism

Sexual sins

- Addictions

- Anger, rage violence

- Control, possessiveness, manipulation

- Emotional dependency

- Fears of all kinds

- Idolatry

- Money extremes, greed & lack

- Not caring for children

Inheritance Can Be Major!

According to Dr. Strydom, *"Inheritance plays a very large role in bipolar disorder. It is inherited from a gene that is passed down from the mother on the X chromosome. (Males have an X chromosome from the mother and a Y chromosome from the father). Females have two X chromosomes – (one from the father and one from the mother). The only way to overcome this is for the Lord to heal the genetics. God created the X chromosome perfect from the foundation of the world, and if the devil, because of generations of sin, was able to come in and mix up the DNA in the genes. God is well able to change it back the way it was. The devil is not more powerful than God. I believe that when we line up with His Word and His conditions for healing, God can fix the genetics… and He does."*

As is made clear in this manual, inner healing and getting the sins of the fathers–and mothers to the cross of Christ–can do wonders to change the impact of inherited and corrupted genes.

Allow me to reiterate Dr. Caroline Leaf's knowledge and understanding of epigenetics. *"The genome has been prominent in general scientific thinking; however, because of the recent discoveries in the growing field of epigenetics, the perceived pre-eminence of the gene is waning. The science of epigenetics describes how gene expression is controlled by mechanisms other than changes in DNA sequence. The mind thinks and produces thoughts. Thinking epigenetically affects DNA and gene expression. Thinking therefore lies within the sphere of epigenetics. Thinking affects gene expression in somatic cells of the brain and the rest of the body. This in turn affects the anatomy (structure) and physiology (function) and subsequently the health of the body. Therefore aberrant (toxic) thinking can adversely affect the normal functioning of the body, leading to particular psychological and somatic disorders and diseases."*

May I hasten to add bipolar disorder!

Specific Diseases

Antidepressants and lithium (the drug of choice used to treat or prevent mania) are not long-term answers to bipolar disorder because they do not deal with the underlying problem. These drugs help regulate but don't heal the roots of the problem.

No Blame Game

We don't blame our ancestry for these things any more than we would blame them for any physical problems we inherited; they are what they are. However, those spiritual, financial, physical, mental and emotional curses are passed down to us (see Exodus 20:5; Deuteronomy 27-28), and their consequences remain with us until we learn to appropriate what Jesus did on the cross to break these iniquities from us:

Christ has redeemed us from the curse of the law, having become a curse for us (for it is written, "Cursed is everyone who hangs on a tree"[a]) (Gal. 3:13 NKJV).

I love Psa. 103 where the Psalmist blesses the Lord with his soul (his mind, emotions and will) because He is forgiving, and note here that through Christ He forgives ALL our iniquities: *...Bless the LORD, O my soul, And forget none of His benefits; 3Who* pardons all your iniquities, *Who* heals all your diseases; (Psa. 103: 2-3).

Jesus' death and provision on the cross was simply a legal transaction because Jesus paid the price to fulfill every legal demand of the law. He kept it in its entirety because He was the perfect, sinless sacrifice that God the Father required to pay for our sins, rebellion, transgression and iniquity. Until Jesus did this, God's wrath remained on every one of us for our sins:

For our sake He made Christ [virtually] to be sin Who knew no sin, so that in and through Him we might become [ᵃ endued with, viewed as being in, and examples of] the righteousness of God [what we ought to be, approved and acceptable and in right relationship with Him, by His goodness] (2 Cor. 5:21 Amp).

Everyone is familiar with John 3:16 (For God so loved the world that He gave His only begotten son that whosoever believes in Him might have eternal life), but what about John 3:36? *Whoever believes in the Son has eternal life,* **but whoever rejects the Son will not see life, for God's wrath remains on them.**

God loves people but is angry at the unforgiven sin in people, plain and simple, and unless we are forgiven and separated from our sins by repenting and believing in Christ's death, burial and resurrection, and appropriating it for ourselves, we will be separated from God for eternity!

Curses Don't Necessarily Mean Profanity!

Besides idolatry, curses and their consequences may come from others cursing us with spoken words (or vice versa) or curses we speak upon ourselves. The Book of James makes it clear how this operates:

… but no human being can tame the tongue. It is a restless evil, full of deadly poison.

With the tongue we praise our Lord and Father, and with it we curse human beings, who have been made in God's likeness. **10** *Out of the same mouth come praise and cursing. My brothers and sisters, this should not be.* **11** *Can both fresh water and salt water flow from the same spring? My brothers and sisters, can a fig tree bear olives, or a grapevine bear figs? Neither can a salt spring produce fresh water* (Jas 3:8-12).

In ancient days a curse was considered to possess an inherent power of carrying itself into effect. Prayer has been defined as a wish referred to God. Curses were imprecations (curses) referred to supernatural beings in whose existence and power to inflict harm; in other words, demons.

Times Have Not Changed

Some people don't believe that curses are still passed down since Jesus died to remove them (Gal. 3:13). However, the key word is "appropriation."

Jesus died for everyone, but only those who *appropriate* His death for their sins are saved. There's no automatic trip to heaven unless sins are repented of, and Jesus is truly believed on. It is the same with curses, yet many people, who don't believe these things, even many Christians, cannot explain why some people and their families–and those who went before them––who have lived righteously, are constantly plagued by never-ending sickness, financial failures, premature death and various and sundry mental disorders!

Some cling to the verse that says the children will no longer die for the sins of the father (Ezekiel 18:20), but we're not talking about death here––just the consequences of unconfessed sin so the covenant blessing can be restored! And until Jesus died on the cross for curses (became a curse), this verse was not effectual, anyway!

Here is one biblical reference to confessing the sins of our ancestry (we are not asking God to forgive them) but do this so the blessings of the covenant can be restored that were lost because of iniquity:

40 *"But if they will confess their sins and the sins of their ancestors––their unfaithfulness and their hostility toward me,* **41** *which made me hostile toward them so that I sent them into the land of their enemies––then when their uncircumcised hearts are humbled and they pay for their sin,* **42** *I will remember my covenant with Jacob and my covenant with Isaac and my covenant with Abraham, and I will remember the land* (Leviticus 26:40-42 NIV).

Daniel, Nehemiah and Ezra also used this same model. Today we call this "Identificational Repentance."

In the New Testament, Jesus became that curse to provide the solution to the sins of the father:

*Christ purchased our freedom [redeeming us] from the curse (doom) of the L a w [and its condemnation] by [Himself] becoming a curse for us, for it is written [in the Scriptures], Cursed is everyone who hangs on a tree (is crucified); (*Gal. 3:13 Amp).

Why Was Crucifixion the Answer?

Consider the fact that crucifixion is, without question, the most humiliating and degrading form of public death ever devised. First of all, it was a very slow agonizing death. Often it would last for days, as the victim died more from suffocation than from bleeding. Furthermore, hanging naked in public along some well-traveled road added immensely to the sense of shame. Fully exposed like a carcass hanging on a rack, the victim experienced long hours of pain and an interminable time of humiliation. Crucifixion was not only ugly it was inhuman.

Crucifixion was a well-known and commonly practiced means of executing criminals in the ancient world. Herodotus, the Greek historian, tells us that the Persians used crucifixion as a form of extreme punishment. Other sources reveal the practice among the Assyrians, the Scythians, and the Thracians as well as among more distant European groups such as the Celts, the Germans, and the Britons. On one occasion, Alexander the Great had 2000 survivors of the siege of Tyre crucified along the shores of the Mediterranean.

In the Roman mind, crucifixion was reserved for rebellious slaves, mutinous troops, vile criminals, and insurrectionists against the state. Roman citizens, especially the upper class, were normally exempt from such an ignominious death no matter what their crime. The reason for this was that crucifixion was viewed not just as a means of death, but also as a means of portraying shame. Therefore only the most despicable were crucified. To be hung on a cross meant more than that a crime worthy of death had been committed. It meant that the accused was considered to be a lowly, vile, reprehensible person, in addition to being a criminal. He was not only bad—he was base.

Hanging the body exhibited the person to public humiliation. The criminal was under the curse of God... the judgment that takes a person's life out of the covenant community as a perpetrator of the worst kind of sin and displays that judgment by the humiliation of hanging his body in public shows that that person is under God's curse. (*The Bible*

Knowledge Commentary, Vol. 3, pp. 134-135)

All this should underscore for us why God planned this before the foundation of the world:

And all that dwell upon the earth shall worship him, whose names are not written in the book of life of the Lamb slain from the foundation of the world (Revelation 13:8). The perfect, sinless Son of God was ordained to suffer and die as the vilest kind of criminal of that day! He was whipped until He almost died, and then carried His cross to Calvary, where He was nailed, scorned, humiliated and publically shamed then put to death for us!

Christ being slain from the foundation of the world illustrates not only that He was foreordained to be slain, but also that the efficacy, or the beneficial effects of that death, are the same as if that sacrifice had been made before the creation of the world. Thus, Old Testament saints were washed clean in Christ's blood the same as we are today. In other words, the efficacy of Christ's sacrifice is not limited by time. God had already chosen who He would save before creation, and had thus already ordained the Savior to shed His blood for them, to make this possible. Their salvation wasn't something, which could be thwarted; it was something that was as good as 'done' from the time that God ordained it!

Prayers for the Brain

We've discussed a lot of things that negatively affect the brain in this chapter. In my research I found some wonderful prayers for the brain. No matter what your state is, and if you're just forgetful like most of us, you will find these handy.

Prayer for Rest

I thank you, Lord, that because of your grace and mercy you are the giver of good gifts. I thank you, Lord, that your Holy Spirit dispels chaos and fear everywhere He goes. I ask you, Lord, to forgive me for the times in my life that I have purposefully chosen chaos and anxiety rather than asking you to deal with my worries and fears.

I repent for the times in my life when I have not accepted your rest, but instead have invited stress, disorganization and confusion. Forgive me, Lord, for anyone I may have hurt by my words and behaviors when I was under stress and swimming in chaos. I ask you to bless those I may have hurt and place them under the shadow of your wings. As a member of my family line, I confess the sins for all those who used drugs, alcohol or medications to force rest upon their bodies and spirits rather than turning to you.

As a member of my family line, I confess the sins for all those who although they knew you, chose pride and selfish ambition over surrender to your Sabbath rest. In the name of Jesus I break, shatter, cut-off and dissolve and destroy all ungodly frequency vibrations, lay lines, tubes and mechanisms that have prevented my brain from receiving your rest. Father, I ask you to tune my brain to your heartbeat. Father, in Jesus' name, I ask you to seal all ungodly dimensions and open up the godly dimensions that lead to you and the revelation of your purposes in my life. I declare that you give only light burdens. I welcome your gentle touch upon my life. In the name of Jesus, I break, shatter, dissolve and destroy the behaviors in my life that have prevented me from observing your Sabbath rest and remembering your healing touch.

Father, in the name of Jesus, I ask you now to come into my brain and transform any thoughts that are not pleasing to you. Seal all cracks in my brain that have allowed chaos and fear to enter. I thank you Lord, and bless your name because you carry my problems and teach me to depend on you. Teach me about the peace and joy of your Sabbath rest. In the name of Jesus, I accept quietness into my heart. Thank You Lord that you are the God of rest!

Prayer written by Jeffrey Barsch *Genesis 1:2-3, Deuteronomy 5:12, 6:6, Psalm 46:10, Matthew 11:28-30, 1 Corinthians 14:40*

Prayer for Attention Deficit Disorder

Lord Jesus, I thank you that your healing power purchased through the cross of Calvary is available for me today. I declare that you created my brain for the purpose of bringing glory to your name. I do not want my brain to be conformed to the patterns of this world; instead I ask for your transforming power to enter all areas of my brain that you might give me the ability to process academic and spiritual wisdom from your Holy Spirit.

I declare that I believe that you created my innermost being and that my brain were fearfully and wonderfully made by your hand. Lord, I repent for all the times I have not regarded my brain and my learning abilities as a gift from you. I ask you to forgive me for the negative thoughts and words that I have spoken against my own brain and learning abilities. I repent of trying to solve my learning problems through my own efforts rather than turning to receive your love, grace and healing touch first. I choose to forgive parents, teachers and friends who have not believed in my mental abilities or who have made learning more difficult for me. In the name of Jesus I now free them from unreasonable expectations I may have placed upon them. Lord, I ask you to remove all generational sin from my family line that may have played a part in my present learning struggles. As a member of my family line I confess the sins of all those, who although they knew you, did not use their brains to glorify you but rather engaged in futile and foolish spiritual thinking. Lord, I confess the sins for those in my family line who had used their brains to misuse the spiritual gifts that you had provided for them.

In the name of Jesus I command the neurons in my brain to function properly. I command in Jesus name that the damaged dendrites in my brain be healed. All axons and synapses will respond to the healing touch of Jesus Christ and function the way they were created to work. I command in Jesus' name that the right and left sides of my brain function normally and in complete balance and that all the academic and creative abilities I have will flow like a river. In Jesus' name I command that the electrical and chemical frequencies in every cell of my brain come into the harmony and balance. In Jesus' name I command Werenicke's Area (speech) and Broca's Area (understanding of language) to function normally. In the name of Jesus I declare that impulse control and lack of attention to task be healed. In the name of Jesus I declare that I have a new academic and occupational future. I break, shatter, dissolve and destroy the lie that says my brain will always remain the same. In the name of Jesus I declare that I will not have a spirit of fear about learning new things. I accept your gift of the spirit of power, love and self-discipline into my brain. Lord, I now ask you to give me the spirit of wisdom and revelation that I might succeed in school and to know you better.

Psalm 139: 13-16, Romans 1:21, 12:2, Ephesians 1:17, Colossians 1:9-13, 2 Timothy 1:7.

Prayer for Impulsivity

The issue of temporal awareness (timing) is a critical issue in the daily life of Attention Deficit Disorder individuals. Impulsivity (responding too quickly) keeps many ADD individuals from receiving information in the learning environment and often makes personal decision making difficult. By speaking this prayer aloud on a daily basis we are asking the Lord to change the timing patterns in the brain and to place His healing touch over all impulsive behavior tendencies. Please pause between the various sections of this prayer to allow the Lord Jesus to bring his healing touch to your brain. Be alert to any Scripture verses or thoughts the Lord might provide to you during your reflection time, record them in your journal for future reference. Prepare your heart to recite this prayer. Ask the Lord for His presence. (Pause For Reflection/Selah) Father, I declare that your majestic presence reigns over all issues of timing in my life. I further declare that you are the author of all time and that you existed before time began. I rejoice in proclaiming that Jesus Christ is the same yesterday, today and tomorrow. All issues of impulsivity and timing I gladly place under your dominion. (Selah/Reflect)

Lord, I repent of all the times in my life when I have made quick decisions without asking your Holy Spirit for wisdom and revelation. I ask you to put your healing touch on my brain so that I can learn to wait, to hear your voice before speaking or making decisions. Lord Jesus, please forgive me for all the times that my words have been spoken impulsively and have hurt other people. I ask today, Lord Jesus, that you would free them from the pain or disappointment of my impulsive words and that you would pour out your blessings on every person that my impulsive words have hurt.

Lord Jesus, I ask you to supernaturally change my brain and slow me down that I might enjoy the daily wonders of the world you have created. Help me think before I speak. Lord Jesus, every time I am in a learning environment, I ask for the power of your presence so that I will understand all the information that is presented and process the information according to your timing. In Jesus' name I break, shatter, dissolve and destroy any generational sin that has kept my brain from receiving your healing touch. In Jesus' name, I ask for correct alignment of all temporal and spatial dimensions in my brain. Lord, return to me the parts of my brain function that have been robbed by the enemy. In Jesus' name, I command that the neurological firing of my brain be changed from random firing to the orderly firing and exact electrical impulses that I was created to receive from you. I ask you, Lord Jesus, to coat my brain in the redemptive blood of the Cross so that my impulsivity might be healed once and for all. (Selah)

I pray from this day forward that I will turn to you first for wisdom and revelation about my brain and my learning problems. I declare that you are Jehovah-Tsebaoth in my life, the Lord of Hosts, the provider of miracles, and the God for whom nothing is impossible. Lord, will you now shower your healing power on the areas of my brain that need your touch. (Selah)

Lord Jesus, I ask you to close all temporal dimensions that lead to demonic realms and to open all temporal dimensions that lead to a greater revelation of your glory. I rejoice that I am seated with you in heavenly places. Lord Jesus, would you now remove the human boundaries of time and space and give me a glimpse of your kingdom and your glory. I yearn to see you. Only the power of your presence can heal my brain. In the mighty and powerful name of Jesus I pray. Genesis 1:1; Ephesians 1:3-4, 2:6; 2 Timothy 1:9; Col. 1:16-17; Hebrews 13:8. **Prayer by: Jeffrey Barsch**

All this has been written to explain how God paid for iniquity through Christ's redeeming Blood. The question is how do people find themselves under curses and seemingly never-ending difficulties and torments since Christ has already paid for them? One of the ways is through entry wounds. Bipolar and many other brain disorders come as a result of these wounds, and they begin early.

CHAPTER 5

Entry Wounds

Satan loves open doors. He looks for any opportunity to gain advantage over people, especially God's people. Ephesians 4:27 says we're not to give the devil an opportunity (literally a place of operation). How so? The Word of God plainly says not to let the sun go down upon our anger. In the vernacular, it means don't go to bed mad! That seems simple enough, but Satan loves to take advantage over anyone to get an edge.

Four Doors

Essentially Satan seeks to afflict and oppress us through at least one of four doors of access: hatred, fear, the occult and sexual sin.

Door #1 Hate

Except for hating sin, hate is a no-no in Scripture, especially in the New Testament. While in one place, the Old Testament actually says to love your friends and hate your enemies; the overall message to Israel was to do good to others, even strangers and aliens. We find a lot of passages in the Old Testament "condoning" hatred, especially in the Psalms, but remember Christ had not come to live in these OT folks, so they only had The Law to keep them straight. They believed "an eye for an eye." But what did Jesus say?

You have heard that it was said, 'Eye for eye, and tooth for tooth.' 39But I tell you, do not resist an evil person. If anyone slaps you on the right cheek, turn to them the other cheek also. 40And if anyone wants to sue you and take your shirt, hand over your coat as well. 41If anyone forces you to go one mile, go with them two miles. 42Give to the one who asks you, and do not turn away from the one who wants to borrow from you (Matt 5:38-42).

Being Kind to Enemies Was Not Just a New Testament Injunction!

Further instruction is found in the Old Testament about how to treat an enemy. Exodus 23:4, "If thou meet thine enemy's ox – "you say "Ah ha, there's my enemy's ox loose" – "or his ass going astray, thou shalt surely bring it back to him again." God's attitude had not changed from the Old Testament to the New. His was and is a God of love. God dealt with His people in different dispensations through ceremonial laws, and the like, but one thing has always been the same: God's heart of love for humankind.

When we're wrong and we hold a grudge, feel vengeance and long for someone to be hurt because of how they offended us, we're fueling hate, and hatred leads to murder:

You have heard that it was said to the people long ago, 'You shall not murder,ᵃ and anyone who murders will be subject to judgment.' **22** *But I tell you that anyone who is angry with a brother or sisterᵇ ᶜ will be subject to judgment. Again, anyone who says to a brother or sister, 'Raca,ᵈ is answerable to the court. And anyone who says, 'You fool!' will be in danger of the fire of hell (Matt. 5:21-22).*

William Barclay, in his commentary on these verses, writes:

"What Jesus is saying here is this: "In the old days men condemned murder; and truly murder is forever wrong. But I tell you that not only are a man's outward actions under judgment; his inmost thoughts are also under the scrutiny and the judgment of God. Long-lasting anger is bad; contemptuous speaking is worse, and the careless or malicious talk which destroys a man's good name is worst of all." The man who is the slave of anger, the man who speaks in the accent of contempt, the man who destroys another's good name, may never have committed a murder in action, but he is a murderer at heart.

Ethically, the teaching is not that the emotion of anger, with or without a cause, stands on the same level of guilt with murder, but that the former so soon expands and explodes into the latter, that it will be brought to trial and sentenced according to the merits of each case, the occasion of the anger, the degree in which it has been checked or cherished, and the like."

Some people read James 4:2 metaphorically, but in some cases people, even Christians will kill because they don't get want they want. Unrepentant anger against someone can lead to murder!

You want what you don't have, so you scheme and kill to get it. You are jealous of what others have, but you can't get it, so you fight and wage war to take it away from them. Yet you don't have what you want because you don't ask God for it (James 4:2 New Living Translation).

A Demonic Entry Way

What's the problem here? Going unchecked, the open door of anger allows a demon of anger to enter into the person to harass, stir up and tempt him to murder. God warned Cain in Genesis that his jealously and anger for having his sacrifice unacceptable was leading to great trouble. "Sin is crouching at your door," God said (Gen. 4:6-7). Later, as we know, Cain killed Abel.

Is anger wrong? No, the Scripture says to "be angry but don't sin" (Eph. 4:27). Anger is a human emotion just like all the others, but most often our anger is unrighteous. Failing to express anger correctly, only leads to stuffing it inside, thereby building a veritable volcano of compounded anger that going to blow its stack on someone!

Anger has support, believe me. Along with it you'll find the emotions and sins of abandonment, disappointment, intolerance, irritability, feuding, frustration, hatred, hostility, murder, punishment, rage, resentment, retaliation, revenge, spoiled child, tempter tantrums and violence. No? Check yourself out the next time you get really angry! These are what are called "associated sins," which demons can exacerbate.

Door #2 Fear

"Do not fear," or its equivalent, appears 365 times in the Bible. That's one warning for every day of the year! Think God is serious about this? After sinning in the garden, Adam and Eve experienced the first negative human emotion: fear.

God: "Adam, where are you?"

Adam: "I heard you in the garden, and <u>I was **afraid**</u> because I was naked; so **I hid**."

This is called the Shame-Fear-Control stronghold. **Shame**: "I was naked." **Fear:** "I was afraid." **Control**: "I hid myself."

This is daily repeated by us humans. We have inherent shame—it sticks to us like Velcro (unless we kill our consciences), we are afraid ("I may be exposed for who I am really am") and we "hide" (wrap ourselves in a pretense of always in control, super cool, "the man," "the woman who has it altogether – looks, brains, sexual appeal, etc.) to ensure we can't be real about who we are. This is a sad commentary on humanness. Most of this is a sham, and it leaks out eventually when we see headlines that the latest "sexist man alive" or "most desired woman on the planet" loses their cool and does something totally insane.

Fear has a number of "supporters." Worry, unbelief, need to control, anxiety, isolation, apathy and alcohol.

According to the American Heritage Dictionary fear is: "An emotion of alarm and agitation caused by the expectation or realization of danger; Extreme reverence or awe, as toward a supreme power." Fear can also have a positive side by causing us to avoid danger, such as that written by King Solomon.

"The fear of Yahweh is the beginning of knowledge... (Prov. 1:7)." The medical and psychological definitions are as follows. "Fright, dread. Primitively, the emotional reaction to an environmental threat; it now also, presents itself frequently as an indicator of inner problems. .... (Taber's Cyclopedic Medical Dictionary). Panic is: "A sudden overpowering terror, often affecting many people [Fr. panique, terrified]." Terror is: "an intense, overpowering fear. [Lat. terror <terrere, to frighten.]" Anxiety in principle is the very same emotion as fear because the physiological responses in the body are similar. Anxiety is defined as: "A troubled feeling; expressing a feeling of dread or fear especially of the future or

distress over a real or imagined threat to one's mental or physical well- being" (Taber's Cyclopedic Medical Dictionary).

Control

Adam and Eve's response to fear was control—do something, anything to control, hide and protect the fact that they were now "naked and ashamed." Without the full understanding of Christ's righteousness in us, we may often feel naked and ashamed. Christ's righteousness is a robe we wear, as we understand ALL he did for us and in us to remove our shame, guilt, fear and control. He loves us with everything in His being, yet our fear leads us to control situations that seem beyond our ability to deal with them.

Let's take rejection, which we discussed earlier that can happen as early as the womb. If we carry rejection, we have to create a mask to "protect" ourselves from the gaze or even ridicule of others. Our control leads us to all kinds of foolish endeavors – anything that will keep people from finding out WHO we are – how rejected we feel inside. Even the new creation (2 Cor. 5:17), those who are born again of the Spirit, has not yet realized in their total being what Christ has done. All attempts to "cover" ourselves lead to striving, insecurity and a sense that we don't belong.

Early wounding, especially abandonment, leads many to attempt to regain security and acceptance by seeking "false refuges" in which to hide ourselves. These attempts can lead us into looking for Mr. or Ms. Right to complete us. We strive with great fear or even panic to do whatever is necessary to attract someone who will make us "complete." Failed marriages and equivocating romances are our lot. Some people have to go through two or marriages or more to realize the truth of what I'm saying here.

The Absence of Fatherhood

The Bible is clear that simple loving and connecting fatherhood can solve many problems—including fear, abandonment and rejection in people's lives, but what happens when fathers fail? Malachi 4:5-6 gives us the answer—a curse will fall upon the land where this occurs:

⁵ Behold, I will send you Elijah the prophet before the great and terrible day of the Lord comes.

⁶ And he shall turn and reconcile the hearts of the [estranged] fathers to the [ungodly] children, and the hearts of the [rebellious] children to [the piety of] their fathers [a reconciliation produced by repentance of the ungodly], lest I come and smite the land with a curse and a ban of utter destruction.

Lest anyone doubt that the curse has fallen upon America, read the statistics following this piece by Mark Hamby. Where fatherhood is present, positive results occur, but where it is absent, negative and sometimes horrible results are produced.

You Have Not Many Fathers

Mark Hamby in his book, *You Have Not Fathers,* asks, *"Where is the power of God in the Church today? Where are the mighty men, the apostles and prophets of yore who spoke and nations trembled? God has taken away His excellence from us so that we will return to His ways. God desires to fully restore the Church to the Kingdom. 'He taketh away the first, that he may establish the second' (Heb. 10:9b). God takes away mature leadership, which results in the loss of excellence in leadership:*

And I will give children to be their princes, and babes shall rule over them. And the people shall be oppressed, everyone by another, and every one by his neighbor: the child shall behave himself proudly against the ancient, and the base against the honorable (Isaiah 3:4-5).

When the people of God refuse maturity in Christ, they are judged by losing maturity and having immature individuals in leadership positions. The fathers are replaced with children.

When Paul tells the Corinthians that they have 'ten thousand instructors in Christ, yet have ye not many fathers' (1 Cor. 4:15), he is referring to the root of their problem: a lack of mature father leadership. Instead of having many fathers, they had ten thousand instructors. The word for 'instructor' here in the Greek is paidagogos, which means 'boy-leader.' This term refers to a servant whose official position was to make sure the children went to school. Thus hired servants unrelated to spiritual inheritance substituted fathers.

Today there are thousands of ministry people who have been educated in the finest schools. Many have supplemented their formal education through audio and video as well as through books and magazines from qualified scholarly sources. Although there has never been a greater flood of biblical material available, there are precious few drops of biblical power manifested. We reach millions with information, but without spiritual relationship, impartational truth is not given and received.

The reason we have not seen a manifestation of power in biblical proportions is because we are not giving and receiving impartation by the biblical pattern. We have ten thousand 'boy-leaders' in Christ, but not many fathers.

One of the results of a fatherless church is oppression. Isaiah said, 'And the people shall be oppressed, everyone by another, and every one by his neighbor: the child shall behave himself proudly against the ancient, and the base against the honorable' (Is. 3:5).

A family without a father suffers financially, socially, and psychologically, as well as spiritually. The pressure on single mothers and fatherless children is oppressive. When a father is not present in a home to train the children in matters of the Lord, the hearts of the children turn to rage and they dishonor authority (see Eph. 6:1-4). Oppression occurs when immature rulers serve as baby-sitters over congregations, leading the people without having any true vision. 'Where there is no vision, the people perish' (Prov. 29:18a)."

There is a "Father Factor" in Our Nation's Worst Social Problems

According to the U.S. Census Bureau, 24 million children in America—one out of every three—live in biological father-absent homes. Nine in ten American parents agree this is a "crisis." Consequently, there is a "father factor" in nearly all of the social issues facing America today. But the hope lies in the fact that children with involved fathers do better across every measure of child wellbeing than their peers in father-absent homes.

For more information on the impact of fatherlessness, see http://www. fatherhood.org/father-absence-statistics for data on the positive impact of father involvement, and data on the effects of father absence on poverty, maternal and child health, incarceration, crime, teen pregnancy, child abuse, drug and alcohol abuse, education and childhood obesity.

Here are just some of the statistics on the presence of fathers in America:

The Positive Impact of Father Involvement

Using a sample of resident fathers in the Early Childhood Longitudinal Study- Birth Cohort (9-month Father Study), researchers examined the connection between father involvement and infant cognitive outcomes in two domains (babbling and exploring objects with a purpose). Results indicate that aspects of father involvement, such as cognitively stimulating activities, physical care, paternal warmth, and caregiving activities are associated with lower chances of infant cognitive delay. Findings indicate that early positive father-child interactions reduce cognitive delay. *Source: Bronte-Tinkew, J., Carrano, J., Horowitz, A., & Kinukawa, A. (2008). Involvement among resident fathers and links to infant cognitive outcomes. Journal of Family Issues, 29, 1211-1244.*

A study using data from the National Longitudinal Study of Youth looked at father-child relationship and father's parenting style as predictors of first delinquency and substance use among adolescents in intact families. The results indicate that more positive father-child relationships are associated with reduced risk of engagement in multiple risky behaviors. Even though having a father with an authoritarian parenting style is associated with an increased risk of engaging in delinquent activity and substance use, the negative effect of authoritarian parenting is reduced when there is a positive father-adolescent relationship. Permissive parenting style also predicts less risky behavior when the father-child relationship is positive. The positive influence of the father-child relationship on risk behaviors appears to be stronger for male than for female adolescents. *Source: Bronte-Tinkew, J., Moore, K.A., & Carrano, J.*

(2006). The father-child relationship, parenting styles, and adolescent risk behaviors in intact families. Journal of Family Issues, 27, 850-881.

There is evidence supporting the positive influence of father engagement on children's social, behavioral, and psychological outcomes. Father involvement seems to reduce the occurrence of behavioral problems in boys and psychological problems in young women, as well as enhancing cognitive development, while decreasing delinquency and economic disadvantage in low-income families. *Source: Sarkadi, A., Kristiansson, R., Oberklaid, F., & Bremberg, S. (2008). Fathers' involvement and children's developmental outcomes: a systematic review of longitudinal studies. Acta Pædiatrica, 97, 153–158*

Research provides evidence that fathers can encourage the development of their children's literacy skills. Fathers can promote children reading skills by reading books to them, engaging their children in discussions about books they read, and encouraging their children to read more books. *Source: Saracho, O. N. (2007). Fathers and young children's literacy experiences in a family environment. Early Child Development and Care, 177, 403–415.*

Here now the negative impact because of the absence of fathers:

Father Factor in Poverty

Children in father-absent homes are almost four times more likely to be poor. In 2011, 12 percent of children in married-couple families were living in poverty, compared to 44 percent of children in mother-only families.

Source: U.S. Census Bureau, Children's Living Arrangements and Characteristics: March 2011, Table C8. Washington D.C.: 2011.

In 2008, American poverty rates were 13.2% for the whole population and 19% for children, compared to 28.7% for female-headed households.

Source: Edin, K. & Kissane R. J. (2010). Poverty and the American family: a decade in review. Journal of Marriage and Family, 72, 460-479.

From 1970-1996, there was a 5% increase in child poverty that was nearly all attributed to the rise in single-parent families, especially never-married mothers.

Source: Sawhill, I. V. (2006). Teenage sex, pregnancy, and nonmarital births. Gender Issues, 23, 48-59.

A study of nearly 5,000 children born to parents in 20 large US cities found that unmarried childbearing helped sustain high poverty rates due to multiple partner fertility and relationship instability.

Source: McLanahan, S. (2009). Fragile families and the reproduction of poverty. Annals of the American Academy of Political and Social Science, 621, 111-131.

Back to Top

Father Factor in Emotional and Behavioral Problems

Data from three waves of the Fragile Families Study (N= 2,111) was used to examine the prevalence and effects of mothers' relationship changes between birth and age 3 on their children's well-being. Children born to single mothers show higher levels of aggressive behavior than children born to married mothers. Living in a single-mother household is equivalent to experiencing 5.25 partnership transitions. *Source: Osborne, C., & McLanahan, S. (2007). Partnership instability and child well-being. Journal of Marriage and Family, 69, 1065-1083*

A study of 1,977 children age 3 and older living with a residential father or father figure found that children living with married biological parents had significantly fewer externalizing and internalizing behavioral problems than children living with at least one nonbiological parent. *Source: Hofferth, S. L. (2006). Residential father family type and child well-being: investment versus selection. Demography, 43, 53-78.*

Father Factor in Maternal and Child Health

Infant mortality rates are 1.8 times higher for infants of unmarried mothers than for married mothers.

Source: Matthews, T.J., Sally C. Curtin, and Marian F. MacDorman. Infant Mortality Statistics from the 1998 Period Linked Birth/Infant Death Data Set. National Vital Statistics Reports, Vol. 48, No. 12. Hyattsville, MD: National Center for Health Statistics, 2000.

High-quality interaction by any type of father predicts better infant health.

Source: Carr, D. & Springer, K. W. (2010). Advances in families and health research in the 21st century. Journal of Marriage and Family, 72, 743-761.

Expectant fathers can play a powerful role as advocates of breastfeeding to their wives. Three-fourths of women whose partners attended a breastfeeding promotion class initiated breastfeeding.

Source: Wolfberg, Adam J., et al. "Dads as breastfeeding advocates: results from a randomized controlled trial of an educational intervention." American Journal of Obstetrics and Gynecology 191 (September 2004): 708-712.

Fathers' knowledge about breastfeeding increases the likelihood that a child will be breastfed. Children who fathers knew more had a 1.76 higher chance of being breastfed at the end of the first month and 1.91 higher chance of receiving maternal milk at the end of the third month.

Source: Susin, Lurie R.O. "Does Parental Breastfeeding Knowledge Increase Breastfeeding Rates?" BIRTH 26 (September 1999): 149-155.

A study of 3,400 middle schoolers indicated that not living with both biological parents quadruples the risk of having an affective disorder.

Source: Cuffe, Steven P., Robert E. McKeown, Cheryl L. Addy, and Carol Z. Garrison. "Family Psychosocial Risk Factors in a Longitudinal Epidemiological Study of Adolescents." Journal of American Academic Child Adolescent Psychiatry 44 (February 2005): 121-129.

Summary

These studies indicate the importance of a good father in the maturation and development of a child. Consider the mental impact upon so many of these! Is it any wonder we are seeing a generation of drug-induced children to young adults whose minds are being claimed by Satanic forces bent on their destruction? It's clear that good fathers produce mentally balanced children who don't suffer the same kinds of difficulties that others do.

Door#3 The Occult

The grand deception for people involved in the occult is that Satan actually wants to help the people trapped in this. All he wants is for souls to be taken to hell with him!

The occult is huge in America and elsewhere today. Occultdangers.com says that *"from a Christian perspective, the word 'supernatural' is action, which goes beyond any created nature, which is attributed only to God. Preternatural, which is finite, goes beyond the structure of the nature of the material universe, and is associated with both holy and fallen angels. Supra-human is that which is above and beyond that of a normal human. By the "occult," we are referring to the pursuit or access of preternatural or supra-human knowledge or powers.*

Occult practitioners are those who attempt to pursue knowledge and power from preternatural or supra-human forces. They seek knowledge by forbidden means outside of God's influence or the natural way that human beings use to obtain it. They also seek forbidden power, producing effects apart from God and in a way that is beyond ordinary human means.

There are several events recorded in the Bible where God speaks against occult-based activities. One of these events occurred during the time when God turned over possession of the land of Canaan to the Israelites, just as they were about to enter it. God prohibited and warned the Israelites not to imitate the evil ways of the Canaanites, who were steeped in occult practices.

When you come into the land which the Lord your God is giving you, you shall not learn to imitate the abominations of the people there. Let there not be found among you anyone who immolates his son or daughter in the fire, nor a fortuneteller, soothsayer, charmer, diviner, or caster of spells, nor one who consults ghosts and spirits or seeks oracles from the dead. Anyone who does such things is an abomination to the Lord, and because of such abominations to the Lord, your God is driving these nations out of your way. You, however, must be altogether sincere toward the Lord, your God (Deut. 18:9-13).

Many people from all walks of life are knowingly and deliberately becoming involved in some form of occult practice. Some of these people are using these occult powers with malicious intent to hurt others. And, then there are those who, through lack of knowledge and understanding of its dangerous nature, unknowingly venture into the world of the occult, thinking there is such a thing as "white magic." No, white magic is black.

The devil can tempt us, but he cannot gain dominion over us unless we open a door to him. Anyone who ventures into occult practice opens a door to diabolic influence and the risk of demonic attacks. These attacks can start off with haunting or poltergeist activity, and could possibly lead to demonic oppression or even possession! **Demonic attacks can affect our mental and physical health.** *They can directly impact our family, marriage, business, social relationships, and ultimately our spiritual wellbeing."*

How to Open a Door to the Occult

There are numerous ways, but here are just a few: astrology, astral projection, consulting Ouija boards, palm reading, Edgar Cayce, Eastern meditation, spiritism, Tarot cards, voodoo, witchcraft, Satanism, horror movies, reading books on the occult, involvement in and as a descendant of members of freemasonry, the Eastern Star and their other associations, clairvoyance, handwriting analysis, and the list goes on (see http://occultdangers.com for an extensive list). Actually, seeking power from anyone or anything outside of Jesus Christ can open an occult door. Occult bondage is extremely difficult, oppressive and sometimes even possessive, depending on how far one goes into it. Innocence is no excuse. Once the unknowing person crosses the line, evil can have its say.

I've met one demon-possessed man in my entire life. It was quite obvious. He was in jail, and I was asked to visit him. I saw demons in his eyes as I peered through the bars. He refused to wear clothes and usually threw himself about against the walls of the jail. The police thought he was just mentally ill, and shipped him off the next day to a mental institution before I could return to minister to him. I did get to ask him one question: "Do you want Jesus to set you free?" He nodded his head yes.

Witch Hunt

King Saul, after God stripped the kingdom of Israel from him, sought a witch for advice (ironically, he had previously banned all witches from Israel), and he later died for it as a result. The devil doesn't play fair. He comes to kill, steal and destroy (John 10:10).

According to Dr. MK Strydom, *"Many psychotic mental disorders, for example, multiple personality disorder, schizophrenia and psychosisin and bipolar disorder, are often an insanity that comes from dabbling in occultism – either personally or in your family tree generationally. Diseases that stem from occultism are a result of separation from God and His Word. When the Spirit of God departs, all that man has left is his own tormented mind or a spirit of insanity from the devil, which will cause psychosis. Here fear, torment and deep mental confusion come in.*

"The first evidence of this is fear and torment. 1 John 4:18 in the King James says, "Fear has torment." We see this in the story of King Saul in the Bible. King Saul was anointed by Samuel to be King, and the Spirit of God rested on him to be king. Then he disobeyed the Word of God and listened to the people instead. Because he was no longer a doer of the Word, and he listened to the people, the Spirit of God departed from him and a spirit of insanity came to him.

"So here we have a king that had insanity and what was causing it was an evil spirit. The evil spirit caused a malfunction in the neurochemistry (chemicals in his brain), which lead to an imbalance in thought so that he was no longer in touch with reality. When David came and met Saul, Saul liked him because when David played his Godly music, he felt better. The reason is because the evil spirit causing Saul's insanity could not handle the anointing of the Holy Spirit and so it departed. When the evil spirit left King Saul, he became sane. So did King Saul have a physical problem with

his brain? No. Was there anything wrong with his head? No. Then why should he have insanity?

"Because something that was invisible had joined him that spoke to him as if it were his own mind and he believed it. When king David left, guess what came back shortly thereafter? The evil spirit of insanity. And all of a sudden Saul could no longer think right. So right here is an example of insanity or what we call a psychiatric problem.

"Eventually Saul committed suicide on the battlefield by falling onto his own sword (1 Chronicles 10 v 13 – 14). That is what insanity will do – it will take you to suicide. The World Health Organization says that there are 10 million threatened suicides globally a year and one million are successful.

Many psychotic mental disorders are often an insanity that comes from dabbling in occultism.

Psychosis not only results from involvement in occultism personally, but also generationally upstream in your family tree.

"There is a doctor in Texas in America, who is now practicing medicine, according to the principles that I am sharing with you. There is a case report, which was published in Henry Wright's book, "A More Excellent Way," where he tells the story of how he dealt with a case of psychosis:

"We have seen the Lord do some pretty awesome things here in the past couple of weeks, but He blessed me with a special one yesterday. I had admitted a Hispanic man about 52 years old who had frankly become psychotic over a one-week period of time. When I entered the room Monday on rounds, I realized that there was no objective medical reason to this man's insanity. He had indeed had two small strokes—one distant and one more recently, according to the CT scan, but this did not account for what I was seeing. He was not able to speak and had not spoken in 15 hours. He was writhing in bed with agitation.

"He would not respond to the family or me at all. I began to sense that the Lord wanted to show His power here, so I asked the family if they went to church. They are Catholic. I then asked if I could pray for him. They said yes. I then began to ask

for the Father's peace for the family and for His Presence in the room. I then took authority over the spirit of insanity and fear and cast them out. He immediately quit writhing in agitation. I left and returned in the afternoon. The family told me that as soon as I had left the room, he began to talk. He is now lucid and speaking quite normally today. I explained to the family that this is a miracle of God."

Witchcraft's Destruction

Sarah C. Corriher, who has extensively studied witchcraft and the occult in England, which is growing in increasing popularity, says, "Many people journey into the occult due to a combination of rebellion and curiosity. When this rebellion occurs in adults, it is usually a response to their feelings of rage toward either society or God. In many cases, God appears unwilling to give them the *power* that they desire; so they turn to other (darker) sources of empowerment.

"In teenagers, this rebellion may either be against God, or against parental authorities. For what rebellion could be worse than to veer down a deceptive path of evil, and for parents to have no clue about their child's safety: either emotionally, or physically? What parental nightmare is worse than having one's own child manipulated, and fed lies against both parents and morality in general, so that their child may commune with Satanic people?

"Angry teens turn down the path of the occult in order to create these fears, and as a type of revenge. In far too many cases; their lives are destroyed in the process. For the teenagers who are reading this: if you truly have bad parents, then you must remember that your best revenge is success. Self-destruction will only vindicate deplorable parents."

The occult is massive. Satan has legitimized it in American through ignorance, as foolish people submit their hearts to his whims. "Psychic Hotlines," getting in to touch with the dead (these are familiar spirits that imitate loved ones who have died), encouraging black magic and witchcraft as harmless fun and other forms of channeling have opened wide the door.

The Beautiful Side of Evil

Once a victim of the occult, Johanna Michaelsen, always seemed to have magical spiritual gifts, but was deceived by very dark forces when she was just a little girl. Even after she dedicated her life to the Lord, the occult had a strong grip on her soul. Johanna's "fellowship" with demons brought her indescribable depression and despair.

For many years she was caught up in the occult, yet she believed that the "angels" who reached out to her were servants of God, not Satan. One demon convinced her that he was Jesus, and she thought she was doing all of these things for the Christ of the Bible.

Michaelsen is a noted author, researcher, lecturer and authority on the occult. Her internationally best-selling autobiography, *The Beautiful Side of Evil*, tells the story of her involvement with the occult, yoga, and Silva Mind Control.

She left the occult 30 years ago and has dedicated her service to Jesus Christ warning others about the dangerously deceptive practices that are sweeping our nation—and our churches.

There are literally hundreds of thousands of people throughout the world like Joanna who once was confused by the seemingly harmless appearing doors into the occult. Relying on their education, human reasoning and sometimes mockery of the Bible's admonitions, they open wide the door to this dangerous involvement. Hell's reach is endless, and its strong grip would be fatal were it not for the saving power of Jesus Christ and people who know their authority over Satan and his schemes.

Door#4 Sex Sins

Sex is the most widely promoted "product" in the world; it's everywhere. It fills most every TV show, movie, magazine and, of course, the Internet. The power and lure of sex in undeniable. It sells and it sells big! Most every advertisement contains some sexual relevance from selling automobiles ("it's the sexy European" – cars are sexy?) to voluptuous woman biting down on a humongous Hardee's burger. All this seems so alluring, as Hollywood purveys it to our eyes and minds. Beautiful people of all types beckon the unwary to partake. It all looks so amazingly beautiful and innocent... God had other plans to discourage involvement, which we can so easily justify. He planned it for marriage and marriage alone to draw a covenant keeping couple together for life, but somewhere before or after "I do," the pull to experience sex often becomes too much.

Porn is Big Business!

Statistics provided by Covenant Eyes, an Internet filtering service, reveals that porn is big business. Just seven years ago, global porn revenues were estimated at $20 billion, with $10 billion coming from US consumers. However, by 2011 both global and U.S. porn revenues had been *reduced* by 50%, due in large part to the amount of free pornography available online. It is estimated that 80-90% of Internet porn users only access free online material.

As far as online pornography is concerned, from 2001 to 2007, the Internet porn industry went from a $1-billion-a-year industry to $3-billion-a-year in the US alone.

Porn is a dangerous business

On average, 17% of performers use condoms in heterosexual porn films. Sixty-six percent of porn performers have herpes, and 7% of porn performers have HIV. Ex-porn star Tanya Burleson says men and women in pornography do drugs because "they can't deal with the way they're being treated" in the industry. A 2012 survey of porn actresses demonstrated 79% of porn stars have used marijuana, 50% have used ecstasy, 44% have used cocaine, and 39% have used hallucinogens.

When hundreds of scenes were analyzed from the 50 top selling adult films, 88% of scenes contained acts of physical aggression, and 49% of scenes contained verbal aggression.

All Types of People Look at Internet Porn

Paul Fishbein, founder of Adult Video News, is right when he says, *"Porn doesn't have a demographic—it goes across all demographics."* After an analysis of 400 million web searches, researchers concluded that 1 in 8 of all searches online are for erotic content.

Who is more likely to seek out pornography online? According to data taken from Internet users who took part in the General Social Survey:

Men are 543% *more* likely to look at porn than females.

Those who are politically more liberal are 19% *more* likely to look at porn.

Those who have ever committed adultery are 218% *more* likely to look at porn.

Those who have ever engaged in paid sex are 270% *more* likely to look at porn.

Those who are happily married are 61% *less* likely to look at porn.

Those with teen children at home are 45% *less* likely to look at porn.

Regular church attenders are 26% *less* likely to look at porn than non-attenders, but those self-identified as "fundamentalists" are 91% *more* likely to look at porn.

Mobile porn is increasing in popularity

After an analysis of more than one million hits to Google's mobile search sites, more than 1 in 5 searches are for pornography on mobile devices.

By the end of 2015, mobile adult content and services are expected to reach $2.8 billion, mobile adult subscriptions will reach nearly $1 billion, and mobile adult video on tablets will triple worldwide.

It is common for teens to see porn.

In a 2010 national survey, over a quarter of 16 to 17-year olds said they were exposed to nudity online *when they did not want to see it*. In addition

20% of 16-year-olds and 30% of 17-year-olds have received a "sext" (a sexually explicit text message).

More than 7 out of 10 teens hide their online behavior from their parents in some way.

35% of boys say they have viewed pornographic videos "too many times to count."

More than half of boys and nearly a third of girls see their first pornographic images before they turn 13. In a survey of hundreds of college students, 93% of boys and 62% of girls said they were exposed to pornography before they turned 18. In the same survey, 83% of boys and 57% of girls said they had seen images of group sex online.

It is Common for Young Adults to Use Porn

About 64-68% of young adult men and about 18% of women use porn at least once every week. Another 17% of men and another 30% of women use porn 1-2 times per month. Two-thirds of college-age men and half of college-age women say viewing porn is an acceptable way to express one's sexuality.

Porn is Destroying Families

The American Academy of Matrimonial Lawyers reports that 56% of divorce cases involve one party having "an obsessive interest in pornographic websites."

According to numerous studies, prolonged exposure to pornography leads to:

a diminished trust between intimate couples

the belief that promiscuity is the natural state

cynicism about love or the need for affection between sexual partners

the belief that marriage is sexually confining

a lack of attraction to family and child-raising

So *what's* the big deal? It wars against your soul:

Beloved, I beg of you, as wayfarers and as foreigners, depart from all these desires of the body that make war against the soul (1 Peter 2:11 Aramaic Bible).

The mind is part of what is considered the soul. According to the Apostle Peter, this war with lust causes one to "boil over."

Skip Moen, "What Boils Over" (posted February 23, 2006, updated on May 15, 2010) said, *"The Greeks knew the underlying essence of lust. Lust is what makes you boil over. Lust is that force that grips you with its power and causes you to explode. Lust is passion unbridled. In fact, the Greek word itself shows us this background. Epi and thumos combine to mean "out of violent movement of the mind" (epithumia). Lust is the volcanic reaction that occurs when your mind says, "I've got to have that now!" It isn't accidental that the word thumos is also associated with wrath and anger.* **Lust drives us insane.**

Every addict knows the power of epithumia, the addictive force that refuses to be denied, that will not be satiated, and that has a mind of its own. That's why addicts often refer to themselves as two people; one who is rational and under control and the other who is a slave to the addiction. Every addict also knows that there is no hope of gaining freedom by just deciding to change. An addict is at war with himself."

James Dobson's Interview with Ted Bundy

At 7 a.m. on Tuesday, January 24, 1989, convicted serial killer Ted Bundy was put to death in the electric chair at Florida State Prison. He admitted that he murdered more than 12 young women, but it is widely believed he may have killed many more. In Bundy's final and exclusive interview, conducted by Focus on the Family President James Dobson, Bundy takes viewers back to his roots, explaining the development of his compulsive behavior. He reveals his addiction to hard-core pornography and how it fueled the terrible crimes he committed. Bundy warns that within our society are men like him, whose violent tendencies are being encouraged by pornography. A controversial presentation, recorded just hours before

Bundy's execution, "Fatal Addiction," is the story of a tormented man, a man caught between the right and wrong he learned as a child and his plunge into the dark world of hard-core, violent pornography.

Often people, rather than allowing the Lord to sanctify their soul, engage in sex sins that war against it, setting them at odds with God. Anyone with any knowledge of the Bible knows it's the central theme of the Old Testament in which God's covenant people constantly fell into the clutches of idolatry and the worship of male and female deities (demons) that were often placated by sex orgies and even human sacrifice.

It continued into the days of the New Covenant and has remained a thorn in the side of most every human being who has taken his or her first breath. So what's the difference between this and Internet porn, sex trafficking, premarital sex and adultery? Nothing—just worse with every climb to another pleasure seeking height! All this nonsense about "consenting adults" is simply nonsense, a cultural excuse for our bad behavior. You certainly won't find the excuse you may be looking for in the Bible because there are no loopholes! The lack of cultural mores in the do-whatever society are destroying lives daily. A quick glimpse at the news provides a morbid view of this ever-unfolding picture.

Truth or Consequences?

The pleasure principle sometimes rules over us, and what happens? Another door is opened for Satan to enter into. Some may escape sex addiction or being overcome with lust, but it isn't likely. At the least we lose our intimacy with God the Father because our spirits were designed for total and complete fellowship with Him, and we absolutely lose sensitivity to His Spirit when we share our spirit with another person outside the marriage covenant:

Do you not see and know that your bodies are members (bodily parts) of Christ (the Messiah)? Am I therefore to take the parts of Christ and make [them] parts of a prostitute? Never! Never! Or do you not know and realize that when a man joins himself to a prostitute, he becomes one body with her? The two, it is written, shall become one flesh. But the person who is united to the Lord becomes one spirit with Him. Shun immorality and all sexual looseness [flee from impurity in thought, word, or deed]. Any other sin which a man commits is one outside the body, but he who commits sexual immorality sins against his own body. Do you not know that your body is the temple (the very sanctuary) of the Holy Spirit Who lives within you, Whom you have received [as a Gift] from God? You are not your own, You were bought with a price [purchased with a ᵇpreciousness and paid for, ᶜmade His own]. So then, honor God and bring glory to Him in your body (1 Cor. 6:16-19 AMP)

Don't you know that anyone who is joined to someone who is sleeping around is one body with that person? The scripture says, The two will become one flesh (1 Cor. 6:16 CEB).

There's more to sex than mere skin on skin. Sex is as much spiritual mystery as physical fact. As written in Scripture, "The two become one." Since we want to become spiritually one with the Master, we must not pursue the kind of sex that avoids commitment and intimacy, leaving us more lonely than ever—the kind of sex that can never "become one." There is a sense in which sexual sins are different from all others. In sexual sin we violate the sacredness of our own bodies, these bodies that were made for God-given and God-modeled love, for "becoming one" with another. Or didn't you realize that your body is a sacred place, the place of the Holy Spirit? Don't you see that you can't live however you please, squandering what God paid such a high price for? The physical part of you is not some piece of property belonging to the spiritual part of you. God owns the whole works. So let people see God in and through your body (1 Cor. 6:16-20 The Message).

One Body, One Flesh

This should scare the living daylights out of anyone who understands the implications of what these verses are saying. For each person with whom you sexually share your body, you become ONE with them! And we wonder why our spirit may be reaching out to everyone we've committed sex with? Why a married man or woman wonders why they are craving someone else, even someone on a screen somewhere or a page in a magazine?!

It's one thing for Hollywood or anywhere else where sex is not valued as holy by the society – they will pay a terrible price! But for Christians who are washed in the Blood of Jesus to do this, it becomes a travesty. I ministered to a man not long ago who had been with 85 different women, not including his wife. The good news for the repentant is that Jesus' Blood can cleanse each transgression, and forgiveness reigns so that the person who has defiled himself or herself can become a virgin once again. Think of this... If your spirit is joined to another multiple others– **what does that do to your mind?**

Toxic Relationships

As humans we all desire relationships. However, they can become toxic. Our dependence upon another person, other than God, to provide for our peace and security becomes a thorn in our flesh. This explains why people who are abused by another will cling to the abuser—for security reasons. Their need for someone is addictive because the brain is demanding that chemistry needs are met! Hurt and rejection repeatedly seem not to matter to the abused. The addiction to some kind of "chemistry high" will go to no extreme to ensure something happens to quell the storm in the mind.

The threat to a relationship causes fear to erupt that demands action on the part of the "needy" one. It is a sad but true scenario. Apparently, the chemistry, previously mentioned, is huge in bipolar disorder because of the sensations produced or lack of them in determining high or low experiences. Much fear and anxiety are produced because of the wounding in relationships, beginning with our mothers and fathers, or those who exercise significant influence over our hearts and minds. Once the deficit occurs in brain chemistry, a search is underway for someone to bring the healing. Usually we look for a man or woman to provide this, which often results in much disappointment and another cycle of "the search."

The Role of Obsession in Open Doors

We can become obsessed with just about anything—sex, alcohol, drugs, sports, cars, food, rock stars, women and men, lifestyles, Hollywood, movies, TV, Christian teachers and preachers, religion (notice I'd didn't write true spirituality), living in certain sections of the country, prejudice, politics, denominations, national pride, war—you fill in the blanks. Who are what could you be obsessing over?

Obsession is defined by Merriam-Webster Dictionary as "a state in which someone thinks about someone or something constantly or frequently especially in a way that is not normal;

Someone or something that a person thinks about constantly or frequently; an activity that someone is very interested in or spends a lot of time doing. The full definition is as follows: a persistent disturbing preoccupation with an often unreasonable idea or feeling; *broadly* compelling motivation i.e. an *obsession* with profits."

Once obsession begins it ties the brain to compulsions and impulsivity, the results in the brain can be startling and highly revealing, as Cambridge University researchers have discovered with Obsessive-Compulsive Disorder (OCD).

Cambridge researchers have discovered that measuring activity in a region of the brain could help to identify people at risk of developing obsessive-compulsive disorder. As the current diagnosis of OCD is based on a clinical interview and often does not occur until the disorder has progressed, this could enable earlier more objective detection, and intervention.

The scientists have discovered that people with OCD and their close family members show under-activation of brain areas responsible for stopping habitual behavior. This is the first time that scientists have associated functional changes in the brain with familial risk for the disorder.

OCD is a debilitating condition that affects 2-3% of the population at some point in life. Patients suffer from recurrent intrusive thoughts (obsessions) that are distressing and hard to suppress. Examples include fears of contamination, or that something terrible will happen to a loved one. They also suffer from repetitive rituals (compulsions), which are often designed to neutralize these thoughts. Examples include hand-washing and checking oven gas hobs. These symptoms cause distress and can occupy hours during the day, interfering with quality of life and the ability to work.

Although OCD tends to run in families, genetic factors responsible for this heritability are not known. Genes may pose a risk for OCD by influencing how the brain develops. Dr. Samuel Chamberlain at the University of Cambridge's Department of Psychiatry used functional magnetic resonance imaging (fMRI) to measure brain activity in the lateral orbitofrontal cortex (OFC).

Located in the frontal lobes the lateral OFC is involved in decision-making and behavior.

Volunteers were asked to look at two pictures on a screen, each image had a house and a face superimposed. The volunteers were asked to use trial and error to work out whether the house or face was the correct target. Volunteers pressed a button to indicate which image they believed to be the target and feedback of 'correct' or 'incorrect' was given on the screen. After the correct target had been identified six times in a row it changed so the volunteer had to learn again. MRI was used to monitor their patterns of brain activity throughout.

Fourteen volunteers without a family history of OCD, 14 people with OCD and 12 immediate relatives of these patients took the picture test. Later comparison of MRI images of their brain activity throughout showed under-activation in the lateral orbitofrontal cortex and other brain areas in both the OCD patients and their family members.

Dr. Chamberlain, who led the study, explains, *"Impaired function in brain Areas controlling flexible behavior probably predisposes people to developing the compulsive rigid symptoms that are characteristic of OCD. This study shows that these brain changes run in families and represent a candidate vulnerability factor. The current diagnosis of OCD is subjective and improved understanding of the underlying causes of OCD could lead to more accurate diagnosis and improved clinical treatments.*

"However, much work is still needed to identify the genes contributing to abnormal brain function in those at risk of OCD. We also need to investigate not only vulnerability factors, but also protective factors that account for why many people at genetic risk of the condition never go on to develop the symptoms."

This research was funded by the Medical Research Council and Wellcome Trust.

/1002721/ScienceDaily_Mobile_Top_Rectangle

Story Source:

The above story is based on materials provided by University of Cambridge. *Note: Materials may be edited for content and length.*

It's interesting to note again that scientists find that an area that seems to be the problem but are unsure of the cause. Genetics or brain formation? But how much of this could be related to the idolatry that follows family lines or fear, or the occult or sexual bondage? Likely the majority of it.

Corinth, America

Corinth of First Corinthians Bible fame, the city referred to here, was well known for its sexual immorality, for the popular "religion" of the day was to "worship" by visiting the Temple of Aphrodite, which had up to 2000 "priestesses," aka, "religious prostitutes!" We shrink back from this fact in judgmental disgust, and yet we find ourselves living in a **"Corinthianized Culture"** in America, a culture in which morality has been discarded and replaced with an open minded, politically correct, anything goes attitude.

Sites and sounds on television today would have resulted in a show in the 1950s being removed from the airwaves and possibly even subjected to criminal charges. While the Internet has many good aspects, it is also a veritable sewer of unspeakable devilish evil, a sewer easily accessible even by children! Make no mistake, believers are at war with the fallen world (James 4:4; 1Jn 2:15-17).

Therefore in this section Paul is giving all disciples of Christ strategic instructions that will enable us to navigate the increasingly murky immoral waters of our post-Christian society. And hey, unless you are living in a corner somewhere, you are not immune to these noxious, defiling influences. As Jesus prayed (Jn 17:17), we need daily to be sanctified by the truth of His Word, yes, even by the washing of the water of His Word Eph 5:26, Jn 13:10).

Enabled by Truth and the indwelling Spirit we need to practice "pure and undefiled religion in the sight of our God and Father" and "keep ourselves unstained by the world" (James 1:27). "Beloved, let us cleanse ourselves (OUR "TEMPLES" inhabited by God!) from all defilement of flesh and spirit, perfecting holiness in the fear of God." (2 Cor 7:1) "If you address as Father the One who impartially judges according to each one's work, conduct yourselves in fear during the time of your stay on earth" (1Pet 1:17).

The bottom line in many cases is what the Scripture refers to as "Hope deferred makes the heart sick." This really speaks of the afflictions against our souls because of the serious delays in life for many of us.

How is this healed? Find out in the next chapter.

CHAPTER 6

Hope Deferred Makes the Heart Sick!

Hope deferred makes the heart sick,

But when desire is fulfilled, it is a tree of life (Prov. 13:12 Amp).

Hope that is deferred afflicteth the soul: desire when it cometh is a tree of life (Prov. 13:12

Douay-Rheims Bible).

This verse explains a lot about life. A great deal of what we expect to happen is delayed, perhaps for hours, days, years or even decades. And let's face it, some things for some people are never realized in this life. In understanding a good bit about what makes people tick or not tick so well, it's occurred to me through my own experiences that this one verse holds the key to a great deal of happiness or much sorrow, and consequently, psychosomatic sickness.

In the Douay-Rheims translation the phrase, "afflicteth the soul," is used. If you study the Hebrew translation of this entire verse, afflicted is dead on the money. How so?

Kingdom of God or the Magic Kingdom?

Many years ago I was riding my lawnmower (I liked to refer to it as a tractor), and the Holy Spirit spoke to me and said, "My people think my kingdom is the Magic Kingdom!" I understood the Lord to say that people have great expectations and dreams, some of which may come from the Lord (spiritual) while others merely come out of their souls – an expression of their own minds and emotions, and, quite frankly, willfulness to obtain. Some people–Christians included–will disobey God to **make** *their* dreams come true! We can use the word   stubborn here because some people are very stubborn when it comes to what they've decided is due them in life. We're often told as Christians "not to let go of our dreams," as if the one delivering the message assumes all our dreams come from the Lord! This can be very dangerous because… what if this thing we've decided is our destiny isn't from the Lord?! We need to know this isn't the Magic Kingdom!

In one sense our ticket to the Magic Kingdom has more to do with human dreams to attain rather than the 21 God-given dreams, as they appear in the Bible, which were directional, prophetic and destiny changing. If our dreams are humanly derived, they may be delayed indefinitely, again with much sorrow. But let's proceed with the idea that some of your dreams are God-given. What happens, however, when dreams, or more correctly, expectations, are deferred? The answer is "afflictions of the soul" that come in many shapes because of the stress that's involved. (We all know that anywhere from 75-90 percent of illnesses are stress-related.) Here's a list of mental possibilities: depression, despair, discouragement, dejection, rage, anger and anger that leads to murder (James 4:2-3), sleeplessness, bitterness, jealousy, indifference, apathy, and suicide, to name a few. On the physical side we could have migraines, all kinds of gastrointestinal difficulties including ulcers, arthritis, high blood pressure, chronic fatigue syndrome, bipolar disorder, adrenal fatigue, skin diseases, heart disease and even cancer.

Recognition

How do you recognize hope deferred? It's relatively simple. Whatever or whomever you've wanted in life, and it/they have always eluded you, no matter what you did or how many times you pursued it/them, you're looking at hope deferred. It could be a sickness that just won't go away, no matter how much prayer, confessing Scripture or fasting you've done. It could be the pursuit of a degree of some kind, financial solvency, a marriage without contention and strife, or that ever-evasive sweetheart you've always desired. This hope or desire could have been life-long or simply existed for a few years, which could seem like hundreds of years!

Hope deferred is a type of "prison" for which seemingly no amount of counseling, psychiatrists seen or prophecies received is the answer; the result could be you're still waiting and hoping. Consider also, some people have such small dreams and visions that hope deferred can't even be recognized, or in the case of some fortunate and very happy people (very small percentage of these), hope deferred is just a small bump in the road, but this is highly unlikely. Usually, well-meaning people (are these Job's buddies?) can present you with knee-jerk often ill-thought out responses to your dilemma. Here are a few, and they are indeed possibilities: "You've got a blocking demon." "You don't have enough faith." "You have a victim spirit." "Remember: Moses was 80 when he got the call" (don't you just love that one?). "You're obviously harboring a terrible sin in your life." You get the picture.

Hard as Nails but Not Quite!

Hope deferred is, beyond a shadow of a doubt, one of the most difficult, troubling, dismaying strongholds to overcome. And, yes, I'd classify this as a stronghold indeed! For one thing if we believe God has something good for us, and it seems out of reach after much trial and tribulation, we may simply discard it as not God's will, or as I wrote earlier, we may become indifferent in between bouts of anger and depression that this simply isn't going to happen! I'm a *Rocky* fan. Yeah, I know these movies were sometimes hokey at best, but I loved the fact that Rocky got clobbered over and over again, only to get his butt off the canvas and say to the baddest dude he was now facing in his dumb-sounding Philadelphia accent, "You ain't so bad!"

I love the biblical phrase used concerning Abraham's faith – "hope beyond hope." This is the kind of hope (expectation) that is needed when hopelessness replaces our *God-given* dreams:

*And without hope he believed in hope that he would be the father to the multitude of the nations according to what is written: "Thus shall your seed be (*Romans 4:18 Aramaic Bible in Plain English).

This verse is an oxymoron at face value, but that's the way of the kingdom of God. In this equation you have human hope, with its flag-waving for a while that if we just try a little harder, things will work out. But that's not what this verse is saying at all! Abraham knew his body was as good as dead so it was IMPOSSIBLE for him (his virility was gone) to have a child and thus fulfill the promise of God that he (Abraham) would become "the father of many nations." Its important here to note that faith is a gift of God (Eph. 2:9), whether it's found in the Old Testament or the New. In effect, Abraham received the gift of faith to trust God (hope beyond human hope) that God would deliver. For us, we need faith in our spirit to believe that hope deferred no longer will be!

…But Joy (or Desire) Realized is a Tree of Life!

Christians have a lot of "refrigerator verses," some of which are not found on refrigerators! One I've heard repeatedly in the last few years is Jeremiah 29:11, which to me, has become almost "shopworn":

For I know the plans I have for you," declares the LORD, "plans to prosper you and not to harm you, plans to give you hope and a future.

This one just rolls off people's tongues so easily in modern day America, but the promise was actually given to those Jews exiled to Babylon, who had to carry out a 70-year sentence of captivity decreed by God. In verses 8-9 false prophets kept telling the Jews, "You'll be going home soon," and the people, who were so anxious for good news, believed them. To the contrary, God told them to "settle in, build homes, and raise kids, etc., because you're going to be here until times up!" This reminds me of hope deferred. We are often not willing to walk out the cost of receiving the promise, which may require a great deal of us as our faith is stretched to the max:

Do not, therefore, fling away your [fearless] confidence, for it has a glorious and great reward. [36] For you have need of patient endurance [to bear up under difficult circumstances without compromising], so that when you have carried out the will of God, you may receive and enjoy to the full what is promised (Heb. 10:35-36 Amp).

I like quick answers from the Lord, but often they are not forthcoming. A preacher-friend once told me, "Soon to God is at least five years!" Was he being cynical after walking with the Lord for 50 years? No, just realistic. I heard of a very well-known prophet who schooled hundreds, maybe thousands in the prophetic gift, who had a prophetic word fulfilled exactly 50 years from the time it was given—on the day of his ordination!

Character Building

When all is said and done in this life, becoming like Christ is more important than anything we ever do. Gifts aren't going to heaven; works will be judged there, but how much we look like Jesus when we stand before the Son of God one day will be the most important thing on God's agenda (Rom. 8:29). Hope deferred, like it or not (and frankly, I've hated it!), builds character. But how is "the tree of life fulfilled" or joy realized? I think there are several important considerations:

Consider it may take a long time as God builds His character in you.

Understand that your own stubbornness concerning His will may be holding you up.

A lack of repentance of the negativity I wrote about earlier—bitterness, anger, resentment, etc., are wall-builders against realizing your dream from the Lord.

Is your dream of human origin, or is it divine? (I often think of people who, say, have a "dream" of winning the 100-meter dash in the Olympics. They kill themselves for years, pushing past every obstacle, to overcome and finally their "dream" comes true. This is all well and good, and I admire this kind of courage and determination, but who got glory in the end? Themselves, their country or God? Do you remember who won the men's 100-meter dash in the last summer Olympics? (I don't but I guess I could Google it.) My point is some "dreams" are for this life only.

What does it take to satisfy your heart? The right job? Marriage partner? Early retirement? All the sex you can stand? Are we like Paul who was after "the high calling in Christ Jesus," or have we accepted something much lower on the shelf, which is much less than what God desires for us?

It may be your dream—even if it's divine—may need to go to the cross to remove the selfishness that's wrapped itself so neatly and carefully around it. Believe me, if it's divine, you'll receive it – the cross won't kill it!

The Tree of Life

In our text verse, the tree of life could be any number of things, but we have to first recall the Tree of Life in the Garden of Eden. It stood opposed to and diametrically opposite the Tree of the Knowledge of Good and Evil. The Tree of Life was a spiritual tree that was the essence of Jesus Christ and what he offers us -- To seek Him first and the kingdom of God, and all the other stuff will be added (Matt. 6:33 Beckham Translation). The Tree of the Knowledge of Good and Evil was a tree that was the essence of the flesh – pride, vanity, ego, "Me, myself and Irene." The choice was made there, and it was horrendous!

The other possibility is the Tree of Life found in Revelation. Note here the qualities of this remarkable tree-- it monthly bears fruit, and its leaves are for the healing of the nations:

Then he showed me a river of the water of life, [a]clear as crystal, coming from the throne of God and of [b]the Lamb, 2 in the middle of its street. On either side of the river was the tree of life, bearing twelve [c]kinds of fruit, yielding its fruit every month; and the leaves of the tree were for the healing of the nations (Rev. 22:1-2).

I believe in overcoming hope deferred, we become like one of these trees of life, bearing fruit for the kingdom of God and offering our "leaves" as healing to those around us. As we consider hope deferred, we must understand the difference between God's expectations and ours.

Hope Against Hope: His Expectations and Ours

"Expectation is the root of all heartache."

— William Shakespeare

A clear understanding or misunderstanding of expectations can make or break us in life. We often fail to distinguish between God's expectations and ours. I think much of this is due to our inability to distinguish between spirit and soul (Heb. 4:12). Our expectations are most often based on past experiences and successes and/or a wishful hope that things will turn out the way we have conceived and planned them in our minds (soul).

Sometimes this soulish thing works, and sometimes it doesn't. If our expectations are high and certain, and they emanate from our own souls, and if the thing doesn't work out, discouragement, despair and sometimes hopelessness and even suicide for some—often follow. And even if we have a clear word from God, delays, detours and "things going south," will kill the hope we once held so tightly in our grip. So much for human hope. On the other hand, a clear realization, grounded in our spirits, can save us a great deal of trouble. We can remain steadfast in trouble rather than coming apart at the seams. Jesus put it this way: *"In your patience possess your souls"* (Luke 21:19).

Life is filled with people who have had grandiose expectations only to find themselves in the soup line of despair. "It wasn't supposed to be this way," we often hear. Face it, hard work and skill don't necessarily provide a ticket to successful living, nor does prayer and "living right" guarantee a country garden in the shade. Today's economy, an unexpected or inexplicable illness, job loss or an inheritance that somehow eluded us can spell emotional, financial and physical disaster.

Reality Bites

Many people, and often Christians themselves, have somehow missed the point that this life doesn't necessarily guarantee smooth sailing.

Reality bites, no matter whose latest CD you bought to ensure "it" won't happen. Present day faith teachers often fail to prepare people for worse case scenarios, but the Bible does because it wasn't written just to please us. Hence, people are sometimes angry and disappointed in God. "Why God?" fills our thoughts and conversations.

I write this as "the ruling monarch of failed expectations," so I can give you the guided tour into the land of depression, despair and hopelessness because of my misinterpretation of the Lord's expectations, his timing and my willfulness and self-centeredness. Clarifying His expectations and ours is indeed hard ground to plow for anyone—even those most sold out to the will of God. We expect victory, and defeat is waiting at the door. We prepare diligently for that new job and fall flat on our faces during the interview. We have "a word" that God is giving us a baby girl, and lo, and behold, bubba crawls out of the womb! We ask for "this cup to pass," only to have to drink the whole thing.

Jerry Lee Lewis sang, "There's whole lotta shakin' goin' on." If you haven't experienced this yet, your turn will come. Hebrews 12:27-29 says the Lord's shaking will shake everything that can be shaken! And this includes governments, business, cultures, ethnic groups, families, the church and us! The reason for this is to leave what can remain—things not seen like our faith and the kingdom. God sometimes allows things to fall to pieces, which don't have His stamp of approval i.e. works built on sand, human endeavors but not born of the Spirit of God, and, yes, our expectations!

Human expectations can be filled with Eros (fleshly self-centeredness), often motivated by our own desires and the three uglies – acquire, possess and control. If you haven't guessed it by now, human expectations need to go to the cross to be stripped of selfish ambition. In the vernacular, you need to let them die, baby! If we don't do this, we'll often fail to grow up and will continue with our roller coaster emotional responses.

The Good News

The good news is found in the opposite of all this, HIS expectations, which is peace and rest, real hope and power. David said, "Find rest, O my soul, in God alone; my hope (expectation) comes from him" (Psa. 62:5). David, through many trials, found that real hope was found only in God Himself and not through his own view of what life was or is supposed to be. Abraham exemplified this best when God asked him to kill his own expectation – Issac – so faith could be tested. Father Abraham had an expectation based on the reality of God's resurrection power. He got something in his spirit that God would raise up Issac—even if he sacrificed him! Whoa!

"Abraham was first named "father" and then became a father because he dared to trust God to do what only God could do: raise the dead to life, with a word make something out of nothing. When everything was hopeless, Abraham believed anyway, deciding to live not on the basis of what he saw he couldn't do but on what God said he would do" (Romans 4:18, The Message).

"Abraham reasoned that if Isaac died, God was able to bring him back to life again. And in a sense, Abraham did receive his son back from the dead" (Hebrews 11:19, New Living Translation).

One of my favorite life verses is Proverbs 16:3 (Amplified). Notice how God can cause our thoughts (expectations) to be made to agree with His will, but we must roll them upon Him!

"Roll your works upon the Lord [commit and trust them wholly to Him; He will cause your thoughts to become agreeable to His will, and] so shall your plans be established and succeed."

If we keep pushing for our agenda without realizing it's not in His will—or at least the timing is wrong—we can be forever perplexed or worse bitter at God because He won't give in to our petitions. The other side of this consideration is that of character building so real love (agape) can be found to endure. After all, this is what this whole trip is about (1 Cor. 13)!

The caveat here is that our ability to distinguish the difference between our expectations and real hope can be very costly and painful. Our inner being will scream "no fair, God!" while He works a deeper work of faith in us that based on a revelation of the Holy Spirit. "But God, that prophet said you would do this!" "Hey, Father, I confessed that scripture until my lips bled." "Lord, I prayed my guts about this in faith, and you didn't answer me!" The real truth is "faith formulas," systematic and humanistic goals aren't necessarily going to find favor in His bigger plans. We often forget the eternal purpose and work of God just might not include our hopes and dreams while we progressively "vaporize" on Planet Earth.

Real hope and expectation come from God. As I have tried to say here, that which is "manufactured" by soulish efforts may work for a while, but we'll learn when stuff starts to hit the fan that only God's hope, which is the anchor of the soul, will work. True revelation comes from God's spirit to ours, and we would be very foolish indeed to waste our lives trusting in our own insights. Real hope offers us three things: joy, peace and power from His Holy Spirit:

Now the God of hope fill you with all joy and peace in believing; that you may abound in hope, and in the power of the Holy Ghost (Rom. 15:13).

What Does God Expect?

This question is usually a doozy for all of us, especially if we're serious about our walk with God. And we should be:

"For we must all appear and be revealed as we are before the judgment seat of Christ, so that each one may receive [his pay] according to what he has done in the body, whether good or evil [considering what his purpose and motive have been, and what he has achieved, been busy with, and given himself and his attention to accomplishing]"

(2 Cor. 5:10 (Amplified).

This appearance isn't to determine our salvation but what we did with God's Son once we accepted Him into our life. This holy fire of God will test the kind of work, its motivation—for His glory or for self-glory—the substance of which the Bible describes as "wood, hay and straw" or "silver, gold and precious stones." The first group of deeds will burn, while the second remains and results in rewards:

"*According to the grace (the special endowment for my task) of God bestowed on me, like a skillful architect and master builder I laid [the] foundation, and now another [man] is building upon it. But let each [man] be careful how he builds upon it,* [11] *For no other foundation can anyone lay than that which is [already] laid, which is Jesus Christ (the Messiah, the Anointed One).* [12] *But if anyone builds upon the Foundation, whether it be with gold, silver, precious stones, wood, hay, straw,* [13] *The work of each [one] will become [plainly, openly] known (shown for what it is); for the day [of Christ] will disclose and declare it, because it will be revealed with fire, and the fire will test and critically appraise the character and worth of the work each person has done.* [14] *If the work, which any person has built on this Foundation [any product of his efforts whatever] survives [this test], he will get his reward.* [15] *But if any person's work is burned up [under the test], he will suffer the loss [of it all, losing his reward], though he himself will be saved, but only as [one who has passed] through fire*" (I Cor. 3:10-15).

I hasten to add that I don't believe the "evil" mentioned in the 2 Cor. 5:10 is about sins committed – once repented of they are forgiven and remembered no more – Jer. 31:34, so why would those be brought up again? The word evil, the word "poneron" in the Greek, can be rendered as "bad." So we could see these as "bad works" as opposed to "good works."

Summarizing the Judgment Seat

My guess is you've not heard many sermons, if any, on these passages, which, in effect, are tied together regarding the judgment seat of Christ. Before we move on to discuss other aspects of "What God Expects," let's consider several things found in these texts.

1) Paul warns that we should, after making Christ our foundation for building our lives, be careful how we build.

2) We should understand that our motivations for service should be done for God's glory and not to impress others or for selfish kingdom building.

3) Our works will be open before God, with no excuses for our lack because He is omniscient and therefore, keenly aware of every reason why we couldn't or didn't build on the foundation of Christ, accordingly.

4) We will receive rewards from the Lord for those works that are categorized as gold, silver or precious stones, according to the quality of our works.

5) And, even though someone's work turns to ashes, he or she is saved.

Fear of the Judgment Seat

By the way, 1 John 4:18 helps those of us who are still dealing with fear about the idea of being judged at the judgment seat of Christ. It says, quite simply, that if we are fearful, we have not yet come to a full revelation of the agape kind of love that is ministered deeply inside of us as we continue our journey:

"There is no fear in love [dread does not exist], but full-grown (complete, perfect) love turns fear out of doors and expels every trace of terror! **For fear brings with it the thought of punishment,** *and [so] he who is afraid has not reached the full maturity of love [is not yet grown into love's complete perfection]"* (I John 4:18, Amplified).

The coming judgment seat is to bring a holy fear in us, not because of possible punishment, but because we can and should grow in love and awesome respect toward His holiness and love for us.

The wrong response to this question "What Does God Expect?" results in performance orientation or "working to please God," a very wrong response for a Christian. The right response reflects a better biblical and revelational perspective. Despite protestations that "faith without works is dead" (more on this in a few paragraphs) a misunderstanding of salvation (God's finished work) verses sanctification (cooperating with God for a changed life), can wreak havoc through anxiety and fear for most believers.

Love and Fear

Think of it this way. Everything in us flows out of two emotional opposites, fear and love. 1 John 4:18 clearly states, "There's no fear in love, but that "perfect love [a God kind of love called agape) casts out fear." So, we are motivated by either fear or love in serving God and others. The more we set our love on God and allow His love to fill us, the less fear we have in this life. In this way, we understand that to the degree we fear, mature love is lacking. Incidentally, our ability to set our love on God is only possible because He first loved us (1 John 4:19).

The way we view God comes into play, too, if fear not love, is our motivator. Jesus told the story of the Parable of the Talents (Matt. 25:14-30) in which three men were given a certain amount of money to invest. He was pleased with the first two because they invested well and got the expected return. The third man "was afraid and hid his talent in the ground," and was called "wicked and lazy." He said, "he knew" the benefactor (God) was a "hard man, reaping where he hadn't sewn." This man had a wrong view of God and rather than acting out in love to do what was asked, he feared and did nothing. If we think God is "hard," it's really our own hard hearts that cause us to feel this way. As we allow God to remove hardness from us, which based on wrong perceptions, we will see Him differently. David put it this way:

"With the kind and merciful You will show Yourself kind and merciful, with an upright man You will show Yourself upright, 26 With the pure You will show Yourself pure, and with the perverse You will show Yourself contrary" (Psa. 18:25,26).

Our Vocation and God's Will

We often ask, "What's God will for me?" (usually we mean vocation), which is likely not as big a deal as we make it). It's true God has equipped us with certain skills/gifts that are both given at birth (motivational), as found in Rom. 12:4-6, and we are also given gifts of the Spirit through the Baptism of the Holy Spirit (1 Cor. 12:4-11). As long as we use these gifts in whatever we do, we are doing God's will. However, just be sure to make your calling and election sure (2 Pet. 1:10). For example, God made me a "secular" teacher (I taught school as a vocation and at other times I trained people in business), but I have the gift of teaching – given by the Holy Spirit). The Lord also has blessed me with a writing talent and the anointing in that as well. In whatever capacity, I have tried to serve and glorify God with these. You should have this understanding, although most likely with different emphases. Incidentally, I've worked at banks, a college, at a nuclear plant, in a large corporation, at a tourist spot and in the medical field. Regardless, I was a PR guy who taught and wrote in all of these, while attempting to serve the Lord in each capacity. As someone wisely said, "Your pulpit is where you are."

Faith and Works

Let's consider the issue of faith and works for a moment. So much has been written over the ages that trying to address this in a few paragraphs is impossible. First, I prefer to call every good work a "grace work." I don't think it's possible for a person to produce good works that are not actuated by grace. Below is a short study on grace/works by Matt Slick of Christian Apologetics & Research:

Ephesians 2:8, 9; Romans 3:20, 28; Galatians 2:16 and James 2:24; Matthew 19:16-21

Saved by grace

(Ephesians 2:8-9) - "For by grace you have been saved through faith; and that not of yourselves, it is the gift of God; not as a result of works, that no one should boast."

(Rom. 3:20, 28) - "because by the works of the Law no flesh will be justified in His sight; for through the Law comes the knowledge of sin... For we maintain that a man is justified by faith apart from works of the Law."

(Galatians 2:16) - "nevertheless knowing that a man is not justified by the works of the Law but through faith in Christ Jesus, even we have believed in Christ Jesus, that we may be justified by faith in Christ, and not by the works of the Law; since by the works of the Law shall no flesh be justified."

Saved by works

(James 2:24) - "You see that a man is justified by works, and not by faith alone."

(Matthew 19:16-17) - "And behold, one came to Him and said, "Teacher, what good thing shall I do that I may obtain eternal life?" 17And He said to him, "Why are you asking Me about what is good? There is only One who is good; but if you wish to enter into life, keep the commandments.""

God does not want a faith that is empty and hypocritical. James 2 is talking about those who "say" that they have faith but have no works. Therefore, people cannot tell if these people are true believers or not, because there is no obvious fruit in their lives. That kind of a faith is useless and is not a saving faith. True faith results in true works.

In Matthew 19:16-17, Jesus was speaking to a Lawyer who was self-righteous since he wanted to put Jesus to the test (Luke 10:25). He asked what he must do in order to obtain eternal life, and Jesus responded with the requirements of keeping the commandments. If a person keeps all of the commandments, it would seem that they could obtain eternal life. However, nobody can keep all of the commandments. Therefore, Jesus' comments to this man show this man that justification can only be by faith since no one can keep all of the commandments. This is why it says in Eph. 2:8 that we are saved by grace through faith. Also, Romans 3:20,28 and Galatians 2:16 tells us that no one is justified in the sight of God by the law; that is, by the works that he can do.

There is no contradiction at all when we examine the contexts. We are justified by faith but that faith must be alive (James 2). The Law cannot save us because we are incapable of keeping it (Matthew 19:16-17). Therefore, salvation is by grace through faith.

Amazing Grace

The point of the matter is whatever is produced by us—good works—is by grace alone. If we could produce them ourselves, then we could boast. There is a very interesting footnote found in the Amplified Version of the Book of Habakkuk between chapters 1 and 2 that summarizes the progression of law and thus human works. It reads:

"There is a curious passage in the Talmud (the body of Jewish civil and religious law) which says that Moses gave six hundred injunctions to the Israelites. As these commands might prove too numerous to commit to memory, David brought them down to eleven in Psa. 15. Isaiah reduced these eleven to six in Isa. 33:15. Micah (6:8) further reduced them to three; and Isaiah once more (56:1) brought them down to two. These two Amos (5:4) reduced to one. However, lest it might be supposed from this that God could be found only in the fulfillment of the law, Habakkuk (2:4) said, 'The just shall live by his faith.'"

A better rendering is, "By faith the just (justified) shall live"! To me, "What Does God Expect?" can be encapsulated within the Micah 6:8 passage referred to above. In this wonderful passage, our loving Father spells out exactly what He requires:

"He has showed you, O man, what is good. **And what does the Lord require of you** but to **do justly**, and to **love kindness *and* mercy**, and to **humble yourself *and* walk humbly with your God?"**

All that we DO for God BY Grace flows like a mighty river from the three things above: 1) **Do justly;** 2) **love mercy and kindness**; 3) humble ourselves and **walk humbly with God**. To do justly means to follow after what is right, which isn't always "fair." God is just and justifier. He is never guilty of injustice, although Satan would tempt us to accuse God of such.

In our earthly walk we often are not given justice, but we are to try to ensure justice is done through us to others. Bill Gothard, a wonderful teacher, once wrote a piece titled "Fairness: the Enemy of Justice and Mercy." In it he shows how God is always just and merciful but doesn't necessarily execute what we term as "fairness." If things were fair, we'd all be in hell! For us to love mercy and kindness, it means we are to treat others in the same way.

A good way to understand the meaning of mercy is to see how it relates to grace: Mercy, not getting what you do deserve / withheld punishment and Grace, getting what you don't deserve / unmerited favor. Mercy is like a judge finding you guilty, but then withholding any punishment. Grace is getting something you could never have imagined, an inexplicable gift. It's like the same judge awarding you $10,000,000.00, *after* finding you guilty! In the parable of the unrighteous steward (Matt. 18:21-35), Jesus shows how intolerable God is of us when we fail to show mercy after receiving it. He throws us in a prison of torment until we have forgiven and show mercy to our offender!

We live in days when even fellow Christians' love can turn cold toward us, but God tells us in Jude 21 to:

"Guard and keep yourselves in the love of God;*expect and patiently wait for the mercy of our Lord Jesus Christ (the Messiah)—[which will bring you] unto life eternal."*

Last, we are told to walk humbly with God. Peter reminds in his first letter that God resists the proud (he's referring to Christians), but gives grace to the humble:

"Likewise, you who are younger and of lesser rank, be subject to the elders (the ministers and spiritual guides of the church)—[giving them due respect and yielding to their counsel]. Clothe (apron) yourselves, all of you, with humility [as the garb of a servant, [k] so that its covering cannot possibly be stripped from you, with freedom from pride and arrogance] toward one another. For God sets Himself against the proud (the insolent, the overbearing, the disdainful, the presumptuous, the boastful)—

[and He opposes, frustrates, and defeats them], but gives grace (favor, blessing) to the humble. ⁶ *Therefore humble yourselves [demote, lower yourselves in your own estimation] under the mighty hand of God, that in due time He may exalt you"* (1 Pet. 5:5-6, Amplified).

"What Does God Expect"? really comes down to these three things, out of which will flow all the ministry of grace that any of us could ever desire and hope to achieve! And, as we stay on this journey, fear will slowly but surely become a thing of the past and love will be the foundation of our lives.

"Hope deferred makes the heart sick, but desire realized is a Tree of Life." I don't know about you, but I'm after that Tree because there was One who hung on another tree, who has already paid for this Godly realization. Are you willing to pursue it no matter what?

Hope deferred can begin *very* early in life, and from the spiritual warfare perspective Satan does his dead level best to steal our hope before we can get grounded in the reality of God's grace and mercy. The next chapter explains how this happens.

CHAPTER 7

Satan Starts VERY Early

Satan starts early by initiating pre-natal difficulties to make a grand entrance. I believe babies have three basic needs in the womb—besides the obvious physiological ones – **security, love and belonging**. If the parents don't provide these, as the child grows, he or she will continue to seek these but likely find them in the wrong places! And, yes, Satan will gladly offer these.

As the child moves into the toddling years, or any growing up stage and into adulthood – so does Satan's diabolical plan or scheme (2 Cor. 2:11). This is any place where a soul or spirit wound occurs. It's interesting that until a child reaches puberty, or around 12, the brain doesn't normally use the chemicals previously mentioned—serotonin, dopamine and norepinephrine—which would allow him to begin to make abstract decisions. Until then he could/should be trained in the absolute principles of the Word of God, which would establish his heart and mind in Godly thinking and reasoning. But this doesn't usually happen in most homes today.

Not Trained in the Ways of Jehovah

The Biblical admonition to train a child up in the way he should go (Prov. 22:6) reads more emphatically in the Hebrew language as "Train up a child in the ways of Jehovah." But thanks

to the likes of Dr. Benjamin Spock, who trained millions of parents to think biblical training was outmoded, we now have many kids with no sense of morality. Recently, I was talking to a young lady, who had already had two children out of wedlock. She said, "Marriage isn't my thing." I said, "It may not be 'your thing', but it's God's thing." Where did this beautiful young lady get this kind of thinking? Why doesn't she understand children born out of wedlock carry a 10-generation curse? (Deuteronomy 23:2). Well, no, because she is essentially biblically illiterate! The most common and most destructive generational curses that come upon families today are the curses of illegitimacy, Incest, murder of innocents (spilling of innocent blood) and witchcraft.

Illegitimacy (born out of wedlock) and incest are the only two curses in the Bible that affect 10 generations, which total about 2,050 descendants from this sinful root. The majority of mankind is affected by these curses to some degree or another, but people don't usually realize what this means, but once exposed, the patterns seen in families are easily recognizable.

Is abstract thinking bad? Not necessarily because the child has to learn to individuate—or make his own decisions about what is right. However, if his parents or guardians have not "trained him up in the way he should go," he will begin to take on a worldly rationale, which fits in fine with societal mores but not with the ultimate reality, the Word of God. Hence he often leaves what he was taught to seek out what secular life and Satan have offered him, which is fraught with pitfalls and reaping what he may have already sown (Gal. 6:7). As he grows older, this "sowing" can bring on a whirlwind of disaster because this person thinks he can sin with impunity.

As a result of this faulty foundation, his brain chemicals, as in the case of "borderline" bipolar disorder, or in the worse case scenario schizophrenia, become "scrambled." He may develop Attention Deficit Disorder (ADD) or some other kind of neurological difficulty.

"Just the Facts, Mam"

According to David Kupelian, award-winning journalist and managing editor of World Net Daily and editor of Whistleblower magazine, the following facts scream at us about Americans in the age of Obama and terrorism:

Suicide has surpassed car crashes as the leading cause of injury death for Americans. Even more disturbing, in the world's greatest military, more U.S. soldiers died last year by suicide than in combat;

Fully one-third of the nation's employees suffer chronic debilitating stress, and more than half of all "millennials" (18 to 33 year olds) experience a level of stress that keeps them awake at night, including large numbers diagnosed with depression or anxiety disorder.

Shocking new research from the federal Centers for Disease Control and Prevention shows that one in five of all high-school-aged children in the United States has been diagnosed with ADHD, and likewise a large new study of New York City residents shows, sadly, that one in five *preteens* – children aged six to 12 – have been medically diagnosed with either ADHD, anxiety, depression or **bipolar disorder;**

New research concludes that stress renders people susceptible to serious illness, and a growing number of studies now confirm that chronic stress plays a major role in the progression of cancer, the nation's second-biggest killer. The biggest killer of all, heart disease, which causes one in four deaths in the U.S., is also known to have a huge stress component;

Incredibly, 11 percent of *all Americans aged 12 and older* are currently taking SSRI antidepressants – those highly controversial, mood-altering psychiatric drugs with the FDA's "suicidality" warning label and alarming correlation with school shooters. Women are especially prone to depression, with a stunning 23 percent of all American women in their 40s and 50s – almost one in four – now taking antidepressants, according to a major study by the CDC;

Add to that the tens of millions of users of all other types of psychiatric drugs, including (just to pick one) the 6.4 million American children between 4 and 17 diagnosed with ADHD and prescribed Ritalin or similar psycho-stimulants. Throw in the 28 percent of American adults with a drinking problem, that's more than 60 million, plus the 22 million using illegal drugs like marijuana, cocaine, heroin, hallucinogens and inhalants, and pretty soon a picture emerges of a nation of drug-takers, with hundreds of millions dependent on one toxic substance or another – legal or illegal – to "help" them deal with the stresses and problems of life.

Back to the Womb

Before all of the above, for some the womb is the beginning of their troubles. For example, if their parents are ambivalent about the child's birth, or worse yet, downright rejecting, the baby in the womb receives this rejection and may decide that his "coming out party" is already being rained on. To add to this, if the child's ancestors have committed iniquity (and we're all under it), and his or her ancestry were involved in such things as freemasonry, which brings many curses, or perhaps those who were involved in the occult, their troubles are multiplied. Now he has inherited curses against his mind or body plus the feelings of abandonment and/or rejection.

Medical science has finally caught up with the Bible in this respect. The Scripture has emphatically stated in many places that the child in the womb is being formed by God, who is highly aware of his surroundings, which we'll look at in a moment.

Thanks to ultrasound and other high-tech tools allowing a peek inside the womb, scientists have discovered a virtual sensory playground in which a baby is living. The baby responds to the voice of his mother or father and other sounds in the room, reacts to light and dark shadows as they move from place to place, tumbles as you switch positions, even tastes sweet or spicy foods you've just eaten. Experts believe these experiences cause physiological changes in the baby's sensory systems that are necessary for normal brain growth.

According to webmd, most researchers studying fetal development say "Mother Nature" and the stimuli your baby naturally receives in the womb from your everyday conversations and activities are good enough to prepare the baby for the outside world. The study of how the human brain develops still is in its infancy, but there's no convincing scientific evidence that deliberate fetal acoustic stimulation, as it's called, influences intelligence, creativity or later development.

The Secret Life of the Unborn Child

Additionally, in their book, *The Secret Life of the Unborn Child*, Dr. Michael Lieberman is quoted by authors Dr. Verny Thomas and John Kelly, as stating that an unborn child grows emotionally agitated (as measured by the quickening of his heartbeat) each time his mother thinks of having a cigarette. She doesn't even have to put it to her lips or light a match; just the idea of having a cigarette is enough to upset him.

Naturally, the baby has no way of knowing his mother is smoking – or thinking about it – but he is intellectually sophisticated enough to associate the experience of her smoking with the unpleasant sensation it produced in him. This is caused by the drop in his oxygen supply (smoking lowers the oxygen content of the maternal blood passing the placenta), which is physiologically harmful to him, but possibly even more harmful are the psychological effects of maternal smoking.

Verney and Kelly say ...*few things are more dangerous to a child, emotionally and physically, than a father who abuses or neglects his pregnant wife. Virtually everyone who has studied the expectant father's role—and, sadly, so far, only a handful of researches have—has found that his support is absolutely essential to her and, thus, to her child's wellbeing. That fact alone makes the man an important part of the prenatal equation. An equally vital factor in the child's emotional well-being is his father's commitment to the marriage. In short, while the external stresses a woman faces matter, what matters most is the way she feels about her unborn child. Her thoughts and feelings are the material out of which the unborn child fashions himself....the mother's attitude had the single greatest effect on how an infant turned out. For more on this, get the book to see the effects of a child in the womb.*

"Fetuses" Found to Have Memories

An article by Dr. Jennifer Harper of the Holy Cross, Holy Cross Medical Group OB/GYN

They weigh less than 3 pounds, usually, and are perhaps 15 inches long. But they can remember.

The unborn have memories, according to medical researchers who used sound and vibration stimulation, combined with sonography, to reveal that the human fetus displays short-term memory from at least 30 weeks gestation - or about two months before they are born. "In addition, results indicated that 34-week-old fetuses are able to store information and retrieve it four weeks later," said the research, which was released Wednesday.

Scientists from the Department of Obstetrics and Gynecology at Maastricht University Medical Centre and the University Medical Centre St. Radboud, both in the Netherlands, based their findings on a study of 100 healthy pregnant women and their fetuses with the help of some gentle but precise sensory stimulation.

On five occasions during the last eight weeks of their pregnancies, the women received a series of one-second buzzes on their bellies with a "fetal vibroacoustic stimulator," a hand-held diagnostic device used to gauge an unborn baby's heart rate and general wellbeing.

The baby's responses - primarily eye, mouth and body movements - were closely monitored over the weeks with ultrasound imaging to gauge "fetal learning" patterns. The researchers found that the babies acclimated themselves to the sounds and vibrations to the point that they no longer bothered to respond - a process known as "habituation." "The stimulus is then accepted as 'safe' "by the babies, the study said.

The team also found that the tiny test subjects actually improved these skills as they grew older, with those who were 34 or 36-weeks old clearly showing that they had become familiar with the hum outside the womb. "The fetus 'remembers' the stimulus and the number of stimuli needed for the fetus to habituate is then much smaller," the study said.

"It seems like every day we find out marvelous new things about the development of unborn children. We hope that this latest information helps people realize more

clearly that the unborn are members of the human family with amazing capabilities and capacities like these built in from the moment of conception," said Randall K. O'Bannon, director of education and research for the National Right to Life Educational Trust Fund.

A call to NARAL Pro-Choice America for comment on the implications of the research were not returned.

The Dutch medical team, meanwhile, said its findings could help obstetricians track the healthy development of unborn babies during pregnancy. The research was published in Child Development, a medical journal.

Scientists have been curious about fetal responses to sound for decades.

The first real study of "habituation" occurred in 1925 when researchers discovered that fetuses moved less when exposed to a beeping car horn. Since then, door buzzers and even electric toothbrushes have been used to help researchers understand the fetal environment - and the response of the unborn to such influences. Beeps and buzzes were not always the tools of choice.

In 2003, psychologists and obstetricians at Queen's University in Canada found a profound mother-baby link. In a study of 60 pregnant women, they found that the unborn babies preferred the voices of their own mothers - both before and after birth.

Sustained Attention, Memory and Learning

The heart rates of fetuses sped up when they heard their mother reading a poem, and slowed down when they heard a stranger's voice - evidence of "sustained attention, memory and learning by the fetus," said Barbara Kisilevsky, a professor of nursing who led the research. The Queen's group has also investigated fetal response to the father's voice, concluding that if men try a little pre-natal vocalizing to their offspring, the newborn will later recognize the father's voice. Speech pathologists like New York City's Melissa Wexler Gurfein are excited about the findings about what babies can know and do in the womb.

"Really what it is saying is that infants are learning and tuning into the speech patterns of their first exposed language(s) earlier than was originally thought," she tells WebMD. "This may suggest the importance of the mother not only to talk

during the last trimester of pregnancy but to continue to talk to her newborn from the moment of birth to help facilitate language development."

David Mendez, MD, says that the best thing that expectant moms can do for themselves and their baby is to maintain a stress - and chemical-free environment. He is a neonatologist at Miami Children's Hospital. *"Talk to your baby as much as possible in a calm and relaxing way,"* he says. Avoid screaming, yelling and other violent language.

The Results of Chronic Anxiety in the Womb

An author and well-known obstetrician, Christiane Northrup shares that if a pregnant mother is going through high levels of fear or anxiety she creates a "metabolic cascade." Hormones known as cytokines are produced, and the mother's immune system is affected, including her child's. Chronic anxiety in the mother can set the stage for a whole array of trauma based results such as prematurity, complications of birth, death, and miscarriage.

The opposite is also true. When the mother is feeling healthy and happy, she produces oxytocin. This is often called the molecule of belonging. The presence of this component creates feelings of bonding and strengthens immunity in the baby. Neurotransmitters moving inside the mother's body create a chemical and physical imprint on the baby's brain and body. The message imprinted is that there is safety and peace. The baby feels secure and taken care of.

The study is "fascinating," says Amos Grunebaum, MD. He is the director of obstetrics at New York-Presbyterian Hospital/Weill Cornell Medical Center in New York City. "People thought that newborns don't learn until they are born, but this well-conceived study that shows that fetuses can learn while in utero," he says. "We knew they could hear sounds, but we can teach fetuses."

This is all wonderful, yes? But God's Word goes beyond all this.

Psalm 22:9-10: Yet you brought me out of the womb; you made me trust in you even at my mother's breast. From birth I was cast upon you; from my mother's womb you have been my God.

Psalm 58:3: Even from birth the wicked go astray; from the womb they are wayward and speak lies.

Well do I know how treacherous you are; you were called a rebel from birth. Is 48:8.

Psalm 139:15: My frame was not hidden from You when I was made in the secret place. When

I was woven together in the depths of the earth, your eyes saw my unformed body

Luke 1:41 When Elizabeth heard Mary's greeting, the baby leaped in her womb,

And Elizabeth was filled with the Holy Spirit. Luke 1:41

As soon as the sound of your greeting reached my ears, the baby in my womb leaped for joy (Luke 1:44).

In light of these things, consider again Dr. Northrup's opinions about how **chronic anxiety** can set the stage for "a whole array of trauma based results such as prematurity, complications of birth, death and miscarriage."

Certainly, if **chronic anxiety** can produce these things within the womb, why could it not produce bipolar disorder? Early in this book, Dr. MK Strydom clearly established the relationship between anxiety and bipolar disorder. Here we have another doctor quoted as saying "complications at birth" result because of chronic anxiety. Is anyone listening?

Looking at this from a different but relative angle, Webmd suggests that pregnant women who are bipolar can worsen their condition because of the pregnancy.

Complications of Bipolar Disorder in Pregnancy

According to Webmd, few studies have been done on bipolar disorder and pregnancy, so not enough is known about the risks of untreated bipolar disorder or the risks and benefits of medications during pregnancy. And the factors that lead to relapse during pregnancy are not clear.

Bipolar disorder, however, can worsen during pregnancy. Pregnant women or new mothers with bipolar disorder have seven times the risk of hospital admissions compared to pregnant women who do not have bipolar disorder.

At least one study has called into question the common belief that pregnancy may have a protective effect for women with bipolar disorder. The study followed 89 women through pregnancy and the year after delivery. When stopping bipolar medications for the period from six months before conception to 12 weeks after, the women had:

Twice the risk of relapse

A 50% risk of recurrence within just two weeks, if they stopped suddenly.

Bipolar symptoms throughout 40% of the pregnancy—or more than four times that of women who continued their bipolar medications.

This article looks at it only from the side of what happens to the mother with bipolar disorder, but what about the baby inside the mother?

God Knows You Before You're Born!

Before conception the Lord knows a child (Jer. 1:5; Psa. 139), but the child has free will and responds to his environment, quite often in a rebellious way. The child's spirit, which already knows the thoughts within his own being, can interpret his surroundings and begin to assess and judge how he or she is being treated:

But, on the contrary, as the Scripture says, What eye has not seen and ear has not heard and has not entered into the heart of man, [all that] God has prepared (made and keeps ready) for those who love Him [who hold Him in affectionate reverence, promptly obeying Him and gratefully recognizing the benefits He has bestowed].

Yet to us God has unveiled and revealed them by and through His Spirit, for the [Holy] Spirit searches diligently, exploring and examining everything, even sounding the profound and bottomless things of God [the [h]divine counsels and things hidden and beyond man's scrutiny] God. **For what person perceives (knows and understands) what passes through a man's thoughts except the man's own spirit within him?** *Just so no one discerns (comes to know and comprehend) the thoughts of God except the Spirit of spirit within him? Just so no one discerns (comes to know and comprehend) the thoughts of God except the Spirit of God* (1 Cor. 2:9-11).

All this says we are much more knowledgeable and capable in the womb that anyone has ever realized. The spirit has no limitations, especially as God empowers, enlightens and frees us to know Him.

To scientists knowledge is based on observable facts, which is extremely limited when attempting to observe the inexplicable, such as faith. The things of the Spirit are most definitely inexplicable but true nevertheless!

The spirit, mind and body are infinitely greater than any human can fathom. The mysteries of God are endless! One thing is certain. There are certain things that carry major and seemingly intractable effects in the way people think of themselves, behave and relate to everyone else. These are called strongholds.

One of the reasons for bipolar disorder continuing impact is a mental stronghold. Understanding and overcoming this stronghold is imperative. In the next chapter we'll take a look at what a stronghold is, how it works and its ultimate affect on thinking.

CHAPTER 8

Strongholds Are Mental Fortresses!

Mental difficulties are certainly not uncommon in our day. It seems most people are struggling with some kind of mental duress, either short-term or something that's been life-long. In some cases drugs bring relief– at least temporarily–but often this kind of assistance can bring more side effects than help. Actually, many people who struggle with bipolar disorder or other mental problems refuse to take medicine. We've tried to look at "roots" here. What actually is the root of the problem? Is there a key overlooked? Let's talk a little about personal strongholds.

John and Mark Sandford of Elijah House International, speaking of personal strongholds, described it this way:

"It is an automatic, practiced and habitual way of thinking. God created us with lives and wills of our own; what we create also has life of its own (habits, fantasies, and ways of thinking). The ways of thinking that we developed before we knew Jesus can resurrect and maintain lives of their own. Although we think of our mind as a friend, we must remember that "a mind set on the flesh is death, but the mind set on the spirit is life and peace' Romans 8:6 "The mind set on the flesh is hostile toward God; for it does not subject itself to the law of God, for it is not even able to do so." Romans 8:7 those who are in the flesh cannot please God (Romans 8:8).

The very first sin was a mental sin. Our childhood ways become practiced ways of thinking, habitual ruts, and strongholds. Like a computer, the mind continues to function as it was programmed (inertia: unless halted, things continue as they are). Once sinfully programmed, the only remedy is death; we must be born anew.

Jesus died. He was crucified on the "mind of man," a place called Golgotha meaning: the skull, the residence of the brain.

The Lord renews our mind. Paul tells us to "be transformed by the renewing" of our minds, that we may "prove what the will of God is, that which is good and acceptable and perfect" (Romans 12:2).

Warfare against the mind is biblical. It is not chasing demons, but rather the act of destroying speculations, every lofty thing raised up against the knowledge of God, and taking every thought captive to the obedience of Christ (2 Corinthians 10:4-5).

Here's an analogy of biblical warfare: A fortress was often built on a hill in an easily defended valley. To conquer it, attacking warriors breached the city wall and burned the city. They accomplished this by hurling burning logs or balls of debris over the walls catching the structures in the city on fire. When the people would abandon the walls to put out the flames the army would scale the walls without resistance from the defenders.

In spiritual warfare, we must hurl the Word of God against the walls of the mind. Truth breaks down walls and takes every thought captive. Our truest warfare is against ungodly ways of thinking.

When dealing with mental difficulties, whether it's bipolar disorder or some other mental problem, we have to consider what thing could have happened to cause the mind to respond the way it does. Certainly bipolar disorder, like most brain disorders, has a beginning, whether we are born with a genetic predisposition, or if there were wounding while in the womb or later on. For those who are seeking an answer to something other than, "I just have to deal with this," understanding and dealing with personal strongholds could hold the key. But how does Satan use darkness to do his dirty work? Isn't he bound in hell? This article by Francis Frangipane provides the answers.

Satan's Domain: The Realm of Darkness

By Francis Frangipane

(En Español)

Many Christians debate whether the devil is on the earth or in hell; can he dwell in Christians or only in the world? The fact is, the devil is in darkness. Wherever there is spiritual darkness, there the devil will be.

Preparing for Spiritual Warfare

For most, the term spiritual warfare introduces a new but not necessarily welcomed dimension in their Christian experience. The thought of facing evil spirits in battle is an unsettling concept, especially since we came to Jesus as lost sheep, not warriors. Ultimately, some of us may never actually initiate spiritual warfare, but all of us must face the fact that the devil has initiated warfare against us. Therefore, it is essential to our basic well-being that we discern the areas of our nature, which are unguarded and open to satanic assault.

Jude tells us, "And angels who did not keep their own domain, but abandoned their proper abode, He has kept in eternal bonds under darkness for the judgment of the great day"

(Jude 1:6).

When Satan rebelled against God, he was placed under eternal judgment in what the Bible calls "pits" (2 Pet. 2:4) or "bonds" of darkness. The devil and the fallen angels with him have been relegated to live in darkness. This darkness does not simply refer to areas void of visible light. The eternal darkness to which this Scripture refers is essentially a moral darkness, which ultimately degrades into literal darkness. However, its cause is not simply the absence of light; it is the absence of God, who is light.

It is vital to recognize that this darkness to which Satan has been banished is not limited to areas outside of humanity. Unlike those who do not know Jesus, however, we have been delivered out of the domain or "authority" of darkness (see Colossians 1:13). We are not trapped in darkness if we have been born of light. But if we tolerate darkness through tolerance of sin, we leave ourselves vulnerable to satanic assault. For wherever there is willful disobedience to the Word of God, there is spiritual darkness and the potential for demonic activity.

Thus Jesus warned, "Take heed therefore that the light which is in thee be not darkness" (Luke 11:35 KJV). There is a light in you. "The spirit of man is the lamp of the Lord" (Prov. 20:27). Your spirit, illuminated by the Spirit of Christ, becomes the "lamp of the Lord" through which He searches your heart. There is indeed a holy radiance surrounding a true Spirit-filled Christian. But when you harbor sin, the "light, which is in thee" is "darkness." Satan has a legal access, given to him by God, to dwell in the domain of darkness. Thus, we must grasp this point: The devil can traffic in any area of darkness, even the darkness that still exists in a Christian's heart.

God's Thresher

An example of Satan having access to the carnal side of human nature is seen in Peter's denial of Jesus. It is obvious that Peter failed. What we do not readily see, however, is what was occurring in the invisible world of the spirit.

Jesus predicted accurately that Peter would deny Him three times. Anyone looking at Peter's actions that night might have simply concluded his denial was a manifestation of fear. Yet Peter was not fearful by nature. This was the disciple who, a few hours earlier, drew a sword against the multitudes who had come to arrest Jesus. No, human fear did not cause Peter to deny the Lord. Peter's denial was satanically induced.

Jesus had warned the apostle, "Simon, Simon, behold, Satan has demanded permission to sift you like wheat; but I have prayed for you, that your faith may not fail; and you, when once you have turned again, strengthen your brothers" (Luke 22:31-32). Behind the scenes, Satan had demanded and received permission to sift Peter like wheat. Satan had access to an area of darkness in Peter's heart.

How did Satan cause Peter's fall? After eating the Passover, Jesus told His disciples that one of them was going to betray Him. Scripture continues, "They began to discuss among themselves which one of them . . . was going to do this thing" (Luke 22:23).

This was a very somber time. Yet, during this terrible moment, "there arose also a dispute among them as to which one of them was . . . greatest" (Luke 22:24). They went from an attitude of shock and dismay to an argument concerning who among them was the greatest! Evidently Peter, the water-walker, who was also the boldest and most outspoken of the apostles, prevailed. We can imagine that Peter's high visibility among the disciples left him with an air of superiority, which was fanned by Satan into an attitude of presumption and boasting. Peter, being lifted up by pride, was being set up for a fall.

Pride caused Satan's fall, and pride was the very same darkness manipulated by Satan to cause Peter's fall. Lucifer, from experience, knew well the judgment of God against religious pride and envy. He knew personally that pride goes "before a fall" (Prov. 16:18 KJV). Satan did not have a right to indiscriminately assault and destroy Peter. He had to secure permission from Peter's Lord before he could come against the young apostle. But the fact is, the devil demanded permission to sift Peter, and he received it.

Submit to God

The trip wire that Satan used to cause Peter's fall was the disciple's own sin of pride. Let us recognize before we do warfare that the areas we hide in darkness are the very areas of our future defeat. Often the battles we face will not cease until we discover and repent for the darkness that is within us. If we will be effective in spiritual warfare, we must be discerning of our own hearts; we must walk humbly with our God. Our first course of action must be, "Submit . . . to God." Then, as we "resist the devil . . . he will flee" (James 4:7).

Satan will never be given permission to destroy the saints. Rather, he is limited to sifting us "like wheat." The good news is that God knows there is wheat inside each of us. The outcome of this type of satanic assault, which is allowed through the permissive will of God, is to cleanse the soul of pride and produce greater meekness and transparency in our lives. It may feel terrible, but God causes it to work for good. Our husk-like outer nature must die to facilitate the breaking forth of the wheat-like nature of the new creation man. Both the chaff and the husk were necessary; they provided protection for us from the harsh elements of this life. But before God can truly use us, in one way or another we will pass through a time of threshing.

Peter's husk nature was presumptuous and proud. His initial successes had made him ambitious and self-oriented. God can never entrust His kingdom to anyone who has not been broken of pride, for pride is the armor of darkness itself. So, when Satan demanded permission to assault Peter, Jesus said in effect, You can sift him, but you cannot destroy him. The warfare against Peter was devastating but measured. It served the purpose of God.

Peter was ignorant of the areas of darkness within him, and his ignorance left him open to attack. But the Lord would ask each of us, "Do you know the areas where *you are vulnerable to satanic assault?" Jesus would have us not be ignorant of our need. In fact, when He reveals the sin in our hearts, it is so He might destroy the works of the devil. Thus, we should realize that the greatest defense we can have against the devil is to maintain an honest heart before God.*

When the Holy Spirit shows us an area that needs repentance, we must overcome the instinct to defend ourselves. We must silence the little lawyer who steps out from a dark closet in our minds, pleading, "My client is not so bad." Your "defense attorney" will defend you until the day you die—and if you listen to him you will never see what is wrong in you nor face what needs to change. For you to succeed in warfare, your self-preservation instincts must be submitted to the Lord Jesus, for Christ alone is your true advocate.

We cannot engage in spiritual battle without embracing this knowledge. Indeed, James 4:6 says, "God is opposed to the proud, but gives grace to the humble." God is opposed to the proud. That is a very important verse. If God is opposed to the proud, and we are too proud to humble ourselves and admit when we are wrong, then God is opposed to us.

James continues in verse 7, "Submit therefore to God. Resist the devil and he will flee from you." When we see this verse, it is usually all by itself as a monument to spiritual warfare. However, it is in the context of repentance, humility, and possessing a clean heart that we find Satan fleeing from us.

We must go beyond a vague submission to God; we must submit the exact area of our personal battle to Him. When we come against the power of the devil, it must be from a heart in submission to Jesus.

There is a recurring precept throughout this book. It is vital that you know, understand, and apply this principle for your future success in spiritual warfare. That principle is this: Victory begins with the name of Jesus on your lips, but it will not be consummated until the nature of Jesus is in your heart. This rule applies to every facet of spiritual warfare. Indeed, Satan will be allowed to come against the area of your weakness until you realize God's only answer is to become Christlike. As you begin to appropriate not just the name of Jesus but His nature as well, the adversary will withdraw. Satan will not continue to assault you if the circumstances he designed to destroy you are now working to perfect you.

The outcome of Peter's experience was that, after Pentecost, when God used him to heal a lame man, a new, humble Peter spoke to the gathering crowd. He asked, "Why do you gaze at us, as if by our own power or piety we had made him walk?" (Acts 3:12) Peter's victory over pride and the devil began with the name of Jesus on his lips, and it was consummated by the nature of Jesus in his heart. The darkness in Peter was displaced with light; the pride in Peter was replaced with Christ.

Adapted from Francis Frangipane's book, *The Three Battlegrounds*, available at www.arrowbookstore.com.

One thing we cannot do is continue to blame others for our predicament, be they God, people or circumstances of life. But many choose to play the blame game, and it's a losing game.

The Blame Game

A singer named Joe South sang a song titled "The Games People Play." The Blame Game is one such game.

Here's how it works: If I can divert attention to someone else and away from my own responsibility or excuse myself for my own sinful or carnal actions or reactions, I can hold off the blame I should take myself. It is typical human behavior, and it often works – at least for a while. There are three components to this scenario: run, hide and shift blame.

The devil knows how to keep this game alive, and constantly tempts us not to focus on our own faults, sins and reactions to hurts done to us by others so pain will remain. Either that, or he causes us to constantly focus on our own faults, sins and reactions to hurt that we become obsessed with these failures. Either way, he wins.

One of the first sins was that of blame. Adam, in his attempt to find an excuse for willfully choosing to eat off the wrong tree, blamed two others: Eve and God. Eve blamed Satan. Nobody wanted to own up to the transgression.

"The wife YOU gave me tempted me, and I ate," Adam said.

"Satan tempted me and I ate," Eve said.

Let's face it. Generally, there's more than one person at fault in any relationship fracas, and in one sense all share blame. In Adam's case, it's true Eve gave him the forbidden fruit, God placed two trees in the garden, and Satan cajoled Eve into taking the first bite. All were guilty but God, who, as Lord, had given Adam and Eve a choice. They weren't robots MADE to obey God. The Scripture is clear that God never tempts anyone (Heb. 2:18). He doesn't desire evil to have its sway over us, and He constantly stands with us to prevent our giving into it, but allowing temptation is simply part of His plan:

"Blessed (happy, to be envied) is the man who is patient under trial and stands up under temptation, for when he has stood the test and been approved, he will receive [the victor's] crown of life which God has promised to those who love Him" (James 1:12, Amplified).

Run, Hide and Shift Blame

The sinful, carnal or Adamic nature lives in every human being, so run, hide and shift blame are our modus operandi until we decide that with the help of the grace of God we won't do this any longer.

If and when we sin, our first move is where? away from God (run). If we could physically hide from God, we would.

Run

Some people think they actually can run from God. One such was the prophet Jonah. When God told him to go to Nineveh to preach repentance, he hopped on a ship that was headed in the opposite direction to run from the Lord. We know the rest of the story – a perfectly designed fish named "Jaws" changed his mind.

Most of our running, however, isn't geographical but avoiding times or situations in which we know God's going to show up or be brought up. A lot of church skipping is nothing more than avoiding the Holy Spirit's dealing. Some people avoid Godly people because they can't stand to be convicted by their lives.

Hide

After the fall, Adam and Eve "hid" from the presence of the Lord, after realizing they were naked. You're probably wondering why they realized they were naked, right? Hadn't they realized they were naked before? No, not in a sinful sense. They were naked and not ashamed (Gen. 2:25). It is theorized that Adam and Eve had a "glory covering," so their focus was on loving God and each other, and not on their nakedness. Everything was copacetic in the garden. Woo hoo!

God asked, "Adam, where are you?" God wasn't asking for a physical location! The question was asked to help Adam identify *where* he was *with* God at that moment. Adam said, "I was naked so I HID myself."

We can hide ourselves in many ways. We can busy ourselves so we don't have to think about God. We can do it with drugs or alcohol. We can develop a permissive philosophy so our sinfulness is justified as in "Everyone's doing it. This can't be wrong." Basically, hiding is lying to ourselves about ourselves.

Shift Blame

A comedian of 60s fame, Flip Wilson, made famous blame shifting with his saying, "the devil made me do it." If we're realistic, we'll admit this is one of our favorites. We can find a passel of excuses or methodologies to blame others for our own sin, faults and failings. The problem with this is that it never allows us the freedom to be set free from our own guilty feelings because we won't 'fess up.

This may all seem quite elementary until we come face to face with it. The Lord made it clear to me that one of the reasons I and others couldn't find freedom from some things was because I/they kept blaming somebody else for the predicament, emotional pain or cyclical feelings. The first couple had two sons, originally, Cain and Able. We know the story. Cain killed Able out of jealousy, and God asked him where his brother was. "Am I my brother's keeper?" replied Cain.   He took no responsibility for his actions, shifting blame to someone else for taking care of Abel.

Abuse by Others

I want to make it clear that suffering at the hands of someone who takes advantage of our size, age, emotional state or vulnerability is wrong and not our fault. The problem lies in our not forgiving the guilty party and continuing to blame him or her for what they did. This will NOT set you free! You WILL become a victim of your circumstances, and fear and anger will rule your life. For those of us who pray/counsel with people who have suffered from physical or emotional abuse, we need to show mercy and comfort. But we must also help people out of their awful circumstances by helping them see the need to stop blaming. If we don't, we allow Satan to steal our true identity.

Identity Theft

The number of identity theft incidents has reached 9.9 million a year, according to the Federal Trade Commission. Every minute about 19 people fall victim to identity theft. It takes the average victim an estimated $500 and 30 hours to resolve each identity theft crime.

This is bad stuff, especially if you are the victim of this kind of abuse. But consider this. The most important identity theft that ever occurs is the one Satan pulls on you to steal who you really are in Christ Jesus:

Praise be to the God and Father of our Lord Jesus Christ, who has blessed us in the heavenly realms with every spiritual blessing in Christ. For he chose us in him before the creation of the world to be holy and blameless in his sight. In love he^b predestined us for adoption to sonship^c through Jesus Christ, in accordance with his pleasure and will— to the praise of his glorious grace, which he has freely given us in the One he loves. In him we have redemption through his blood, the forgiveness of sins, in accordance with the riches of God's grace that he lavished on us. With all wisdom and understanding, he^d made known to us the mystery of his will according to his good pleasure, which he purposed in Christ, 1 to be put into effect when the times reach *their fulfillment—to bring unity to all things in heaven and on earth under Christ (Eph. 1:3-10).*

A good friend of mine, who has traveled the US and world for more than 42 years as a teacher-evangelist, says that self-worth is the biggest problem in the body of Christ. If you consider the above, you would have to wonder how this happens. It's easy really. It's called lies since birth.

We Believe What We Hear and Experience

From conception the human spirit begins to believe truth or lies, primarily lies, because there is usually little defense for the child being formed at that point. The Lord in His omniscience formed the human spirit before the brain in an effort to jumpstart our lives in the right direction, but the enemy of our souls had other plans.

Science is continuing to verify what God taught us in His Word about the miracle of formation in the womb – what we can know, understand and even judge. Thus a child being formed can be blessed or cursed by what he or she hears and experiences. "I bless you with the joy of the Lord and the knowledge that you are infinitely loved!" Or, "I don't want this child!" "We cannot afford this baby right now!" "It's your fault for wanting this blankety-blank child!" These words sink deeply into our innermost being:

"The words of a talebearer are as wounds, and they go down into the innermost parts of the belly" (Prov. 18:8 KJV). Interestingly, some translations for heart in the Scriptures are "chambers of the belly." In other words, we could conclude that different aspects of the heart are affected by the words that are spoken to us.

Clarke's Commentary on Proverbs 18:8: The words of a talebearer - וגרנ ירבד dibrey nirgan, "the words of the whisperer," the busybody, the busy, meddling croaker. Verba bilinguis, **"the words of the double-tongued."** - Vulgate. The wordes of the twisel tunge - Old MS. Bible. "The words of a slanderer." - Coverdale.

The Spirit is Primary

God made us with a human spirit, soul and body (1 Thess. 5:23), with the spirit to be in the lead role. The Adamic Fall caused the soul (mind) to take the lead, reversing God's plan for dominion. Whereas once we were conditioned to seek and hear God's leading through our spirits, the focus now became human reasoning and analysis. As Arthur Burk says, "The spirit in most people is like a stickman, and the soul is like a sumo wrestler!"

God made us such an incredible species, but because of the aforementioned, we succumb to lies about who we are and settle for less than optimum lives promised by God. Our real identity that of Royal Bloodis stolen from us on a regular basis, until we believe what is being said to us in the spirit realm.

God made our incredible brains, and He loves them. I never cease to be amazed at the brilliance of some people, while at the same time regretting their spiritual darkness and lack of wisdom that is found in God's Word. Even with these terrific minds, God's intent was to be able to talk to us, lead us and direct us via our spirit, and there is nothing in the Bible that intimates He stopped communicating with us in this manner.

"⁹But, on the contrary, as the Scripture says, What eye has not seen and ear has not heard and has not entered into the heart of man, [all that] God has prepared (made and keeps ready) for those who love Him [ᵉwho hold Him in affectionate reverence, promptly obeying Him and gratefully recognizing the benefits He has bestowed].

¹⁰ Yet to us God has unveiled and revealed them by and through His Spirit, for the [Holy] Spirit searches diligently, exploring and examining everything, even sounding the profound and bottomless things of God [the ᶠ-divine counsels and things hidden and beyond man's scrutiny].

*¹¹ **For what person perceives (knows and understands) what passes through a man's thoughts except the man's own spirit within him?** Just so no one discerns (comes to know and comprehend) the thoughts of God except the Spirit of God"* (I Cor. 2:9-11 Amp).

In effect, we only know who we are by revelation of the Holy Spirit. Nobody on this planet can tell you who you are but Him. People can boast about you and tell you all kinds of sweet things, which you may not believe, no matter how much you want to, but God through His Spirit, will brand that truth inside you, sometimes with one mighty revelation! But generally, we are so hardheaded and hard hearted, we defend ourselves against the truth because we don't want to believe it!

Subnormal Lives

A preacher I heard once said, "We live such subnormal lives that normal is abnormal." How true is this? We don't believe the real truth about who we are so we can't even live the *Normal Christian Life* (Watchman Nee 1957). The choice is to live this! Lies lower our expectations to subnormal, and we wonder why life is so dismal?

We can allow identity theft or choose to believe God's Word that there is something better for us. It's our choice.

David Was Different

King David sinned when he took more than a passing glance at the UFO (Unclad Female Object), namely Bathsheba. His lust led to adultery and the murder of Uriah the Hittite, Bathsheba's husband, who was one of David's mighty men of war (2 Sam. 11).

David apparently lied to himself about what he had done, but when confronted by Nathan, who told him a story about a rich man who had taken a ewe lamb away from a poor man, David cried, "This man should die!" Then comes Nathan's famous line, "You are the man!"

This allegory was enough for David to clearly see he had been found out – Scripture says, "the Lord sent Nathan."

David acknowledged his sin, repented of it, but the consequences led to the death of his first child with Bathsheba.

Psalm 51 recounts David's sin with Bathsheba, but here we find a different response. "In verse 4, David says to God, "Against you, and you alone, have I sinned; I have done what is evil in your sight. You will be proved right in what you say, and your judgment against me is just" (New Living Translation (©2007).

Were there others to blame in this situation? Personally, I don't think Bathsheba was naive enough to think the king wasn't checking her out, as she lay sunbathing on her roof below his. Scripture says she was "beautiful." She was probably in Sports Illustrated's latest swimsuit issue that had just hit the Jerusalem's scrolls.

I can just hear most of us under these same circumstances:

"Lord, Bathsheba shouldn't have been lying out naked as a jaybird in front of me. "It wasn't my fault. It was Eve's fault – I mean Bathsheba's. You should rebuke her for that."

"God, it was that demon of lust again. That thing gets me every time I look at woman with no clothes on."

"Lord, if you had just gotten me those super dark sunglasses when I asked you to, this wouldn't have happened."

Blaming others: It's as Easy as 1,2,3

Blaming others is easy to do. In the deliverance ministry, a lot of people never truly get set free because they want to blame others or demons for their situation, and again, there may be some truth about both of their involvement.

However, if you continue to focus on blaming the person who hurt you, your pain will remain. Demons most often have to have had something to work with, or they wouldn't have gotten hold of the person needing deliverance. I hate demons, but putting the blame entirely on the demon usually won't set you free. Again, God looks for truth in the situation. Truth blows the devil's cover!

Blaming God

I put this in a different category because it's SO major in people's lives. "Why did God let...?" "God took my wife/son/daughter, and I'll never serve Him again." "Where was God during all this hell that happened to me?" These are typical questions or statements about how God is to blame for whatever happened to us. We can develop an inner rage at God (Prov. 19:3). After all, He knows everything before it happens, so why didn't he prevent it? The overall answer to this is I don't know, and usually, neither does anyone else.

Some have referred to this as "the God of allowance." He doesn't cause problems and difficulties, but neither does He necessarily prevent them. He knows "all things can work together for our good to those who love (agape) God and are called, according to His purpose" (Romans 8:28).

This we do know. God is perfectly holy and just and always does what is right and righteous. It may not seem to us that this is true, especially at the outset. From a human and especially Christian perspective, we know that this is true if we believe the Scripture. On the other side of the coin, emotionally, we may remain incensed at the Lord for a long, long time because we are not honest about the way we feel. Getting real will help you get on with your life and enjoy it; honesty is the key.

Honest to God

God doesn't lie, and His Spirit, the Holy Spirit, is the Spirit of truth. You can't lie to Him and expect Him to be with okay it. He wants the truth, the whole truth and nothing but the truth, so help *you*. Playing church, and acting like everything is "okay" when it's not, won't set you free. Since God knows everything about everyone all the time, He doesn't need you to explain things to him. "Well, God, you just don't know my brother, Phillip. He's been a jerk all my life."

God is only after the truth from our mouths about how we feel about others and Him. Anything less than the truth won't get you there. He can take it, believe me. He won't be shocked by anything you tell Him. But you'll feel a "block" with God as long as something isn't brought into the open. And experiencing real freedom sometimes requires confession to another human. Why? Because it's a pride killer!

James 5:14-16 says we sometimes need to confess our faults one to another and pray for one another, and if we have committed sins, they will be forgiven, and healing will result. If you confess something to a person you're ashamed of or not proud of, for goodness sake, choose a mature believer you can trust and not a blabbermouth!

God knows who's to blame in your situation. He will always vindicate the righteous, and He may not want your help to get the job done. We so often want God to avenge us, but if we decide He's not going to do it to our satisfaction or quickly enough, we do it ourselves.

"Don't hit back; discover beauty in everyone. If you've got it in you, get along with everybody. Don't insist on getting even; that's not for you to do. I'll do the judging," says God. "I'll take care of it" (Romans 12:19, The Message (MSG)

The Blame Game is a losing game. In summary, you become a victim of your own circumstances, and bonded, in a sense, to the person who may have mistreated you. Personally, I decided that my Father is able to do exceedingly abundantly above all I could ever ask or think (Eph. 3:20). Letting go of blame is peace, joy and the Holy Spirit, and it "sets God free" to move on your behalf! God can uncover up covered up places in our deceitful selves so we can "walk in the light as He is in the light" (1 John 1:7).

How the Carnal Mind Defends Itself

Our mind wants to rule us. When the mind fell under the law of sin of sin and death (Rom. 8:2) in the garden, it became independent of God's way of thinking. From that point the mind set up its own fortress to ensure it stays in control. Romans 8:5-7 says the carnal mind is at war with God or, as the King James Version says, it's enmity:

5 *For they that are after the flesh do mind the things of the flesh; but they that are after the Spirit the things of the Spirit.* **6** *For to be carnally minded is death; but to* *be spiritually minded is life and peace.* **7** *Because the carnal mind is* **enmity** *against God: for it is not subject to the law of God, neither indeed can be.*

The Oxford Dictionary defines it this way: the state or feeling of being actively opposed or hostile to someone or something: synonyms: hostility · animosity · antagonism · friction · antipathy.

So you can see clearly that without the mind being renewed and transformed by the power of the Holy Spirit and the Word of God, it remains against God. This explains the struggle we all have in replacing the antithetical thought processes with those that agree with the Bible. As human beings we tend to go in the opposite direction of where we really need to go – in God's direction. Hence we HAVE the very serious difficulty to move forward.

Healing the Mentally Disturbed

Jesus came to save us from our sins and ourselves. The Scripture says he went about doing good and healing all who were physically sick and mentally ill:

*"In two places Matthew speaks of "lunatics" (from the Greek word meaning "moon-struck" because mental aberrations intensified during a full moon or luna in Latin). The first passage, Mt 4:24, was just before the Sermon on the Mount: "His fame spread to all of Syria, and they brought to him all who were sick with various diseases and racked with pain, those who were possessed, lunatics, and paralytics, and he cured them" (all Scripture quotations are from the New American Bible). Here Matthew includes all kinds of illnesses **and distinguishes between mentally ill people** (lunatics) and possessed people. Jesus heals every kind of illness, including the mentally ill"* (excerpt from "Is there a Scriptural Approach to Mental Health" by Robert T. Sears, SJ, PhD, www.familytreehealing.com.

The Power of the "Old Rugged Cross"

We Christians are often naive about the power of the cross to heal and transform the mentally-emotionally afflicted. When Jesus died, His Blood was shed to cleanse the past and future of everyone who would receive it. Hell was defeated, the grave overcome, physical healing was made available, and our souls (ourselves) were given healing for oppression from torment beyond the scope and ability of humankind to deal with it. Faith is required to access this amazing power that is available to every hungry person on Planet Earth. There is nothing this Great God and Savior Jesus Christ cannot do, and that includes the severing of the ties to generational curses of the mind!

It is awesome to know that through this one act we have been forgiven once for all sins and have passed from death to life without condemnation (John 5:24). Upfront we need to understand the Blood of Jesus is for SINS, the cross for the SIN nature and the power of God through the spoken word that brings victory over tormenting spirits. These spirits will attack as long as they have something to work with, but once their ground of operation is removed (our fleshly responses), they have to leave. Obviously, sometimes we must command them to! Inner healing often uncovers this ground of operation that remains hidden as long as we are in darkness about it (not aware of it), thus giving Satan and his demons room to work. The Holy Spirit gives us light! God in His sovereignty and love may "set up" situations that cause us to see these problems so He can heal us.

Most Christians understand God's forgiveness for the Penalty of SINS (eternal life) because of the cross but have often not been taught that it via the work of the cross Christ also conquered the Power of SIN, thereby giving us victory over it. This power was broken because Jesus Christ condemned sin in the flesh (Rom. 8:3) or the Adamic nature in us that we inherited from the first male human. **It is very important to understand that the SIN nature produces sins**. Trying to get victory over habitual sins is like fruitlessly trimming the branches of a tree (sins) when the tree (sin nature) has to be cut down at the roots to kill it. Not comprehending this produces a continuous cycle of sins, condemnation, repentance, a temporary victory and the repeat of this agonizing experience. The sin nature cannot be improved on or "reformed." Jesus said what is flesh is flesh and what is spirit is spirit.

In other words, the flesh doesn't change — you can't reform it. That's man's answer — God's answer is crucifixion.

Hard Place

Getting the carnal mind to the cross requires a great deal of courage. It all depends on someone's view of what happens after this life. Most give little thought to the judgment seat of Christ. I've heard so few messages on this in my life, it is unbelievable. Here's a taste:

John 3:16 and John 3:18

As silly as this sounds, some people envision doing well and pleasing God if they "haven't killed anybody." Just kidding, of course. Despite this outrageous thought, most folks are constantly wondering if God really loves them, if their behavior is pleasing to Him, or if He wants to fling a "bolt of lightning" their way. The first answer is yes, the second is sometimes, and the third one is not right now, at least not at everyone.

Let me explain. The Bible is clear – and it's marked on the faces of football players – that God sent Jesus because He loved the world and that whoever believes in Him will have everlasting life (John 3:16). The following verse, 17, says God sent Jesus into the world <u>not</u> to condemn the world but THROUGH Him it may be saved. This is good news. This takes care of "Does God love me?" The answer is clearly yes.

Is He pleased? Yes, sometimes. Sometimes? Yes – if our life is a "faith walk." I get this answer in Hebrews 11:6:

*"It's impossible to please God **apart from faith**. And why? Because anyone who wants to approach God must believe both that he exists and that he cares enough to respond to those who seek him" (The Message).*

Here's another one about pleasing or not pleasing God:

"Now the just shall live by faith; but if anyone draws back, my soul has no pleasure in him" (Heb. 10:38 JB Phillips)

So, yes, we are loved always because that's His nature, but faith in Christ is the way God is "accessed" and "pleased." This is the whole message of the New Testament. People who believe there's another way to God have to base their philosophy on something other than the Bible because it "ain't" there.

How many Christians consistently walk in faith? Certainly, we should have faith for eternity–that God will take us to heaven–but faith for everything else? Do these little or big anxious, worrisome thoughts bug you, or do you take them by faith to God? Fear and faith are opposites. They cannot coexist.

Before I continue in this vein and on to grace works, I want to address the third part of the questions above – the lightning bolt reference. While John 3:16 is the headline verse for most people, John 3:18 isn't:

"Whoever believes in him is not condemned, but whoever does not believe stands condemned already because they have not believed in the name of God's one and only Son."

I've heard people say all my life that "you're damned if you do and damned if you don't." Well, this is a "damned if you don't verse." A lot people think doing nothing with the decision about Jesus is ok. They're not "bad people" – they just don't do anything about God's Son. They don't seek to know, understand, repent or believe in Jesus' finished work on the cross. This is tragic and unacceptable to the God of the Bible. Doing nothing is the same to God as being against Him (Matt. 12:20).

Strongholds are very difficult to deal with. Another way they are established is through trauma. Trauma blasts away at our insides, penetrating to the deepest parts of us. Just how deep? Right down to the cellular level, and it is sometimes there that the "accuser of the brethren" (Rev. 12:10) has buried a hatchet. Chapter explains how.

CHAPTER 9

Trauma and the Accuser

As we have discussed here, open doors allow Satan to afflict us, most often mentally. The oppression of the mind is his chief weapon to harass, accuse, condemn, beguile, deceive, berate, belittle, and attempt to cause such disruption in our mental faculties that we can become mentally ill. I don't write here of those who are mentally ill because of some birth defect or otherwise physical abnormality but what we may suffer in our daily lives from trauma or very serious life-altering situations. As David Kupelian wrote earlier, mental duress and illness have many Americans in a tailspin, with a dependence on drugs to get through the day (pg. 55).

Tribulation is Now!

Jesus said, "In the world you will have tribulation" (John 16:33). The Greek word for tribulation is "thlipsis," which means pressure (literally or figuratively): – afflicted, (-tion), anguish, burdened, persecution, tribulation, trouble. Note that the verse clearly states that we all have it … not might have, not will have it (as though we are not having it now) nor does it *imply* potential tribulation. Everybody experiences it one way or another. Jesus said, "In the world you will *have* tribulation." You get it by being human!

According to the web site www.trauma-pages.com/trauma.php (David Baldwin's web resource for all things trauma) states, "Traumatic experiences shake the foundations of our beliefs about safety, and shatter our assumptions of trust."

Many people feel insecure as a result of things that happened that make them feel unsafe. Molestation is just one of those things.

According to Jim Banks of House of Healing Ministries, invariably, sufferers of some physical and/or emotional difficulty have experienced significant emotional and/or physical trauma at some point in their lives, which has detrimentally affected their ability to recover from the normal, but difficult circumstances of life, and remain stable.

Removing the physical effects of trauma can greatly help an individual achieve or regain the capacity to heal and grow in many areas. It can also eliminate the daily torment of the long-term effects of trauma, both emotionally and physically.

"In the healing process, the crucial issue is building enough capacity to stay relationally connected to God over a sufficient amount of time for us to allow the process to be completed. Unfortunately, trauma affects us on many levels, emotional, spiritual and physical. Medically, the understanding and treatment of the effects of trauma has been limited primarily to the emotional. And medication seems to have been relegated to insulation from the pain. Traditional medicine seems to recognize that our bodies have many little understood capabilities, and one of them is the retention of the memory of trauma at a cellular level, but treatment has not been effective in reversing its effects," Banks says.

Christ's Trauma on the Cross Provided Our Healing

Arthur Burk, founder of Plumbline Ministries, (www.plumblineministries.com) has an understanding that trauma itself is a specific scheme of the enemy to gain access to us for purposes of future torment and emotional torture. His take on it is that when Jesus was on the cross, the darkness that overtook the scene that day was neither a storm, nor the aftermath of a localized earthquake, as many Biblical scholars have tried to reason. But instead, it was every demon in hell coming to take its last best shot at Him with intentional torment and torture. It is little wonder that his death took comparatively so little time on the cross.

Jesus Paid It All!

All pain and suffering Jesus experienced on the cross was for the removal of our sins or done to facilitate our healing, and this includes the trauma we experience. Consequently, Jesus' death on the cross was complete atonement in another aspect of human life in that He took upon Himself all the trauma, torture and torment intended for you and me. We do not have to suffer that again. It is Arthur's belief that the principle behind this scheme of the enemy is to cause trauma **before the cross became effective in the life of an individual for one of two purposes***: 1) make it difficult for a person to enter into their full identity 2) for the purpose of causing future torment.*

Trauma in the Womb

This is one reason Satan seeks to act early. If he can create havoc in the womb or in the early years, much of what happens stays beneath the conscious level of awareness.

The only way that "before the cross became effective" is remotely possible is to remove some portion of the individual to another dimension, time or place and hold it captive there. This would again reiterate Satan's scheme to traumatize an individual and remove them to another dimension.

Dr. Tom Hawkins, founder of Restoration in Christ Ministries, (www.rcm-usa.org) has noted as a result of ministry to numerous Satanic Ritual Abuse (SRA) victims that portions of their identity/being can be stuck/captured/imprisoned/delayed in other dimensions, times or spaces through intentionally enforced trauma, which to my mind confirms Arthur's assertion that a trauma victim's identity can be messed with by intentionally introducing, or taking advantage of, events that effectively delay development.

A Multi-Dimensional World

Further, Hawkins states, that people live in a multi-dimensional world but are generally only cognizant of four of them; height, width, depth and time. But theoretical scientists working with String and Superstring theory tell us that there are at least 11, and maybe as many as 23 dimensions!

Banks reminds us "we are made in the image of God (Genesis 1:27), and God is light (1 John 1:5 and John 1:1-9) and are a children of light (Luke 16:8). Scientists tell us that if each organ is broken down to the lowest common denominator, it will all be a similar type of cell; same DNA as the whole person but encoded such that it will perform well within the context of that organ. If we break that cell down further, we find a number of atoms. Each atom can be further reduced to its component parts; neutron, proton(s) and electron(s). These elements vibrate at a specific frequency, which is in accord with the individual's DNA. Scientists further tell us that if each individual's DNA strand is un-twisted. it can be played as a melody on a piano; more vibrations."

The Devil's in the Details

When the enemy messes with us through our own sinful activity or cursed generational (family) issues, our DNA can be altered by attaching junk to the strand (the science of epigenetics) or through trauma; our "song" can be changed from a major key to a minor one, simply by slightly altering our frequency. Although our DNA can't be changed, and our DNA is passed on to our children, things riding on it can have a profound effect in a single generation. How can that be done? By removing one small part of us to another domain or dimension.

All this may seem too weird until you realize the complexity of the human being. Scientists estimate the average human being has 50 trillion cells in their body. Many different kinds of macromolecules are used to build cells, which in turn can be organized into tissues. Tissues form organs, and several organs may have interrelated functions in a cohesive organ system, such as the digestive system. A complex organism contains multiple organ systems with different functions. Multiple organisms of a single species may form a group, called a population. Many populations of different species form diverse communities, and communities that share the same geographical space are part of a larger ecosystem. The Earth's biosphere is made up of many diverse ecosystems.

We should not wonder why then some part us is captured during trauma that can keep us from realizing exactly what happened to maintain our imbalances.

So How Do We Set Things Back in Order?

First, by applying the principles of Jesus Christ's Atonement to the issues of the effects and the residue of trauma in the life of a trauma victim. Jesus' substitutionary death in our behalf says we do not have to suffer the subsequent torment that trauma victims usually report.

Banks prescribes the healing comes through several steps for counselors to take:

1. Through specific questions (an interview), determine the traumatic events for the client from childhood into adulthood; physical, emotional, spiritual, sexual. Include such things as divorce/deaths/loss of a key loved one, childhood accidents and injuries, rape, abuse, surgeries, frequent moves, moves at key times, major rejections, abandonment, car accidents, major illnesses, broken bones, surgeries and invasive medical procedures, attempted suicide, near death experiences, etc. Anything that potentially had a major negative (traumatic) effect on them. Make a list if you need to.

2. First of all, tell your client what you are about to do, and get their permission to do it. If they will not give you permission to take authority over their being/body for a few minutes to cut some things off, you do not have the authority to continue. If your client agrees, in the name of Jesus Christ, take authority over their body (I often use the term "being," which tends to be more inclusive) and command out of it all of the effects of everything that made it on the list, down to the cellular level; all memories of any incident on any level, the results of all trauma; fright, terror, chemicals (drugs, poisons or toxins) the body has either produced naturally and hung on to as a result of trauma, or that were ingested or injected, excess enzymes produced, anesthesia and anesthetics, etc., produced prior to, during and after the incident. This would include fear induced during and following significant medical procedures and surgery(s).

Require that it come out without harm or injury. Bless their lymphatic system and other systems to safely remove all wastes, toxins, poisons, or any other product or by-product of trauma from the body. Include anything that is naturally a foreign agent in the body, that were bonded to, or that the body produced in excess connected with the traumatic event.

3. Take authority over their body, and command out of it all of the long and short-term effects of trauma, injuries, stress, tension, worry, anxiety, fear, wounding, etc. Be certain to include the memories of all abuse, defiling touch, incisions, invasive medical procedures, rejection, abandonment, beatings/bruises, harsh words or curses spoken by parents or other significant authorities, etc. I recently prayed for a woman who's intercession induced secondary trauma to her through attempting to help carry the burdens of others.

In the event of particularly defiling activity such as rape or initial homosexual encounters, command out of their body the memory of all smells, feelings, tastes, sounds, vibrations and touch connected with those events. Do not hurry through this part. You will find that your client may feel things leaving them as the get progressively more relaxed. I have had several clients actually fall asleep toward the conclusion of this section and many more unable to walk out of my office immediately afterward because they are so relaxed.

4. This is important; Ask the Lord to disconnect them from any and all 2nd heaven entities; principalities, powers, dominions, thrones, rulers, etc., that have gained access to them through the traumatic events they suffered, for the purpose of future torment. Ask the Lord to shut down all pathways, portals, and means of access to them for communication or influence.

According to Psalms 115:16, "The heavens are the Lord's heavens; but the earth he has given into the hands of men." From this scripture I deduce that there are 2nd heaven entities above our pay grade that the Lord himself should be asked to deal with, but we have been given authority over those demonic entities that touch/affect earth. Those are our responsibility. I have dealt with them as a higher order of evil, such as a dark power, ruler, throne or dominion and experienced much success with breaking all their tormenting activities by asking God the Father to deal with them. They seem to come out or disconnect whether they are demons (earth bound) or 2nd heaven entities of a higher order. This step alone seems to cut off all tormenting dreams in 95% of those for whom I have used this tool. And if this is all you are able to pray due to time or opportunity, it will go a long way toward establishing freedom for them.

As Dr. Paul Cox of Aslan's Place Ministries (www.aslansplace.org) teaches, ask the Lord if there is a specific place where portions of them have been imprisoned; ie, Sheol.

5. Take authority over all pathways, portals, and means of access, marks or markers, or any means of connectivity placed upon them physically or spiritually to track them or gain access to them for purposes of torment, and shut them down in the authority given to you in the name of Jesus. Cancel all assignments of familiar spirits made against them as a result of traumatic incidents. If your client has been frequently tormented by violent or sexually oriented dreams, this will usually kill them. But if you are uncertain or just want to cover the ground, ask the Lord issue a "cease and desist order." If these tormenting dreams persist, and you have tried a number of other ministry avenues and feel you have exhausted your efforts, you might want to try a technique called "Convening The Court of Heaven" from Psalm 82, created by Dr. Tom Hawkins, founder of Restoration in Christ Ministries, (www.rcm-usa. org). A teaching CD set is available from his ministry that covers this tool clearly.

If they have had violent or tormenting dreams, ask them if there is a theme or pattern to what happens to them in the dreams. Sometimes this will give you a clue as to other issues you need to deal with in a subsequent ministry session.

6. Ask the Lord that if there is any portion of their being that has been delayed, trapped, captured or imprisoned in another time, another space, dimension or place, as a result of trauma, would He please cause it to be released and rejoined with their core being in this current time, space and dimension. I also ask the Lord to reunify those portions with the core person. If prompted by the Holy Spirit, walk them through a reunification of these fractured parts by walking them through each dimension or through each year of their lives.

See Isaiah 61:1-2, "The Spirit of the Lord GOD is upon me; because the LORD hath anointed me to preach good tidings unto the meek; he hath sent me to bind up the brokenhearted, to proclaim liberty to the captives, and the opening of the prison to them that are bound; 2 To proclaim the acceptable year of the LORD, and the day of vengeance of our God; to comfort all that mourn;"

(Remember that prisoners are there because of something they have done. Captives are imprisoned through no fault of their own.)

I have on several occasions had the Holy Spirit have me walk them slowly forward from the age of one, two or three years, year by year, until we reached their current chronological age, pausing when prompted between years to allow the Holy Spirit to re-integrate them. More recently, I have included the period from conception to birth as well when their birth mother experienced trauma herself or planned to abort the child. I also asked Him to mature each reintegrated portion to the client's current age. This doesn't seem to take any more time, but I believe it is worth the effort. I have not had the opportunity to use this tool in behalf of an abused child, but I have no doubt that it would be equally as effective as it is with adults, and perhaps even more so. It is always proper to coach your adult client to be aware of his/her body and report to you the changes they sense or feel as you are walking them through each year of the process. Don't get in a hurry.

7. Pray that the Lord will reestablish the connection between the hemispheres of the brain. Often heavily traumatized clients live predominately out of the left hemisphere of their brain and need the right side to be stimulated. Pray that the Lord will reestablish and synchronize both explicit memory and implicit memories and to reactivate any connections required to retrieve memories needed for complete healing.

8. If prompted, I will place my hands specifically in the area near the amygdala and then the hippocampus and ask the Lord to restore them, repair them or enhance them so that their healing can progress rapidly. There are five specific organs in the human brain that are damaged by wounding and trauma. These will have to be addressed later in order to assure complete healing.

I usually ask if I can place my hands of the head of my client while praying this section of the tool, and it usually accompanied by a strong anointing. So don't freak out if this happens to you as well.

Ask the Lord to reestablish for them the appropriate sleep patterns the Lord designed for them, and to establish for them a sweet undisturbed, rejuvenating, regenerative rest. Proverbs 3:24 "If you lie down, you will not be afraid; when you lie down, your sleep will be sweet."

9. Ask the Lord to begin or reestablish Godly dreams, visions and angelic visitations in the night seasons, both to enlighten, instruct and direct them. I have had numerous clients report that following the ministry session that they fell asleep immediately, stayed asleep and were not awakened by dreams the entire night for the first time in years. The immediate restoration of sleep patterns happens for 90% of my clients. And reestablishment of Godly dreams for only about 70% initially. I believe this is because of the reestablishment of sound sleep, which has usually been deprived for years.

10. Ask the Lord to begin to dismantle all automatic human responses gained as a result of trauma; i.e., abnormal fright responses, triggers, fears and phobias, etc. Pray over their brain for the Lord to rebuild, reestablish, recreate any electrical or chemical any connections broken or improperly reconnected, as a result of trauma so that the individual can operate once again within normal limits of high and low stimulus, and can remain in control emotionally when the stimulus exceeds those limits. I have had numerous clients report that following the ministry session that they no longer have most (or all) of their long-term exaggerated fright responses. This is a very common experience.

11. Then instruct the client to instruct his/her human spirit each evening before going to sleep to turn its face to the Father during the night, while the body and soul are out cold, and receive everything he/she needs for the coming day. Psalms 16:7 "I will bless Jehovah, who has given me counsel; Yes, my heart instructs me in the night seasons."

Jim Banks of House of Healing Ministries

P.O. Box 15514 Asheville, NC 28813

www.houseofhealingministries.org

How Trauma Causes Imbalanced Thinking

Traumatic events can trigger such fear in people that their thinking becomes unbalanced and unstable. If unforgiveness is at the core —and it usually is—Satan bores a hole into the conscience to suggest the person believe they are "crazy." His goal is self-rejection and the creation of a false personality or "mask" to cover up feelings of instability. As we investigate further in this manual, shame-based living over something that occurred long ago about something we remember, or even that which is sometimes buried in the subconscious, can lead to tremendous daily and sometimes debilitating fear that we can't put our finger on. It's what's called "floating anxiety," which often seems to have no rhyme or reason.

The Accuser Goes to Work

Once Satan's accusations begin, and don't forget one of his names is "the Accuser" (Rev. 12:10), his persistent lies can bear such torment (fear has torment – 1 John 4:18) that it can make it unbearable for the afflicted. If the traumatic events occur very early in life, as we have seen, the impact can be compounded over many years of one's life so that the lies have become imbedded in the personality and so that fear reigns even more, causing more and more instability. Obviously the brain chemistry can undergo serious alteration, causing up and downs, severe mania and depression. If not treated, this can lead to suicide.

If we add curses to the mix, we have an incalculable combination of conditions bearing down on the psyche. Within the litany of curses and blessings found in Deuteronomy 27 and 28, one stands out when we focus on mental illness. Incidentally, all these curses mentioned in these chapters are incurred for the sin of idolatry. Remember, also, these are passed from generation to another.

"
The Lord will smite you with madness and blindness and dismay of [mind and] heart" (Deut. 28:28).

Fear factor

The stronghold of mental illness has a number of associative demons that harass, torment and bind one's mind into a state of extreme difficulty and instability, including attention deficit disorder (ADD), alzheimer's disease, bipolar disorder, confusion, distraction, forgetfulness, hallucinations, hysteria, insanity, mind binding, mind blocking, mind racing, obsessive-compulsive disorder, paranoia, schizophrenia, senility and stress disorder. These illnesses, of course, have a myriad of reasons for their existence, and certainly cannot be laid solely at the door of the demonic.

Love and fear

When you boil it down, everything comes down to these two things: God's unconditional agape love can heal anyone of anything. His power is amazing. However, fear can keep us bound in a "multitude of sins."

Above all things have intense and unfailing love for one another, for love covers a multitude of sins [forgives and ᵃdisregards the offenses of others] (1 Peter 4:8 AMP).

There is no fear in love [dread does not exist], but full-grown (complete, perfect) love ᵃturns fear out of doors and expels every trace of terror! For fear ᵇbrings with it the thought of punishment, and [so] he who is afraid has not reached the full maturity of love [is not yet grown into love's complete perfection] (1 John 4:18 AMP).

No Easy Task

Overcoming this stronghold, like any other, is no easy task. It takes great courage and perseverance. Once recognized, however, it can be defeated, but most often people will not make the attempt to do this because they have accepted their plight as inevitable, and Satan wins. One way he wins is to ensure you walk in shame-based living. Bipolar disorder is a condition that is full of shame. We'll explore this in our next chapter.

CHAPTER 10

Shame Off You!

At the bottom of all things is abandonment. Psychiatrists called this "the primary wound." It doesn't really matter if it's a physical or emotional abandonment; it opens a very extensive wound in the soul of anyone. Way down in the inner being people discover they've often been left to fend for themselves, whether from birth or later own. They may feel they are "on their own" in this world to embrace self-reliance because "nobody really cares for me." The Psalmist put it this way:

I pour out my complaint before Him; I tell before Him my trouble. ³ When my spirit was overwhelmed and fainted [throwing all its weight] upon me, then You knew my path. In the way where I walk they have hidden a snare for me. ⁴ Look on the right hand [the point of attack] and see; for there is no man who knows me [to appear for me]. Refuge has failed me and I have no way to flee; no man cares for my life or my welfare. I cried to You, O Lord; I said, You are my refuge, my portion in the land of the living. Attend to my loud cry, for I am brought very low; deliver me from my persecutors, for they are stronger than I. Bring my life out of prison, that I may confess, praise, and give thanks to Your name; the righteous will surround me and crown themselves because of me, for You will deal bountifully with me (Psa. 142:3-7).

Feeling alone most of their lives, people often strike back to become that independent soul who needs no one, when in fact, they are in desperate need of the love of many. Abandonment's "cousin" is shame. This one starts early, too, to make the person feel they are "hopelessly and fatally flawed," and nothing can help them—not even God. This can be so subtle, but shame is part of The Fall and is part and parcel of being a human. It, too, started with the first couple:

God: "Adam, where are you?"

Adam: I was naked and ashamed so I hid myself."

Chester and Betsy Kylstra, who have been teaching on these things for years through their ministry, Restoring the Foundations, say this about shame, in *Overcoming the Hidden Joy Stealer*:

There is a "killer" on the loose, a deceptive one, that creates powerful strongholds in Christians everywhere destroying their joy unless it is identified and exposed. We call it the Shame-Fear-Control Stronghold or SFC. This multifaceted stronghold will also destroy their self-confidence and rob them of their destinies; and it destroys unbelievers, too. Go with us as we expose this stronghold and help you overcome it.

Perhaps you know people who are affected by this stronghold. Right now it is killing their emotional lives while its victims curiously try to protect it from being exposed. Such is the nature of this stronghold, which binds its victim with the shame of being found out until he musters the courage to receive his freedom. If you or someone you love are among its victims, in order to be free, you must learn to identify the fruit of the stronghold, understand its operation, and then apply God's strategy to defeat and demolish it. Let's examine its trail of evidence. (Editor's Note: This article used by permission from Catch the Fire www.revivalmag.com)

Clues of the Killer's Presence

The "SFC Killer," which may affect as many as 80% of the people you know, hides deep within our personalities, masquerading as part of who we are. Ask yourself these questions to see if you or someone you know has its symptoms.

Do you know anyone who constantly feels unworthy, inadequate, intimidated or just plain "bad"? These negative emotions indicate the presence of shame. But don't feel alone, in this age of abuse, fatherless families, emotional neglect, and abandonment, it seems that many people struggle with these issues. Many people have even taken on "shame" as a personal identity.

When we are looking for the presence of shame in a counselee, we usually ask him, "Do you have an endless refrain that 'plays' in your thoughts? Are you continually thinking thoughts like, I am different, I am defective, I am embarrassed, I am guilty, I am inadequate?" If so, shame has become a part of your identity? But the presence of shame is only the beginning. Shame is often allied with fear.

Ask yourself, is fear included in my frequent mental refrain? Am I afraid of being exposed, or abandoned, or rejected? Do fears like these dominate my thinking so that they have become my continual companions, deeply embedded within my personality as "normally abnormal" parts of my identity?

If so, you may have developed a strategy for survival. Do you control other people, or yourself, or perhaps the situations around you in order to minimize any risk of having the shame exposed? Have you developed "walls" where you permanently display a "Keep Out" sign? If you feel threatened by someone, do you resort to aggressive and bullying behaviors in order to intimidate them? These are only a few of the telltale signs that had their ugly beginning in the Garden of Eden.

In the Beginning

The Shame-Fear-Control (SFC) Stronghold started in the Garden of Eden, with Father Adam and Mother Eve. When both Adam and Eve tasted the forbidden fruit, it produced a terrible effect. "Then the eyes of both of them were opened, and they knew that they were naked; and they sewed fig leaves together and made themselves loin coverings." (Genesis 3:7)

Then when God came to walk with them that day, instead of wanting to be in His company they hid from Him.

When God confronted them, Adam said to God, "I heard the sound of Thee in the garden, and I was afraid because I was naked so I hid myself." (Genesis 3:10) Adam and Eve's shame over their sin led to their fear of being exposed. In order to hide their shame, they covered themselves with the fig leaves and hid themselves. The fears of exposure, of being found out, and of facing their failure, all joined forces to give "legal ground" to the stronghold of control.

Unfortunately, these strongholds are still with us today. They come down our family lines as ancestral sins, those wicked behaviors that we learn from our ancestors and become habits we develop in our own lives. Left undetected and unconfessed, these sins cause us to reap the curse-like effects of shame, fear, and control. They form bonds with other sins such as the fear of abandonment and occult involvement to keep us trapped as they intertwine with our positive, God-created qualities. Because they become so much a part of us, they deceive us into believing that we are one with them.

Revelation

The day the Lord revealed the "inner" workings of the SFC to us, we were excited. We were praying with a counselee and had already progressed through the preliminary stages of cleansing from sins of the fathers and resulting curses, ungodly beliefs, and soul/spirit hurts helping her to recover the "legal ground" she had unwittingly given over to the devil.

(Ephesians 4:27) We were ready to bring freedom from demonic oppression to our counselee.

We explained to her the evidence we saw in her life of oppression by the evil triumvirate, shame, fear and control, and that these were somehow cooperating together and strengthening each other for her destruction. She asked, "How are they able to do this?"

Up to that moment, we had not known the answer to her question. Yet we found ourselves explaining the answer in a word of wisdom from the Holy Spirit that surprised us. He showed us how we give "place" to each stronghold, how the different strongholds reinforce each other, and how they remain hidden. Most important of all, He showed us how to disassemble and demolish the SFC Stronghold.

The Truth Shall Set Us Free

The only way to freedom is to realize and act on the truth. This requires a major paradigm shift in our thinking. We need to change what we think of as "I" because "I" has been distorted by demonic strongholds so that we don't even know our true God-created personalities. For most of our lives, our true identities have been buried in the bowels of a castle-like prison held captive within the walls created by our fears.

It is important to accept the fact that we have believed a lie about our true identities. This lie declares that the real "me" is shameful, has a mindset of fear, and a modus operandi of control. Rather than believe a lie, it is time for us to believe the truth about who we are, that we have a God-ordained identity, that He has destined us for "sonship." It is time to believe that Jesus Christ did indeed take our shame on the cross (Hebrews 12:2), and that He has opened the prison door. It is time to do all that we need to do to receive His freedom. It can be done, and many Christians have already received their freedom.

Strategy For Freedom

The first step in defeating any enemy, even a demonic stronghold, is to understand his weak points, in this case, shame. Shame can be easily destroyed if the SFC victim will make a paradigm shift and treat this stronghold as his enemy rather than as part of himself. He must move from a defensive posture to an offensive one, from hiding to active warfare against shame.

Next, he must make the decision to battle the SFC Stronghold until the victory is total, no matter how long it takes. This is a battle unto death. In the past, shame killed its victim. Now, the demonic stronghold must be destroyed and eliminated.

If the person infected with shame then identifies one by one the places where he has been ashamed, he can then disassemble the stronghold by confessing its presence and its underlying sins. He can then demolish the stronghold by replacing it with believing what God says about him and can achieve victory in a short time. Making fast progress here depends on the victim's willingness to continually submit to the process as it did with the Israelites as they took possession of the Promised Land. "Little by little I will drive them (your enemies) out before you, until you have increased enough to take possession of the land." (Exodus 23:30 NIV)

God has great things for us, as we appropriate His promises like the one in Isaiah 61:7 (NIV). "Instead of their shame My people will receive a double portion, and instead of disgrace they will rejoice in their inheritance; and so they will inherit a double portion in their land, and everlasting joy will be theirs." If we really let Jesus heal us, we will "never be put to shame." (1 Peter 2:6 NIV)

(Chester and Betsy Kylstra are the founders of Restoring the Foundations, based in Hendersonville, NC. Their book, *Restoring the Foundations*, explores emotional healing as an integrated approach to ministry. They founded the Healing House Network, a safe place where leaders can come for ministry and training. For more information on the Shame-Fear-Control Stronghold, be sure to get a copy of the three CD set by the Kylstras, Shame-Fear-Control and the single CD - Breaking Free from Life's Destructive Patterns, found at http://stores. rtfresources.org/audio.

Guilt-Ridden

As one famous teacher wrote, "Most Christians can't get from the church to the parking lot without feeling guilty about something." This speaks loudly to the huge subtleties of shame-based living and a conscience that shouldn't be guilty:

[22] *Let us all come forward and draw near with true (honest and sincere) hearts in unqualified assurance and absolute conviction engendered by faith (by [n]-that leaning of the entire human personality on God in absolute trust and confidence in His power, wisdom, and goodness), having our hearts sprinkled and* **purified from a guilty (evil) conscience** *and our bodies cleansed with pure water* (Heb. 10:22 Amp).

Didn't God wash the conscience of a believer who's received His Son? Yes, but many of them haven't realized that deep cleaning within their own being because of the many "guilt events" that have happened in their souls since they climbed out of the womb. Since people were born with a sense of shame, having come from the loins of Adam, the SIN nature carries with it shame—until we allow Jesus to completely deal with this by the power of His cross! Abandonment, shame and guilt are cumulative!

Abandonment is Cumulative

Abandonment contains all our loses, disconnections and disappointments from the early death of a parent to a teenage breakup, to being shown up by a sibling. All these events and similar ones make us more susceptible to heartbreak as adults when we are abandoned.

The abandonment wound, stored in the limbic brain, is easily triggered. You feel a raw nerve twinge when you fail to receive recognition at work, a friend forgets to invite you to a party, or a special date never called back. When being left is the trigger, core abandonment fears erupt. Stress hormones course through our bodies, leaving the strongest among us desperate and feeling dependent. Rather than dissipate, this fear tends to incubate. Its insecurity burrows deep within us where it sabotages our relationships.

The fear of being left makes it more difficult to let go and desire for our ex to come back to take away the hurt and rejection. The rejection creates nagging conflict; closure remains incomplete. We feel unjustly dismissed, and we long for an opportunity to vindicate the hurt. We are left alone to grapple with the broken pieces. Mixed with our rage is a desire for our ex to come back to take away the hurt and rejection.

One of our big problems is the "eye gate, ear gate" in which we pour the world's values into ourselves.

Brain Rot

Surveys in the past few years have shown that the average Christian in America, besides being a regular churchgoer, had far too much in common with the average person without Christ! They watched the same TV shows, movies and read many of the same books. In other words, most Christians, especially those who had attended public schools, were secularly educated in the same value system that everyone else was.

Hollywood and television produce a lot of entertainment, but how much is edifying to the mind? Probably a small percentage. Most shows are geared toward entertainment, which can range to not so bad to horrendous.

The University of Michigan reported these findings:

Does TV Affect a Child's Brain Development?

With television programs—and even a cable channel—designed and marketed specifically for babies, whether kids under two years of age should be watching becomes an important question. While we are learning more all the time about early brain development, we do not yet have a clear idea how television may affect it. Some studies link early TV viewing with later attention problems, such as ADHD. However, other experts disagree with these results. One study found that TV viewing before age three slightly hurt several measures of later cognitive development, but that between ages three and five it slightly helped reading scores.

The <u>American Academy of Pediatrics</u> takes a "better-safe-than-sorry" stance on TV for young children:

"It may be tempting to put your infant or toddler in front of the television, especially to watch shows created just for children under age two.

Of course violence and sex make up the majority of what is viewed by adults. The University of Michigan found these grim facts:

What about TV and Aggressive or Violent Behavior?

Literally thousands of studies since the 1950s have asked whether there is a link between exposure to media violence and violent behavior. All but 18 have answered, "Yes." The evidence from the research is overwhelming. According to the AAP, "Extensive research evidence indicates that media violence can contribute to aggressive behavior, desensitization to violence, nightmares, and fear of being harmed." Watching violent shows is also linked with having less empathy toward other.

An average American child will see 200,000 violent acts and 16,000 murders on TV by age 18.

Two-thirds of all programming contains violence.

Programs designed for children more often contain violence than adult TV.

Most violent acts go unpunished on TV and are often accompanied by humor. The consequences of human suffering and loss are rarely depicted.

Many shows glamorize violence. TV often promotes violent acts as a fun and effective way to get what you want, without consequences.

Even in G-rated, animated movies and DVDs, violence is common—often as a way for the good characters to solve their problems. Every single U.S. animated feature film produced between 1937 and 1999 contained violence, and the amount of violence with intent to injure has increased over the year.

Even "good guys" beating up "bad guys" gives a message that violence is normal and okay. Many children will try to be like their "good guy" heroes in their play.

Children imitate the violence they see on TV. Children under age eight cannot tell the difference between reality and fantasy, making them more vulnerable to learning from and adopting as reality the violence they see on TV.

Repeated exposure to TV violence makes children less sensitive toward its effects on victims and the human suffering it causes.

A University of Michigan researcher demonstrated that watching violent media can affect willingness to help others in need. Read about the study here: Comfortably Numb: Desensitizing Effects of Violent Media on Helping Others.

Viewing TV violence reduces inhibitions and leads to more aggressive behavior.

Watching television violence can have long-term effects:

A 15-year-long study by University of Michigan researchers found that the link between childhood TV-violence viewing and aggressive and violent behavior persists into adulthood.

A 17-year-long study found that teenaged boys who grew up watching more TV each day are more likely to commit acts of violence than those who watched less. Even having the TV on in the home is linked to more aggressive behavior in 3-year-olds. This was regardless of the type of programming and regardless of whether the child was actually watching the TV].

Media feed the mind of a growing child and an adult with ungodly beliefs. This, coupled with a secular world bent on teaching morals without spiritual grounding, will likely produce cynicism toward real spirituality. Unless there is an experience with the living God that backs up the truth the child or adult has heard, his faith is based solely on what he hears and absorbs. God never intended Scripture alone as the sole foundation for one's spiritual life: He wanted an encounter with the living God!

You study the scriptures thoroughly[1] because you think in them you possess eternal life,[2] and it is these same scriptures[3] that testify about me, **5:40** *but you are not willing to come to me so that you may have life* (John 5:39-40, Net Bible).

This encounter allows us to embrace the totality of the Word of God, the written word as well as the Living Word, Jesus Christ!

If we identify ourselves as Christian, we often refer to ourselves as "believers," but how much do we believe in the Bible? And how much do ungodly beliefs affect our lives? Obviously it can deeply affect our brain chemistry, creating a veritable highway for bipolar disorder. Building new Godly beliefs to replace the older and often rutted places of unbelief and knowledge is imperative. That's why it's so important that we examine how this is done in the next chapter.

CHAPTER 11

Godly and Ungodly Beliefs

We all have Godly and ungodly beliefs. What we believe *does* matter. Either we believe God's Word and the truth about His nature and character, or we don't. For many years the evangelical church has placed heavy emphasis on the Word of God. Some think it's infallible, and others doubt portions of it. I've never quite understood why people pick and choose. Why would they think one part is true, and the other parts are not? Jonah, no? and Job, yes? Jesus' words, yes? and Paul's words, no? Scripture says, "ALL scripture is inspired of God":

Every writing which is written by The Spirit is profitable for teaching, for correction, for direction and for a course in righteousness, (2 Tim. 3:16 Aramaic Bible in Plain English).

The emphasis on believing the Bible is absolutely necessary for a solid faith, but believing in God's character is also imperative. Let's be real. Sometimes we're clinging to scriptures that aren't working as quickly as we thought they should. So we cave. But what about God's infallible nature and goodness? Regardless of whether the scripture we are holding onto is working at the moment, God is still God, and He cannot lie! When scriptures *seem* to fail us, we can trust God's character.

God did this so that, by two unchangeable things **in which it is impossible for God to lie**, *we who have fled to take hold of the hope set before us may be greatly encouraged* (Heb. 6:18 NIV).

In other words, He's going to come through, whether it's the way we claimed or thought or not! The Bible is so full of God's promises, that it is not really possible to count them. Some people have tried and come up with about 3000. Others have counted 7000. Herbert Lockyer wrote a book called *All the promises of the Bible* and claims to list 8000!

Whether there are 3,000, 7,000 or 8,000, there's a great deal of God's truth and promises to hold on to. The question is not, how many promises are available to us, but how much do we REALLY believe and use to replace the ungodly beliefs we grew up with. These beliefs are formed by family, education, culture, friends and others whose opinions and beliefs may absolutely run contrary to the Word of God.

The Cycle of Belief

According to the Kylstras, beliefs are formed from our experiences, particularly in the first six years. When we experience something that is highly negative, we may begin to believe our experience is reality. This leads to an expectation that what we have experienced will happen again, which forms behavior, or at least our perception that this is the way life will go. All of this is based on our experience, whether it's good or bad. For some people many negative experiences set them on a course of negativity toward life, or as psychologists called it, "a self-fulfilling prophesy." Of course positive experience can set us on another track, that of a positive outcome. More on this later.

Changing the way we think, or transformation of the mind, requires a change is our belief system. Many people, after experiencing a truckload of negative experiences, begin to see that they have believed the wrong things! After many years of bad experiences, they turn to God for answers found in His Word. Or they remain the same, living out what they deem that life has "ordained" for them, and they continue on the same track until they die. It's amazing what it requires human beings, being as stubborn as we are, to decide that *Father Knows Best*. Remember: the carnal mind (that part of the mind without the Holy Spirit's influence) will continue to set itself against God and His truth. Strongholds develop in us that can be very hard to pull down:

[4] For the weapons of our warfare are not physical [weapons of flesh and blood], but they are mighty before God for the overthrow and destruction of strongholds, [Inasmuch as we] **refute arguments and theories and reasonings and every proud and lofty thing that sets itself up against the [true] knowledge of God;**

and we lead every thought and purpose away captive into the obedience of Christ (the Messiah, the Anointed One) (2 Cor. 10:4-5 Amp)

If we choose to believe God by the power of the Holy Spirit's intervention, we begin to realize that believing God's Word works! This takes a lot of work, something even a lot of Christians don't do because of the discipline that's required.

Whoever loves discipline loves knowledge, but whoever hates correction is stupid (Prov. 12:1 NIV).

Casting out a demon and sometimes forgiving can be fairly easy, but changing the way we believe can be quite difficult. Consider that you have believed a certain thing all your life, and it is completely at odds with the Scripture. Changing your thinking and believing may be the hardest thing you've ever done! It can be done, however.

Perfect ungodly belief (This information was used by permission from Chester and Betsy Kylstra's book, *Restoring the Foundations*).

Sounds ridiculous, doesn't it, but this encompasses how many people feel about themselves based on the experiences (belief cycle).

Perfect ungodly belief is one that appears to be absolutely **true** *based on the* **facts** *of our experiences and yet is absolutely* **false** *based on* **God's truth are the following:**

No one loves me.

I am all alone.

I am defective.

God doesn't love me.

How UGBs Are Formed

1. By hurtful experiences...

Childhood years — UGBs result from hurts (from words or deeds), traumas, and negative experiences (neglect, abuse, death) **Examples:** *"I am not important because* *my dad does not have time for me." "Significant people in my life will not be there for me when I need them." These UGBs will become incorporated into the very core of the hurt from which this child begins to live his life. These lies embedded within his hurt will powerfully affect his life* **until he learns how to get his hurt healed**

2. By Repetition of Hurts

Family repeated statements, especially ones about ourselves. For example, "You will never amount to anything." "Don't be a baby" or "Don't be a coward!"

Or there can be problems throughout our adult years in business, marriage, church, accidents, natural disasters or tragedies. All these can cause us to believe lies about ourselves, others and **God.**

3. From the Natural Mind of Mankind

It seems logical and appealing, but they reek with the worldly standards of man. The phony idea of the self-made man and worldly success, seeking popularity more than what is righteous and just. This is the natural, unsanctified mind, attempting to handle and make sense out of life's hurts and traumas that is chiefly responsible for the negative belief system that we have. Because of our unredeemed belief system, God "insists" that our minds be renewed.

4. By Family Heritage

We "inherit" our beliefs in politics, life, religion and relationships, and we build our prejudices; and even our parent's "pet peeves."

5. **By Unintentional Parental Teaching.** *The motives may be good, comfort or protecting and even encouraging.*

The Belief Expectation Cycle

Our system of believing is established by the experiences, positive and negative. These experiences lead to our beliefs, which cause us to expect certain things to happen. Our behavior results from these expectations, which lead to more experiences. For example, let's say the first date you have as a teenager ends in disaster, and the girl or guy is rude to us. This could establish a belief that the next date could end in the same way. If it is repeated, we may begin to expect that ALL future dates will turn out badly.

Our behavior from then on could be to shy away from dating – period.

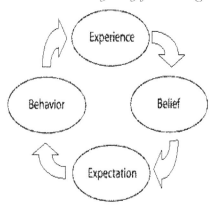

Replacing Ungodly Beliefs With Godly Beliefs

We all have ungodly beliefs, those negative ideas about ourselves, based on what we have just discussed. For example, we may believe that we are "no good" because it is repeated to us early in life by a parent, a teacher, a coach or some other significant person in our life. How can this be changed to a Godly belief?

Write the UGB down

A declarative statement of fears, resentments, unbelief. Let's say something like "I'll always be a financial failure."

Leave 4-5 blank lines between statements.

Write the Godly Belief next to UGB. The Godly belief, or the opposite of the UGB, should read something like, "God is helping me to become financially stable."

Hints for writing GBs:

Use scriptures to support GBs. In the one above, you might choose from among many one that positively reinforces God's desire for you to better yourself financially, such as Deuteronomy 8:18:

Remember that God, your God, Gave you the strength to produce all this wealth so as to confirm the covenant that he promised to your ancestors—as it is today. (Deuteronomy 8:18: The Message).

Ministering to UGBs

Confess – the sin of believing the UGB

Forgive - the ancestors (fathers and mothers)

Forgive - Anyone else responsible

Repent – Living a life based on the UGB

Forgive – yourself

Renounce the ungodly belief

Affirm and receive. Declare the Godly Belief and receive the truth from God's word.

It's wonderful to be able to replace ungodly beliefs with Godly ones, but what – or should I say – Who makes this possible? Who made your brain and who can heal the difficulties found within? His name is Jesus, and He's your healer, but "accessing" Him is the key to change.

CHAPTER 12

"Accessing" Jesus

You have probably realized by now if you have been attempting t o be healed of a particular thing, especially our subject matter, bipolar disorder, that prayer alone will *likely* not heal you. Also by now you may have given up (perhaps not if you're reading this) and relegated yourself to the "that's just the way life is" category.

While prayer is very important in the life of any Christian, few find help without tuning into and "accessing" the Presence of Jesus Christ to receive the help they need, instead of relying on Bible reading, Bible studies, Scripture memory, witnessing or being faithful in church as substitutes for the person of Jesus:

You have your heads in your Bibles constantly because you think you'll find eternal life there. But you miss the forest for the trees. These Scriptures are all about me! And here I am, standing right before you, and you aren't willing to receive from me the life you say you want (John 5:39, 40 The Message).

The Power is in the Person!

Over the years, I have learned one thing: counseling or teaching alone will never completely heal anyone! It helps greatly to give people insights they've never considered, but to be healed or delivered you have to seek the help of the ONLY ONE who can help you – Jesus Himself! My goal in ministry is to "get out of the way" to allow Jesus to move as He pleases to help the person seeking help. This is especially hard for someone like myself who had been teaching/counseling people for 37 years. The mind of a person, no matter how biblically sound or persuasive it may be, is not an alternative to the power that He has to heal and deliver:

And my language and my message were not set forth in persuasive (enticing and plausible) words of wisdom, but they were in demonstration of the [Holy] Spirit and power [^a] a proof by the Spirit and power of God, operating on me and stirring in the minds of my hearers the most holy emotions and thus persuading them] (1 Corinthians 2:4 AMP).

If anyone could have demonstrated his own power to deliver or heal, it would have been the Apostle Paul who penned these words above. The more "helpless" we become, the more powerful He is in us to bring what is needed to the hurting world:

But he said to me, "My grace is sufficient for you, for my power is made perfect in weakness." Therefore I will boast all the more gladly about my weaknesses, so that Christ's power may rest on me. 10 That is why, for Christ's sake, I delight in weaknesses, in insults, in hardships, in persecutions, in difficulties. For when I am weak, then I am strong (2 Cor. 12:9-10).

Becoming "Weak"

I dare say most people have no desire to become "weak." God's desire is for His power to move through us, but often our "soul power" gets in the way. We try to become strong in ourselves! This is the reason God *allows* such things as Paul experienced in the above verse, and if we want what God desires, we will face tribulations that push us to the point of giving up, being broken, feeling forsaken, betrayed and any other kind of difficulty so that His power is "perfected in weakness."

T. Austin-Sparks has said:

"Whether we are able yet to accept it or not, the fact is that if we are going on with God fully, all the soul's energies and abilities for knowing, understanding, sensing and doing will come to an end, and we shall 'on that side' stand bewildered, dazed, numbed and impotent. Then, only a new, other, and Divine understanding, constraint, and energy will send us forward or keep us going. At such times we shall have to say to our souls, 'My soul, be thou silent unto God' (Ps. 62.5); and 'My soul, come thou with me to follow the Lord.' But what joy and strength there is when, the soul having been constrained to yield to the spirit, the higher wisdom and glory is perceived

in its vindication. Then it is that 'My soul doth magnify the Lord, and my spirit hath rejoiced in God my Savior my Saviour" (Luke 1:46). The spirit HATH, the soul DOTH - note the tenses.

So that unto fullness of joy the soul is essential, and it MUST be brought through the darkness and death of its own ability to learn the higher and deeper realities for which the spirit is the first organ and faculty."* (*Quotes from: WHAT IS MAN by T. Austin-Sparks).

Soulish Power

Watchman Nee, the great Chinese missionary and teacher, warned that in *The Latent Power of the Soul* that in the latter days, people would seek to eat more from the Tree of the Knowledge of Good and Evil rather from the Tree of Life (Jesus). Even Scriptural knowledge can be a "hindrance," as we rely far too much on knowledge rather than on knowing the Son of God.

Many years ago I walked into the church where I was attending to pick up my Bible from the pew where I had left it. Standing there alone in the sanctuary, the Lord said to me so clearly, "You don't know as you ought to know." At that time I was cramming every Christian book I could get my hands on into my wee brain so I knew exactly what God was saying to me: Head knowledge without God's love in us and living through us is a far cry from what He wants. Here is the scriptural reference:

If anyone imagines that he has come to know and understand much [of divine things, without love], he does not yet perceive and recognize and understand as strongly and clearly, nor has he become as intimately acquainted with anything as he ought or as is necessary (1 Cor. 8:2 Amp**).**

Deliverance and healing of any kind often evade us because we're led to believe that if we get enough knowledge, that will do the trick; it won't. This is the great tragedy of the American church. All our preaching, teaching and packing pews for the kingdom are not getting the results we seek, and many in the Body of Christ are crippled, hurting and STUCK because we are not seeking the PRESENCE of Christ!

Prayer Alone Didn't Work

I had an experience several years ago that branded me for life. Panic struck. Before panic hit, I was one praying dude and in the Word regularly. I'm talking a couple of hours a day and usually all day long intermittently praying. God didn't intend for prayer to work every time, or He wouldn't have taught us about stillness and meditation. Listen to David as he describes the magnificent power of stillness:

"For God alone my soul waits in silence; from Him comes my salvation.² He only is my Rock and my Salvation, my Defense and my Fortress, I shall not be greatly moved. ³ How long will you set upon a man that you may slay him, all of you, like a leaning wall, like a tottering fence? ⁴ They only consult to cast him down from his height [to dishonor him]; they delight in lies. They bless with their mouths, but they curse inwardly. Selah [pause, and calmly think of that]! ⁵ My soul, wait only upon God and silently submit to Him; for my hope and expectation are from Him. ⁶ He only is my Rock and my Salvation; He is my Defense and my Fortress, I shall not be moved" (Psa. 65:1-6 Amp).

The panic and accompanying fear were so dark and foreboding that I felt I couldn't breathe. My family called the paramedics because I thought I was having a heart attack. The medics told me I was okay and getting plenty of oxygen, but I couldn't believe it. The night rolled into day, as I walked in my yard all night to calm myself down. My feet felt like they couldn't touch the ground. All I did was quote scripture from about midnight until 5 am! Finally, I checked myself into the hospital in the wee hours and stayed there two days until I settled down. It was as close to hell as I ever want to get!

Panic hit me several times after my initial experience before I learned to overcome it in the Presence of the Lord. I would steal away from my family when I felt the same foreboding, enveloping fear and panic enfolding its heavy cloak over me. In this experience, I learned to shut up, sit down and wait on the peaceful Presence of Jesus, and He immediately swallowed up panic in His love! In a matter of minutes, He stilled the storm in me! From that point on, I practiced stillness and meditation most every day to offset whatever fears and anxieties were trying to penetrate my soul.

Most Christians glibly speak about "waiting on the Lord," but few understand the depth or meaning of the significance. Most can't sit down long enough to quiet their souls to learn the discipline to do this incredibly important thing. David said his salvation (his daily protection and direction) came from the Lord. Many wanted to kill him, but what did he do? He silently waited upon the Lord!

God exhorts us in Isaiah 30 with a message for Christians who "run on swift horses that are not my Spirit." Here's a short part of that chapter:

"¹⁵ For thus said the Lord God, the Holy One of Israel: In returning [to Me] and resting [in Me] you shall be saved; **in quietness and in [trusting] confidence shall be your strength.** *But you would not, ¹⁶ And you said, No! We will speed [our own course] on horses! Therefore you will speed [in flight from your enemies]! You said, We will ride upon swift steeds [doing our own way]! Therefore will they who pursue you be swift, [so swift that] ¹⁷ One thousand of you will flee at the threat of one of them; at the threat of five you will flee till you are left like a beacon or a flagpole on the top of a mountain, and like a signal on a hill. ¹⁸ And therefore the Lord [earnestly] waits [expecting, looking, and longing] to be gracious to you; and therefore He lifts Himself up, that He may have mercy on you and show loving-kindness to you. For the Lord is a God of justice.* **Blessed (happy, fortunate, to be envied) are all those who [earnestly] wait for Him, who expect and look and long for Him [for His victory, His favor, His love, His peace, His joy, and His matchless, unbroken companionship]!"** (Isa. 30: 15-18 Amp).

Waiting on the Lord

Wade Taylor wrote in "Waiting Upon the Lord" that there are two steps in this process of "*waiting upon the Lord.*"

"Blessed is the man that hears Me, <u>watching daily at My gates, waiting at the posts of My doors</u>. For whoso finds Me finds life, and shall obtain favor of the Lord." Proverbs 8:34-35

In the first step, we look toward the gate (door) in worshipful anticipation, waiting for His presence to be manifested to us. When the Lord responds, we can begin to "wait upon Him," acknowledging His presence as being with us, and then actively "cooperate" with Him in whatever way He may lead or direct.

If there was ever a time when we need to be led by the Holy Spirit - our being in the right place, at the right time, with the right word, it is today. We are to be good stewards of this "calling" by keeping ourselves available so we can hear and become a vessel through whom the Lord can speak.

Unless we maintain a sensitivity to hearing His voice, we will miss. Today, as we approach the end of the Church Age, the Lord is increasingly knocking upon the "heart door" of our spirit. He is speaking a "present word" to all who are listening and responding. This is the unity for which He prayed - His voice becoming as the voice of "many waters."

"And in the midst of the seven candlesticks one like to the Son of man, clothed with a garment down to the foot, and girt about the breasts with a golden girdle. His head and His hairs were white like wool, as white as snow; and His eyes were as a flame of fire; And His feet like to fine brass, as if they burned in a furnace; and _His voice as the sound of many waters_" (Revelation 1:13-15).

Like David, Enemies Surround Us!

We are faced with many enemies, whether they're physical, financial, familial, or work-related. Stress can be overwhelming! In the physical, terrorists are gunning for America. Today, as I write, we were placed on highest alert. ISIS and those of their ilk hate us and "ride on swift horses." Will we allow ourselves to trust in our technology, our weapons and our American ingenuity to save us? We are foolish if we do! for "Unless the LORD builds the house, the builders labor in vain. **Unless the LORD watches over the city, the guards stand watch in vain**" (Psa. 127 NIV).

In years past when Americans worshipped the one true God, Jesus Christ, and honored Him by our adoration, bowing our heads at football games, and unafraid of speaking in public unashamedly of His name, He "guarded the city." But since our courts have unwisely ruled in the name of ungodliness in the name of "fairness" and "law," banishing the name of the Lord from public life and mocking His statues, we will find ourselves in great peril now and in the future, as we did on 9/11, except much worse. He can't, *He won't, protect a nation that forgets Him:*

"The wicked shall be turned back [headlong into premature death] into Sheol (the place of the departed spirits of the wicked), even all the nations that forget or are forgetful of God" (Psalm 9:17 Amp).

America is no exception. The protection of this country may come down to individuals who understand what I have written here. We cannot continue to "ride on horses that are not of His Spirit."

There are a lot of things we should be doing, but missing God's Presence by not spending time there is really unwise. The promises of maintaining our place there is imperative for becoming unshakeable, bold, loving and remaining at peace when the storms prevail. If we fail to do this, believe me, panic and maybe even death (panic attacks can cause heart attacks in otherwise healthy people by inducing spasms in the coronary arteries) are waiting in the wings!

Drive-Thru Christianity

Rather than seek the still small voice of calm and His promised rest, most Christians favor drive-thru Christianity.

I love drive-thru fast food. It's convenient, fast (sometimes) but usually not good for us, and neither is drive-thru Christianity. My favorite drive-thru chow is Chick-fil-A, but I can devour a good hamburger (the way God intended it) in spite of their omnipresent cows' protestations. I gave up tofu for Lent.

The Bible is clear: we reap what we sow. God, who's a wonderful Father, has always expected His kids to give Him His due. In the Old Testament, the Israelites paid dearly for their sin of forgetting where their blessings came from. Instead they got caught up in stupid idols made of wood and stone like their pagan neighbors:

Leviticus 26:38-45 clearly demonstrates this principle, 38 *"you will perish among the nations; the land of your enemies will devour you. 39 Those of you who are left will waste away in the lands of their enemies because of their sins; also because of their fathers' sins they will waste away. 40 "But if they will confess their sins and the sins of their fathers—their treachery against me and their hostility toward me, 41 which made me hostile toward them so that I sent them into the land of their enemies—then when their uncircumcised hearts are humbled and they pay for their sin, 42 I will remember my covenant with Jacob and my covenant with Isaac and my covenant with Abraham, and I will remember the land. 43 For the land will be deserted by them and will enjoy its Sabbaths while it lies desolate without them. They will pay for their sins because they rejected my laws and abhorred my decrees. 44 Yet in spite of this, when they are in the land of their enemies, I will not reject them or abhor them so as to destroy them completely, breaking my covenant with them. I am the LORD their God. 45 But for their sake I will remember the covenant with their ancestors whom I brought out of Egypt in the sight of the nations to be their God. I am the LORD."*

Stupid Sheep

God loves people but hates sin, and we all sin a lot. But it appears to me, after many years of seeking God, that He's more inclined to be upset with His creation for their lack of seeking Him than the sins we commit. The greatest error people make is "going astray." In the Bible, we are compared to trusting but stupid sheep that leave the shepherd in search of greener grass, which always leads to wolf attacks!

All **we like sheep** have gone astray, **we** have turned everyone to his own way; and the Lord has made to light upon Him the guilt *and* iniquity of us **all** (Isa. 53:6).

Going astray means we follow the dictates of our own hearts in determining what's good for us. We think it's drive-thru Christianity, a "Kid's Meal" 30-minute sermon, grab bag prayers and counting on

Somebody else's recommendation for the food we eat (counseling). Before you go off on me, I counsel and have for at least 37 years, but if I have a seeker wanting counseling – someone who really wants to change – and not a parasite, things work a lot better. It doesn't take long to tell if someone is just trying to pull something from me or whether they're truly a God-seeker. Mary, the mother of God's Son, knew the difference:

49 For He Who is almighty has done great things for me—and holy is His name [to be venerated in His purity, majesty and glory]! 50 And His mercy (His compassion and kindness toward the miserable and afflicted) is on those who fear Him with godly reverence, from generation to generation and age to age. 51 He has shown strength and made might with His arm; He has scattered the proud and haughty in and by the imagination and purpose and designs of their hearts. 52 He has put down the mighty from their thrones and exalted those of low degree. **53 He has filled and satisfied the hungry with good things, and the rich He has sent away empty-handed [without a gift]** (Luke 1:49-53 Amp).

Sermonettes Make Christianettes

Part of the problem lies with the desire for most Christians to grab a bite from their television sets instead of eating at the King's Table. It's better than nothing, but if you want the four-course meal with good wine, you have to get in touch with the Host, who'll gladly supply. Have you ever been to a church where you've gone in starving to death and gotten a gluten-free cracker?

Christian teacher and author Dudley Hall said there's a difference between hungry, in which somebody needs food, and "hongry," meaning if "I don't get some food soon, I'm gonna die!" In Christianity today we find a lot of church swapping or hopping. The Sunday buffet has grown stale, so we look for something where we get more for our dough. Although this is true in many cases, some of God's people are simply looking for a church where Jesus in the main course and not programs, a better daycare or singers who put the Mormon Tabernacle Choir to shame.

"Sister Bertha Better Than You"

We're not talking self-righteousness here but becoming a more mature believer who can stand the heat when it0 gets hotter – and it will get much hotter. One of the funniest songs I ever heard was Ray Stevens' "Mississippi Squirrel Revival" (if you have a religious spirit, you won't like it). Anyway, "Bro." Ray tells the tale of how a crazy squirrel on steroids gets loose in the "First Self-Righteous Church" in Pascagoula, Miss. The end result is revival, where even "Sister Bertha Better Than You" repents. Although hilarious, it is really tragic that a squirrel, and not God, brings revival. That's called "doing church without God."

This reminds me of my friend Steve Sampson's book, *Enjoying God and Other Rare Events*. Of course, Steve was being tongue-in-cheek, but doesn't it describe most Christians' relationship with the Lord? It does if we're eating drive-thru Monday-Saturday, and sometimes on Sunday. I grew up in beautiful downtown Chickasaw, AL, near Mobile. Chickasaw is about three miles from where International Paper Co. used to be. At certain times when the wind blew our way, IP smelled like a pig's sty. This is akin to a Christian meeting where religiosity reigns and not Jesus. The discerning can smell it a mile – or three miles off.

In Search of Outback

The Bible equates our walk to those who drink milk (new believers), eat bread (further down the Christian road) and "strong meat" that is for the mature believer. God expects only what is possible for us, given our years of knowing Him, exposure to truth and whether we really wanted it or not. Let's face it: there are some believers who have been in this for years and who are still wearing spiritual diapers:

[11] *Concerning this we have much to say which is hard to explain, since you have become dull in your [spiritual] hearing and sluggish [even* [*slothful in achieving spiritual insight].* [12] *For even though by this time you ought to be teaching others, you actually need someone to teach you over again the very first principles of God's Word. You have come to need milk, not solid food.* [13] *For everyone who continues to feed on*

milk is obviously inexperienced and unskilled in the doctrine of righteousness (of conformity to the divine will in purpose, thought, and action), for he is a mere infant [not able to talk yet]! ¹⁴ *But solid food is for full-grown men, for those whose senses and mental faculties are trained by practice to discriminate and distinguish between what is morally good and noble and what is evil and contrary either to divine or human law"* (Heb. 5:11-14 Amplified).

You Are What You Eat

This old saying is also true of your spiritual life. I love Krispy Kreme doughnuts, especially as they come hot and poppin' fresh out of that assembly line of calories. But if I ate those babies every morning instead of a good meal, I'd look like the Pillsbury Dough Boy. (Okay, I may be close, but I've lost about 20 pounds lately.)

In reality, the Bible says we are what we think (Prov. 23:7), but spiritually speaking, that depends on what we "eat." God said through Isaiah that we are to make sure we eat what is good and not spend our money on junk food:

Why do you spend your money on junk food, your hard-earned cash on cotton candy? Listen to me, listen well: Eat only the best, fill yourself with only the finest. Pay attention, come close now, listen carefully to my life-giving, life-nourishing words. I'm making a lasting covenant commitment with you, the same that I made with David: sure, solid, enduring love (Isa. 55:2-5 The Message).

Eating well means spending time with the Lord Himself, prayerfully considering His Words that do not pass away, and allowing the nectar of His truth to fill our insides with a quality of life that is unbeatable.

Survivalist Mentality

I'm no prophecy expert, but I can read, and my eyes are wide open – and things are getting worse. What we're faced with is a dilemma of magnanimous proportions that is affecting the whole world. Something's gotta give. One thing is true: We need the full meal of God's offering – His Word, His Son and His incredible Holy Spirit – if we're to survive, and not only survive, but enjoy the Presence of God on a daily basis. Anything less will not be enough. Without getting hold and working toward a single mind concerning what God says is true, we can become double-minded, a debilitating condition that the Bible describes as instability.

Many bipolar people are, in effect, double-minded. This means their brains and minds are at war with the other side of their thinking. We'll examine this next.

CHAPTER 13

Bipolar Disorder and Double-mindedness

⁵ If any of you is deficient in wisdom, let him ask of ᵘ the giving God [Who gives] to everyone liberally and ungrudgingly, without reproaching or faultfinding, and it will be given him. ⁶ Only it must be in faith that he asks with no wavering (no hesitating, no doubting). For the one who wavers (hesitates, doubts) is like the billowing surge out at sea that is blown hither and thither and tossed by the wind. For truly, let not such a person imagine that he will receive anything [he asks for] from the Lord,⁸ [For being as he is] a man of two minds (hesitating, dubious, irresolute), [he is] unstable and unreliable and uncertain about everything [he thinks, feels, decides].

James 1:5-8 (Amp)

James is clear in this text that a person with "two souls" is in a bad fix. He or she is blown about continually and tossed by the wind like the waves of the sea. This person is a state of constant flux, uncertain about life, getting almost nowhere with God, who has told us repetitively throughout His Word that we're to be single-minded. Jesus went so far as to say that we should let us yes be yes and our no be no because that which is caught between the two is evil:

But let your word 'yes be 'yes,' and your 'no be 'no.' Anything more than this is from the evil one (Matt. 5:37 Holman Christian Standard Bible).

Teacher and author Bob Mumford defines freedom as the ability to say yes or no.

Anyone with bipolar disorder is at the core of his being double-minded. His mind is constantly wrestling with emotional mood swings, high and low. Medicine, no doubt, helps many people tremendously, but they are never fully under control and may remain abusive or destructive toward others and themselves and may even commit suicide. As we have seen, the brain chemistry at some point in life became–whether from genetic defects at birth or through trauma–"disheveled" and not functioning normally.

Transformation of the Mind

God's desire is that all would become single-minded. To put it another way, He wants us think like He thinks rather than draw from the complex set of humanistic, rationalistic reasoning to figure it out for ourselves. The wisest man who ever lived, except for the Lord Jesus Christ, was King Solomon. He had this to say about our deviation from keeping things simple in life:

"Behold, I have found only this, that God made men upright, but they have sought out many devices" (Eccl. 7:29).

In the original creation Adam simply trusted God to teach him the right way to live. He was innocent of evil and never gave it a thought. He walked with God and was in total bliss. God further added to his blissfulness by providing a wife to love and accompany him. Until The fall… After this his thinking was drawn from the carnal side of his brain and mind, rather than his spirit, and we know the rest of the story.

When we're born we inherit from Adam the carnal mind. Although brilliant in some respects, even after the fall, God hates the carnal mind because it's set against Him:

5Those who live according to the flesh have their minds set on what the flesh desires; but those who live in accordance with the Spirit have their minds set on what the Spirit desires. 6The mind governed by the flesh is death, but the mind governed by the Spirit is life and peace. **7The mind governed by the flesh is hostile to God; it does not submit to God's law, nor can it do so** (Rom. 8:5-7 NIV).

Jesus' Death and the Carnal Mind

When Jesus died on the cross, He nailed our carnal mind to the cross with Him so they we could have power over it because, in reality, it's dead:

Knowing this, that our old man is crucified with him, that the body of sin might be destroyed, that henceforth we should not serve sin (Rom. 6:6 KJV).

The "body of sin" includes the carnal mind, but prior to this, Jesus had crushed into His skull the crown of thorns, which drew cleansing Blood for our minds from His. Since He has done all this for us, we are told in the same chapter to "reckon it so." In the South we use this term as a way of saying, "Yep, I agree with that." This is what Romans 6:10-11 is stating in this passage – agree that the carnal self (old man) is dead and now powerless over us:

"For the death that He died He died to sin, once for all; but the life that He lives, He lives to God. Even so, consider [KJV "reckon"] yourselves to be dead to sin, but alive to God in Christ Jesus." (Romans 6:10-11)

Living this out is a chore; you can count on it. It takes a great deal of desire to think like God thinks, daily dealing with that carnal mind and its devices. And, yes, the enemy of our souls wants us to continue to cling to the notion that we are helpless to think what we think, but we're dealing with the "father of lies" here (John 8:44).

The new spiritual man we've been given must be nurtured, though. It has to be filled with His thoughts to us and about is. Romans 12:2 calls this the transformation (literally metamorphosis) that Miriam-Webster says is: a major change in the appearance or character of someone or something. The spiritual mind is indeed a major change in appearance and character! This change from the old carnal way of thinking to the spiritual mind is a lifelong journey of attaining the mind of Christ (1 Cor. 2:16). God gives us this mind when we are born of the Spirit of God, but it has to be constantly filled with the Word of God to reach the change God expects from us.

Lovers of Self and Self-Centered

One person whose" case study" appears in this book told me unequivocally that her clinically diagnosed bipolar disorder was essentially nothing but self-centered behavior. As she became God-centered and trusted

Jesus for her complete healing, she was healed of bipolar disorder. Why are there so many people today claiming to be bipolar? The following Scripture sums it up:

3 But understand this, that in the last days will come (set in) perilous times of great stress and trouble [hard to deal with and hard to bear]. *2* **For people will be lovers of self and [utterly] self-centered,** *lovers of money and aroused by an inordinate [greedy] desire for wealth, proud and arrogant and contemptuous boasters. They will be abusive (blasphemous, scoffing), disobedient to parents, ungrateful, unholy and profane.* *3* **[They will be] without natural [human] affection (callous and inhuman),** *relentless (admitting of no truce or appeasement); [they will be] slanderers (false accusers, troublemakers), intemperate and loose in morals and conduct, uncontrolled and fierce, haters of good.* *4* *[They will be] treacherous [betrayers], rash, [and] inflated with self-conceit.* **[They will be] lovers of sensual pleasures and vain amusements more than and rather than lovers of God.** *5* *For [although] they hold a form of piety (true religion), they deny and reject and are strangers to the power of it [their conduct belies the genuineness of their profession].* *Avoid [all] such people [turn away from them]* (2 Timothy 3:1-5 Amp).

Please notice several things that stand out about this passage concerning people of the Last Days:

They love themselves and are utterly self-centered. Their world is themselves! My friend Steve Sampson, who has written 12 books, titled his first one about the Jezebel Spirit, *I Was Always on My Mind*. Apropos for anyone who utterly self-centered, wouldn't you say?

2. They don't have natural affection. Romans 1 delineates this further by declaring that the people mentioned in that chapter burn with desire for people of the same sex.

24 Therefore God gave them over in the sinful desires of their hearts to sexual impurity for the degrading of their bodies with one another. 25 They exchanged the truth about God for a lie, and worshiped and served created things rather than the Creator—who is forever praised.

Amen. 26 Because of this, God gave them over to shameful lusts. **Even their women exchanged natural sexual relations for unnatural ones. 27 In the same way the men also abandoned natural relations with women and were inflamed with lust for one another. Men committed shameful acts with other men, and received in themselves the due penalty for their error** (Rom. 1:24-27 NIV).

They love sensual pleasure more than God. When we choose to take part in and love sensuality more than obeying God, we are committing a grievous error – whether we call it "an affair," "a commitment," or "living together" out of wedlock; it is really called by one name – idolatry. The very sad part of this scenario is that the people involved, possibly Christians, are unaware that they're gradually losing sensitivity to the Holy Spirit, as their own personal spirits become hardened to God. The downward spiral is usually lack of church attendance, falling away from Bible studies and avoiding people who may convict them by word or by character. As they give way to pleasure, it becomes all-consuming and is very difficult to break from because of the obvious physical pleasure the situation provides.

Overcoming the Spirit of Narcissism

Note: My good friend David Davenport (http://teshuvahtzion.com) graciously contributed this article that was written on his blog. He captures this subject quite well, and I can imagine you, as my reader, know someone who fits this category to a T!

At this stage in history; for anyone to deny that we are in the Last Days, is to reveal a gross measure of ignorance and a corresponding lack of spiritual discernment. We are in fact in the last days, and the above excerpt of scripture underscores but one of many excerpts of scripture which are unfolding before our eyes.

Lovers of self

Here in the West, to be a "lover of self" in the context of the prophecy above, is to be a Narcissist, by way of contemporary and generalized definition. The essence or roots of narcissism is a *spiritual* dynamic however, versus that of a clinical, secular designation. The secular designation therefore, is that of an attempt to define what is in actuality a *demonic stronghold*–the more advanced stronghold of which we will discuss shortly (Covert Narcissism).

Demons only inhabit a person when they've received a figurative license or invitation to do so. And in the instance of narcissism, I have observed the invitation and/or license to typically come through 3 primary avenues, as reflective of my protracted experience not only as a counselor, but also as a self-inflicted victim at one stage in my life.

These 3 avenues are as follows:

That of a deep and unhealed wound wrought of neglect, abandonment and/or rejection.

That of the deeply-seated and prolonged suppression of unresolved sin, and, correspondingly, unresolved guilt, which is exacerbated by demonic condemnation.

The very dangerous state of "lukewarmness" as a Believer, spoken of in Revelation 3:16. For it is as we steadily ignore the gentle prodding of the Holy Spirit to cultivate intimacy with the Lord ongoing, and we thereafter resist His subsequent chastening, that we are released to our own devices and subject to a specific form of judgement in the form of mental illness spoken of in 2 Thessalonians 2:11: *"...for this reason God will send upon them a deluding influence..."*.

The initial context of this verse speaks to non-Believers who continue to believe what is false. I tend to believe it speaks more pointedly of those who instinctively *know* that what they are embracing is false. I have equally observed this dynamic played-out in the lives of thousands of Believers as well, over several decades.

In the case of the rejection and abandonment wound, narcissism serves initially as a form of self-preservation, which takes on the form of serving and affirming one's *self*–in the absence of such from others. Over time, self-absorption grows. As it does, the door to our soul that was initially only slightly ajar, is ultimately flung wide-open, following which the demon of narcissism (i.e., obsessive love of self, in its base form) waltzes-in, unpacks its bags, sets-up camp, stretches its legs, and cultivates a multifaceted stronghold.

"Meism"

In the case of the prolonged suppression of unresolved sin, and corresponding terminal guilt and associated condemnation; one is predisposed to fabricating a hyper-spiritual exterior, whereby a person perpetually sells the world on their divine attributes and their super-human qualities, thus disarming any potential question otherwise. One thereafter perpetually seeks to draw attention to themselves, affording a perpetual spotlight under which they may continue to sell their hyper-spiritual state to the world about them.

As long as they continue to successfully sell all others about them, they successfully defer any potential scrutiny or questioning as to what may lay beneath. Over time, the person ultimately "closes the sale" on their very *selves*–whereas the fabricated superficial or hyper-self becomes their reality. At this stage, gross self-absorption ensues, along with deeply entrenched deceit and delusion.

And lastly, in the case of those straddling the fence of their faith, and marinating lives of lukewarmness by attempting to allow wanton carnality and marginal faith in Christ to "sleep in the same bed" together; a blanket invitation is released for the tentacles of 2 Timothy 3:1-7 to envelope their lives. For the present reality is that the spiritual war being waged about us is far more dangerous than the average Believer can fathom. And until we resolve to perpetually cling the Lord in daily intimacy with Him; while also through corresponding necessity, "dying daily" to our carnal selves; we willfully wander out from under the protective "shadow of His wings" (Psalm 91), and stumble into enemy fire–not unlike that of willfully wandering into enemy machine gun fire on a contemporary military battlefield. The end result of which is that of being riddled with bullet-like seeds of demonic infestation.

Deliverance from Narcissism

Deliverance from the above variations of narcissistic strongholds typically occurs in one of two ways: Firstly, and following the acknowledgement of one's condition and the resolve to repent; opting to team with someone in deliverance ministry, to cast-out the roots of this mangy critter, followed thereafter by a willful turning (*teshuvah*) in the opposite direction. And secondly, through *self*-deliverance. James 4:7 says that "*...if we resist the devil he will flee.*" This is the essence of self-deliverance—resisting (starving) the demon until he gets tired and moves on to the next house.

Self-deliverance is quite simple. Below I will outline some cursory steps for performing such:

Steps to Freedom:

Establish a schedule of concerted fasting and prayer, perhaps for a few days leading up to a pre-scheduled time for your self-deliverance. During this brief time of fasting and prayer (ideally a period of 3 days or more), and which can be a partial-fast; pray that the Holy Spirit reveal the tentacles of this stronghold, that you will have a focused inventory of what to renounce as you perform self-deliverance.

As you engage your self-deliverance session, begin by taking communion, and reading John 6:51-58 (from a physical bible—will explain why, in a moment). As you ingest the elements, ask the Lord to further free you from the Tree of the Knowledge and Good and Evil, and to further *attach* you to the Tree of Life—Y'shua (Jesus).

3) After first reading the excerpt from John, follow such with the elements. Leave your bible open to this passage, and press it against your heart. Hereafter, close your eyes, and proceed to breathe-in deeply, in through the nose, and out through the mouth.

As you maintain the above posture, and with your eyes closed, picture in your mind's-eye the Cross of Christ, and thereafter focus upon that image. As you do so, verbally renounce the Spirit of Narcissism, while continuing to breathe deeply, in through your nose, and out through your mouth. Declare to it the authority of the Blood of Y'shua, and His Cross. You can use the name of Jesus if you wish; I simply prefer Y'shua for deeply personal reasons, but of course Y'shua and Jesus are the same Person, and the demons know Him by both names (smiling).

4) As you repeatedly exhale, the many tentacles of the Spirit of Narcissism will loosen, and will be expelled. This process generally does not take more than 15 minutes or so. They often exit by making a person repeatedly yawn, belch, sneeze, cough or even flatulate.

5) Following this session of communion and renunciation, do business with the Lord, by asking the Holy Spirit to invade those places in your spirit and soul which were previously manipulated by the demonic; invite Him to take full-habitation of your heart, and to thereafter guard-against re-habitation. Ask Him to water the seeds of the *authentic* Fruit of the Spirit in your heart (Galatians 5:22-24), which will counter the counterfeit components that were previously at work. The key is that to *replace*, not to keep *vacant* (see Matthew 12:43-45). Our goal is to welcome the full habitation of the Holy Spirit's working in our hearts, not to "sweep" our hearts clean, leaving them empty, as thereafter the "critters" will waltz right back, and wreck the house worse than before.

Inside Out vs. Outside In

Wholly counter to the above approach to self-deliverance, secular psychology and psychiatry seeks to remedy narcissism with a cognitive approach, which attempts to free a person from the outside-in, through a change in thinking and outward behavior, when in fact the issues resides in our heart(s), and to be more specific: our heart-*wound(s)*. The only true freedom from such a stronghold is that from the *inside-out*, by addressing the *spiritual* component—which *governs* our cognition.

It is because of the above "ships passing in the night," that tens of millions of people in the West have submitted themselves to secular counseling and therapy, as well as psychotropic meds, for much of their adult lives perhaps, to thereafter discover that near the end of their lives they had never been set-free of the strongholds their therapists had artfully masked through secular-humanistic "therapy" and medication, all the while reaping the spoils of insurance billing revenues. Hello?

One of the more advanced forms of narcissism is categorized by secular therapists as "Covert Narcissism." In general terms, the secular definition does a fair job of defining the characteristics of such. However, and again, their approach to addressing such is wholly useless in weeding-up and casting-out the demonic tentacles of such, which are very crafty about hiding within the deep recesses of our hearts during secular therapy, only to reappear down the road.

David Davenport (http://teshuvahtzion.com)

Spiritual Warfare and Deliverance from Bipolar Disorder

As I have tried desperately to make clear in this book, deliverance from bipolar can be **extremely difficult** because of the tremendous wounding that happens, and that often quite early in life. Satan and his minions take advantage of this wounding and attempt to set up a beachhead in the wounded person's life. Through rejection or perceived rejection, the mind begins to overly protect itself. For some this protection primarily results in depression in which the person becomes passive and withdrawn.

Others may attempt to protect themselves through angry rebellion against everyone who has wounded them or against society as a whole. If they move alternately in either direction because of rejection and rebellion, a double-minded spirit moves in to create chaos and instability. On "lesser scale" the two poles (bipolar) begin to rule over this person, and on a grander scale, they become schizophrenic. To understand this more fully, I recommend the reader get a copy of *Pigs in the Parlor* by

Frank and Ida Mae Hammond. The Hammonds address in grand detail how this process takes place. Also James Winkler in God Wink Blog - https://jamswinkler.wordpress.com/2009/10/19/mpd-schizophrenia-and-other-forms-of-mental-illness/ covers this briefly but effectively.

Deliverance may come very slowly, or if the person's desire is strong enough, more rapidly, but generally the woundedness and the resulting defensiveness inhibits deliverance and the healing of brain chemistry. This is why inner healing is such an important part of deliverance. Casting away demons is only one side of the coin. If the person goes unhealed, the spirits will return to the unhealed areas of the heart and mind. Jesus put it this way:

When an impure spirit comes out of a person, it goes through arid places seeking rest and does not find it. Then it says, 'I will return to the house I left.' 25When it arrives, it finds the house swept clean and put in order. 26Then it goes and takes seven other spirits more wicked than itself, and they go in and live there. And the final condition of that person is worse than the first (Luke 11:24-26).

"Religion" May Be Our Worst Enemy

"Religion" could become the wounded person's worst enemy because religious pride builds a wall against truth that sets people free. The Pharisees excelled in this! Religion in this sense is keeping rules and acting out the Christian life, rather than submitting to Jesus as Lord and allowing Him to lead in every decision. The religious road is one of three roads or "avenues" people take in life.

We'll call this "EROS Avenue." What is it, and how does it affect us will be discussed in the next chapter. This condition actually fights against the unconditional love of God that everyone should know and receive. Without this we are left to fend for ourselves in an ever-maddening society that seems bent on self-destruction. God never made people to be self-focused but God and others focused. The result of EROS is an ever spiraling down into a self-aggrandized pit of depression and hopelessness, often the hallmark of those afflicted with bipolar disorder.

CHAPTER 14

Going Up Eros Avenue

Most of our troubles begin early. As I have written previously, in utero wounding (prenatal) or early childhood hurts sends us up one of three roads: worldly, religious or agape. My educated guess, after being a Christian for many years, is you, the reader, are on one of the three, and you could be headed up the religious or worldly, or maybe both at the same time?

Since our brains play a large part in our choices, we have to understand that our inclination is to first go the way of the world if we have no religious training. This only makes sense. I grew up in church, which I'm not sure at times, other than exposure that there was and is a God, who runs the universe, was not very helpful --, at least it seemed that way at the time. Church to me was boring, but I enjoyed all the Bible stories about Daniel, David and Goliath, etc. I was something of an altar boy, knowing a good bit about the Bible, but my experience was primarily "head knowledge."

Unfortunately for me my hormones were growing faster than my brain cells, and girls became much more important than "religion." Girls were prettier to me, smelled better and were more comforting that what I was getting at church. I was hooked.

I guess I wasn't much different than most guys, or I suppose girls my age. Nothing much was happening there at church, and the excitement of girls was just too much. I was headed up EROS Avenue.

Most people are acquainted with the original meaning of EROS. Here's what I found about EROS and the goddess Aphrodite. APHRODITE was the great Olympian goddess of beauty, love, pleasure and procreation. She was depicted as a beautiful woman, who was usually accompanied by the winged godling Eros (Love). Her attributes included a dove, apple, scallop shell and mirror. In classical sculpture and fresco she was often depicted nude.

Actually, Eros is defined as the sum of life-preserving instincts that are manifested as impulses to gratify basic needs (as sex), as sublimated impulses motivated by the same needs, and as impulses to protect and preserve the body and mind—called also *life instinct*.

The original meaning of Eros was essentially self-centeredness, as the definition above spells out.

Going Up Three Roads

People go up three roads: the worldly road, the religious road and few, the agape road. Those going up the worldly road could stay there all their lives seeking pleasure by self-seeking, "barhopping" and ultimately thinking life is all about their pleasure. This usually ends in deep disappointment with these people wondering what life was all about before they go toes up. But some find religion.

The Religious Road

Most of the world is headed up this world from Christendom to Buddhist to Muslim. This can be a highly disappointing road as well, as people keep striving to find happiness or contentment as they serve a god who seems like He can't be pleased. Denominationalism (I tried several) often focuses on doctrines established by their progenitors, who may or may not have the true gospel at heart. Often these same ones, who once began with a deep and consecrated focus on the Lordship of Jesus Christ, wind up with errant doctrines that depart erratically from their founders and the Bible. Not to be unkind, but I was served once as a United Methodist pastor, and I find that often today many of these churches have departed from a true love for Jesus to embrace modernism or doctrines that have nothing to do with traditional faith.

The religious road often has nothing to do with Jesus the person, but is empties one of his or her excitement and fervency to God in a personal relationship.

Don't Give Me that Old Time Religion!

You may be old enough to remember the old song, "Give Me that Old Time Religion." Well, don't give me that.

At least not the kind I grew up with. That religion was powerless, ritualistic and based more on tradition than on the Bible. It didn't change me. The church people were sweet, but it seemed that God was distant, detached and kept safely "in a box."

This brand of Christianity seemed to work okay during "Happy Days" when the major concerns were drinking too much beer, smoking and deciding if we needed a nuclear fall-out shelter. Personally, I didn't know one person who bought one (LOL!). As a friend recently joked, "During fire drills we moved peacefully to the outside of the school building, but during nuclear bomb drills, we were told to get under our desks" (wow, that was insightful).

Regarding church, when I was around 15, I found girls much more interesting. It's sad that I can't remember one sermon I heard from that time until I "found" the Lord in graduate school. I can well understand why kids leave the church. In many cases, it's as dull as dirt and void of the central focus of our faith–Jesus and the power of the Holy Spirit– relying more on clever intellectual sermons based on correct doctrine. I love correct doctrine, but heads full of theology do very little for troubled hearts. Why not both?

Woodstock and All That

After "Happy Days," things began to change: Woodstock, the hippie movement, "free love," the LSD dropout drug culture, New Age, Eastern mysticism, legalized abortion, prayer-less schools, promises by the Left to fix it all with socialistic programs, Vietnam, terrorism, super debt, STDs and suicides. Now we have the Ebola virus and ISIS (excuse me, ISIL) moving across Iraq and Syria murdering and collecting vast amounts of wealth and weapons. Scary stuff, right?

Every day I work with people, mostly Christians, whose faith, because of many of the things above, have been shaken or is at the point of hopelessness. In most cases, these searching people are true believers who want to love God with all their hearts, but they have accepted the truncated gospel, one that doesn't call for transformation or change through pain. Somebody forgot to tell them that through much tribulation, we enter into the kingdom of God:

"We must through much tribulation enter into the kingdom of God" (Acts 14:22).

"God's people have their trials. It was never designed by God, when He chose His people, that they should be an untried people. They were chosen in the furnace of affliction; they were never chosen to worldly peace and earthly joy. Freedom from sickness and the pains of mortality was never promised them; but when their Lord drew up the charter of privileges, He included chastisements amongst the things to which they should inevitably be heirs. Trials are a part of our lot; they were predestinated for us in Christ's last legacy." – Charles Spurgeon

Because the average believer doesn't get what Spurgeon says here, they end up with a lot of "why is this happening to me?" queries, as if faith is supposed to protect us from difficulties. Romans 8:37 says, "IN all these things, we are more than conquerors."

The Damage of the Truncated Gospel

The truncated gospel began when the church attempted to reach the masses back in the 60s and 70s. We condensed the gospel to four or five verses – "just believe this, and you're saved." I'm okay with that. Saved for heaven is one thing, but being deeply changed is another. When their stuff hit the fan later on, many of these people didn't know why this should be happening to them. After all, they were believers. Somehow the church didn't get the message to these perplexed believers across the country that the whole New Testament is about being conformed to the image of Jesus!

Part of the problem, also, lay with the prosperity gospel that has emphasized that God wanted all His people materially blessed. This whole teaching, which is so appealing to the flesh, got out of bounds, and believers got sucked up into debt up to their eyebrows, as they constantly pursued a "faith formula." The truth of the matter is the New Testament's main message is one of spiritual change and not necessarily that of material wealth. God is a blessing God, but He ain't Santa Claus. We got confused about needs and wants, with wants getting a higher priority.

When Bill Clinton said, "It's the economy, stupid," he wasn't just provoking the masses for his re-election; he was speaking about the American economy as THE PRIORITY in life and not character of the one running the show. Now our trust in government is at an all-time low because we elected many lying politicians who primarily seek lifelong re-election at any cost. We got "change" all right.

Compartmentalizing Jesus

Most of the church is still getting that "old time religion" on Sundays, but faith in many cases has become compartmentalized: Jesus is good for heaven, but you need a psychiatrist for the other things that ail you. Yet it is the depth of truth that the gospel brings to us, including dealing with evil and entrenched unbelief, which sets the captives free. The whole idea of just wanting Jesus to save you for heaven without the desire to save you from yourself leads to catastrophe, first as individuals and later as a nation.

The real "Old Time Religion" was full of Holy Spirit power! These were visitations of the Holy Spirit because He was given freedom to work among the people who were fully seeking His Face. The real deal saw people filled with Him and set free! As a black sister used to sing in a church where I attended, "He'll Do It Again," but only if we desire that kind of experience in our churches. Anything short of this, and this country will be run over by our enemies. – from within and from without.

Face it, America is slowly dying not because its citizens got lost in the maze of dumb pop culture, dumbed down education, sports idolatry and the idea that we trusted our elected officials to do the right thing – which most of them didn't. All these have contributed to our current state. But the real reason societies like ours crumble is because they lose the most important element of all – honoring Jesus Christ as Lord of all. In America, where there are churches on every corner, we are warned by the Scripture, *"To whom much is given, much shall be required"* (Luke 12:48). Regretfully, in many ways we stand empty-handed when God has called for much.

Restoring the Foundations

I've been doing prayer counseling with people since around 1980, and I've found a lot of good things that work. Sometimes counseling is the answer, but I think we're counseled out for the most part! Quite frankly, people talking about their stuff leads to the same people talking about more their stuff without really nailing the problem.

A program called "Restoring the Foundations" (RTF) is the hammer that drives the nail into the heart of the difficulty or sin. RTF (www.RestoringTheFoundations.org) is a four-step prayer-counseling model that goes to the roots of people's denials and difficulties. And, if they're ripe for healing and deliverance, they experience something fresh and new in their lives. My ministry continues to see amazing breakthroughs in people's lives during one of these 3-hour sessions!

Does Anybody Really Know What Time It Is?

We need a clear picture of where we are in time. As people become more perplexed, confused, scared and desperate, they will turn to the thing/ person that will meet their needs. If it's an antichrist-type personality or a dictator who promises them a free lunch, and they've never decided that Jesus is Lord of all, no matter what happens, they will succumb to this person or system, becoming, in effect, antichrist in their attitudes and choices themselves. Many people have already made that decision.

If I understand the Book of Revelation at all–and sometimes I have my doubts after reading the latest "Revelation Made Easy" book–the end of all this is a choice: Jesus or Barabbas. But as a friend of mine always used to say to assure everyone, "I read the end of the Bible, and we win!"

The Agape Road

Before we point the finger at anyone, it's a good thing to look in the mirror at ourselves. We may find "The Seven Giants of EROS" staring back at us. The who? We are all familiar with the term "erotic," as it refers to sex, as in Aphrodite, but the truest meaning is that of selfishness, our greatest problem, and the first peril listed in the Scripture above … "lovers of self (and utterly) self-centered."

Writer/teacher Bob Mumford, author of The Agape Road, helps us see the giants in us that must be conquered if we are to conquer self, our biggest spiritual enemy! These giants are fierce and can display some of the worst human behavior, given the right (or wrong) situation. When I have shared these with many friends through the years, I often hear a groan or an "oh, my!" coming from them. We may abhor them, but they are all too real in many of us. The Agape Road is a road that leads to a full-fledged love for Jesus. What is the meaning of agape love?

Agape, and its verb form agapao, is one of the several Greek words for love. The Bible also mentions phileo, or brotherly love, and refers to eros, erotic love. The Greeks also spoke of storge, which is a love between family members.

Agape love is a little different. It is not a feeling; it's a motivation for action that we are free to choose or reject. Agape is a sacrificial love that voluntarily suffers inconvenience, discomfort, and even death for the benefit of another without expecting anything in return. We are called to agape love through Christ's example: "Therefore be imitators of God, as beloved children. And walk in love, as Christ loved us and gave himself up for us, a fragrant offering and sacrifice to God" (Ephesians 5:1-2).

We are to agapao God (Matthew 22:37), our neighbor (Matthew 22:39), and even our enemies (Matthew 5:43-46). We are not to agapao money (Matthew 6:24), darkness (John 3:19), or men's approval (John 12:43).

The New Testament has over two-hundred references to agape love. Here are a few.

Matthew 24:12: With increased lawlessness in the end times, concern and caring for others will fade.

Luke 11:42: The legalism of the Pharisees, even their sacrifices, did not reflect a love of God.

John 13:35: The Christian life is characterized by sacrificial agape love.

John 15:9-10; Romans 13:10: When we agape love God, we show it by obeying His commandments because His commandments teach us how to love others.

John 15:13: The greatest demonstration of love anyone can give is to die for his friends.

John 17:26; Romans 5:5; Galatians 5:22: Agape love comes from God, not our own effort.

Romans 5:8; Revelation 1:5: It was agape love that caused Jesus to sacrifice Himself for us.

Romans 14:15; 1 Corinthians 8:1: It is not loving to lead another into sin.

Colossians 3:19: Men are called to show agape love to their wives.

James 1:12; 2:5: Love of God will result in rewards in heaven.

2 Peter 2:15; 1 John 2:15: It is possible to sacrificially love something that is not godly.

Although 1 Corinthians 13 is known as the chapter on love, there is no book that speaks more about agape than 1 John. Two important themes come out of 1 John. The first is that it is inconsistent and false to claim we agape love God while not agape loving other believers. We cannot love God without loving brothers and sisters who also love Him. The second is that it is inconsistent and false to claim we agape love God if we don't obey Him. It is impossible to love God while ignoring what He says. The two are inextricably connected, as Galatians 5:14 says: "For the whole law is fulfilled in one word: 'You shall love your neighbor as yourself.'"

What stands in the way of agape? As you attempt to walk on the Agape Road, you will encounter what Bob Mumford has termed the Seven Giants of Eros.

The Seven Giants of Eros

Look Good – Over-concern for appearance or image rather than character. Look Good is not just concerned with outward appearance, but with creating a reputation that is not established in truth. It involves an improper or illegal search for originality, uniqueness in dress, language, automobile, skills, etc. It will pay any price and exerts a tremendous amount of effort to preserve its image. (Matthew 6:1)

Feel Good – The pure pleasure principle. Feel Good avoids pain and discomfort at any cost, is committed to personal pleasure or gain, and is given to the senses or is sensual. It controls the emotions, mind, and heart and is the source or first cause of all compulsive and addictive behavior. (James 4:3)

Be Right – The inability to admit that we are wrong. A "know-it-all" paralyzed by the domino theory – if wrong once, how can we be sure we have ever been right? Because the mind rules the emotions, Be Right is focused, controlled, and overly committed to his or her own evaluations, ideas, and concepts. The fear of being wrong or challenged makes them increasingly rigid – a form of stubbornness and rebellion. Be Right often uses anger and rage as protective mechanism to prevent being discovered. (Job 40:8)

Stay in Control – Demands to have his hands on the steering wheel – He always wants to be in control because then everyone is safe and the results are guaranteed. Because he thinks he is god, Stay in Control must determine the outcome of everything for everyone. He experiences anxiety regarding the future because it may be just beyond his control. Stay in Control refuses to take no for an answer. He is a control freak determined to have everything and everyone that touches his sphere of life within his power and subject to his influence. (Esther 1:12)

Have a Hidden Agenda – He is covert with words of peace and a heart of criticism. Hidden Agenda is like a snowball with a rock in it. With this Giant in operation, we lie in ambush with undisclosed motives, watching for weakness and vulnerability, ready to spring the trap, which has been disguised and then set with lies or half-truths. We hide one thing in our hearts while proclaiming another. This Giant is a user; it seeks to use life, people, and every situation to advance his own interests. (Matthew 10:26-27)

Take Personal Advantage – This Giant uses others to accomplish its own agenda. It is constantly maneuvering for title, position, or recognition. When he is not the center of attention, he suffers envy and pain. We ask "what's in it for me?" and will help others only if it directly benefits us. Selfish ambition. (Jude 1:16)

Remain Undisturbed – Unwilling to be inconvenienced. Undisturbed is not as blatant as the other six – he is insidious, secretive, subtle, and sophisticated. This Giant disguises himself as the need for stability, perhaps as the need to preserve his reputation or the honor of respectability when more is asked of him than he wants to give. Undisturbed says, "I will follow you, but I cannot follow you that far!" It is that subtle difference between admiration for Christ and identification with Him. (Jeremiah 48:11 and Luke 10:30-35)

Like Goliath of old, these seven menacing behemoths are ugly, treacherous and challenge the Armies of God as never before! True, they are worldly, conniving and totally bent on using others to the best of their abilities. But the real sad part is they are found smack dab in the middle of every church, where they divide and conquer unity!

Giant Killing

Since these giants are manifestations of the carnal nature in us, the only way to kill these giants is to apply the finished work of Jesus on the cross. The Scripture is clear: When Jesus died, we died with Him, and all these ugly traits in us (Rom. 6:6, 6:11). Even though spiritual salvation will get us to heaven, these giants remain until they are dealt with one by one, as we are faced with life's situations in which the giants, in effect, come alive in all their maliciousness, when we feel our self-life needs "protecting."

Steps to Take:

Recognition – To see patterns and how they are affecting our lives and those of others.

Repentance – Choosing change, determining to stop patterns by bringing judgments and expectations to death on the cross in prayer.

Prayer – Specific, focused and Spirit led.

Prayers of forgiveness – Pray out loud, "I choose to forgive Mom, Dad, Husband/Wife, others. Forgive me, Lord, for resenting/hating...

Prayers of death – To demolish strongholds/structures of judgment & expectancy, habits, attitudes & reflexes by taking them to the cross (Gal. 2:20; Gal 5:24).

Prayers of resurrection and life – "Lord, restore (be specific) or say reverse the old pattern; restore to new life and give a new heart in the place where the old heart has ruled."

One of the biggest problems most Christians have is that they "made a decision for Christ" at some point but never became a true follower. Christ's admonition that everyone who comes after me must first deny himself, take up his cross and follow me (Luke 9:23) has gone unheeded

By the majority of people who name the name Christian; hence the condition of America today as we know it – secularly minded. Can you see how the lack of Christian influence in a so-called "Christian society," where there's a two churches on every corner, could possibly bring the kinds of results we've discussed? "To whom much is given, much is required" Or as The Message puts it:

The servant who knows what his master wants and ignores it, or insolently does whatever he pleases, will be thoroughly thrashed. But if he does a poor job through ignorance, he'll get off with a slap on the hand. Great gifts mean great responsibilities; greater gifts, greater responsibilities! (Luke 12:48 The Message (MSG)

So what's the difference between a decision and a disciple? We'll find out in the next chapter.

CHAPTER 15

Decisions and Disciples

Being "saved," "born again," or "believing on Jesus" is a free gift and will get you to heaven (John 3:3; John 5:24), but walking as a disciple in the kingdom in the here and now experience will cost you something—yourself.

Here is the rub. Most people and believers want to make a "decision" for Christ but not become a disciple, confusing this sometimes with the 12 who lived with Jesus while He walked this earth. A decision for Christ, which is what we have often heard in religious circles, often leaves the person feeling happy (for a while), while not realizing that a decision will leave your primarily living for yourself.

There's an age-old debate over whether a person can enter heaven by simply believing, or does he or she have to become a disciple. By the way, the word disciple means "a learner," which was more than just learning things in Bible days – they followed!

The New Testament was originally written in the Greek language. If you have an English Bible, it has been translated from the Greek. The word believe is translated as belief (a noun – pistis) or believe (a verb - pisteo). These Greek words can mean "believe, depend, obey, trust or assurance." It's interesting that in the Book of James he says, "the demons believe and tremble."

You believe that God is one; you do well. So do the demons believe and shudder [in terror and horror such as make a man's hair stand on end and contract the surface of his skin]! (James 2:19 Amp).

Intellectual Assent

Whenever it is argued that faith is more than a mere intellectual assent (i.e., that faith must also include surrender/commitment to the Lordship of Christ), reference is hastily made to the demons' faith mentioned in v 19. It might even be said that Jas 2:19 forms the preeminent argument for the perspective that true faith comprises more than a superficial, intellectual "faith."

Throughout the Bible, God placed a two-letter word on every kind of decision people would make concerning their desire for more than just getting to heaven.

That two-letter word is if, as in "*If anyone would come after me, he or she must deny themselves, take up their cross and follow me*" (Luke 9:23). We can easily add to church rolls with the sweet message of salvation with no commitment, but when you start calling for the cost of discipleship, the numbers get much smaller.

Conditional sentences are "If ..., then ..." statements. They make a statement that if something happens, then something else will happen. The 'if ' clause is referred to as the 'protasis' by grammarians. It comes from the Greek words 'pro' (meaning before) and 'stasis' (meaning 'stand'). So the 'protasis' means 'what stands before' or 'comes first' as far as these two clauses are concerned. The 'then' clause is termed the 'apodosis'; it is what 'comes after' the protasis.

The "if " is important because if a person becomes a disciple of Jesus Christ, they have made a serious decision that their life now belongs to God to do with as He pleases. It's a one-time decision but a lifelong struggle. This discipleship is a process in which the follower goes through myriads of change in their interests, passions, and choices, but it doesn't come without a great deal of pain and suffering. It "ain't no" picnic.

"*If we died with him, we shall also live with him: if we suffer with him we shall also reign with him*" (2 Tim. 2:11-12).

The Self-Centered Refuse to "Die"

The dying here has to do with the dying of the self-life in us, and not necessarily physical death, as with a martyr, although this definitely has happened to many Christians and still does throughout the world. Jesus said that whoever loses life (self) for my sake will find it, but whoever saves his life (self) shall lose it (Matt. 16:25). This statement is the essence of what it means to be a disciple of Christ—you lose your self-life.

The Kernel of Wheat

This is tantamount to the verse that says if a kernel of wheat doesn't fall into the ground and die, it abides alone, but if it dies, it bears fruit. People who hold on to their self-life die alone -- they are ultimately lonely people because they are self-centered, and Numero Uno with them is protecting their self-life at all costs! Additionally, "fruit-bearing," bringing forth spiritual fruit in others, is either non-existent or sorely lacking.

"Very truly I tell you, unless a kernel of wheat falls to the ground and dies, it remains only a single seed. But if it dies, it produces many seeds" (John 12:24 NIV).

Incidentally, the Lord Jesus knew that leaving the old self in charge was a horrendous mistake, so He crucified it with Himself:

"Let us never forget that our old selves died with him on the cross that the tyranny of sin over us might be broken—for a dead man can safely be said to be immune to the power of sin (Rom. 6:6 JB Phillips)."

How many committed Christians do you know who are self-centered? I mean they focus on themselves, their lives, their success, their appearance, their status, etc. I imagine you can think of a bushel of them. You probably have little doubt that they "know the Lord," but their self-centered focus smells like a possum that was just run over by a Mac truck.

Decisions Not Disciples

In the "Bible Belt," where I live, we have a lot of religious sayings. "He made a decision for Christ last night." This means the guy "trusted Christ" (more jargon), but the real question is will he become a disciple of Christ? Will he give himself up for God's purposes, or will he let the old self stay in charge?

In the "Bible Belt" you can often meet people who have grown up with a list of "don'ts." I heard someone say that growing up in his family they definitely knew what they were against but weren't too sure what they were for! At my high school, we had one local pastor who stood against square dancing! Apparently, he felt square dancing led to pre-martial sex – LOL!

We sometimes think "giving your life to Christ" means we have to go to Africa. It usually doesn't. I say usually because I heard one evangelist say he wouldn't give his life to Christ because he didn't want to go there. He finally decided to do it, and guess what?--he went to Africa eight times-- and loved it! The truth is "giving yourself to Jesus" simply means we give up control of ourselves to the Heavenly Father's direction through the power of the Holy Spirit. This isn't a once-for-all decision—it's an everyday occurrence!

We often quote the Great Commission, some of the last words of Christ to the disciples before He returned to heaven (Matt. 28:19-20). The key part in His words was "making disciples of all nations," not making converts.

If we had obeyed this one thing, the world probably would have already been won by now.

Change is Painful

Change into a disciple is painful because the old self wants to continue to assert itself. Consequently, the one who really follows Jesus will experience various kinds of suffering – emotional, physical, mental and spiritual, so this self is rendered meek and servant-like. This suffering allows the person's spirit to have control over him and more easily submit to the Lord. God made us a tripartite being – (human) spirit, soul and body. If the spirit is in charge, the rest will follow. In our growth as a Christian, God takes the "acorn" that was planted in us when we were born of the Holy Spirit and makes us into an oak tree. This can take years! The pain we go through creates for us, in us, an everlasting weight of glory:

For the suffering of this time, while very small and swift, prepares us great glory without limits for the eternity of eternities"(2 Cor. 4:17 Aramaic Bible in Plain English (©2010)).

Suffering and its intensity varies from person to person. Some people experience little physical suffering, but their mental difficulties wreak havoc on them. Relationships falter and sometimes end, and those can be some of the most painful experiences of all. Others experience losing a close friend or many family members within a short period of time. Whatever a disciple incurs is working out that "eternal weight of glory." Either that, or for some people's suffering is wasted on them (1 Pet. 2:20) since they may suffer for the wrong reason or find no meaning in suffering for righteousness sake.

The Release of the Spirit

In *The Release of the Spirit*, Watchman Nee puts all this suffering in perspective. *"ANYONE who serves God will discover sooner or later that the great hindrance to his work is not others but himself. He will discover that his outward man and his inward man are not in harmony, for both are tending toward opposite directions. He will also sense the inability of his outward man to submit to the spirit's control, thus rendering him incapable of obeying God's highest commands. He will quickly detect that the greatest difficulty lies in his outward man, for it hinders him from using his spirit.*

Many of God's servants are not able to do even the most elementary works. Ordinarily they should be enabled by the exercise of their spirit to know God's word, to discern the spiritual condition of another, to send forth God's messages under anointing and to receive God's revelations. Yet due to the distractions of the outward man, their spirit does not seem to function properly. It is basically because their outward man has never been dealt with. For this reason revival, zeal, pleading and activity are but a waste of time. As we shall see, there is just one basic dealing which can enable man to be useful before God: brokenness."

Suffice what Bro. Nee said by considering that in The Fall we gave away ourselves to a downward spiral through "Daddy Adam." The spirit of man, once his loving connection to God, was severed. The soul of man, which was intended to be his servant, took advantage of this and became the master. In other words, knowledge and experience through the senses (soul works) was now the rule of the day. Suffering is one of the ways God uses to release the spirit to become the master again.

"I See That Hand"

I don't know about you, but if God, at the beginning of this journey, had asked for a show of hands of everyone who wanted to suffer for him, I would have kept my down. I guess that's why in most churches the preacher's use of "I see that hand" only means you want heaven or you need help. I can hear it now: "Ok, church, everyone who wants to die the death to your selfishness come forward." Out of 200, two make their way to the front, and one of them was pushed!

You may think I'm being a bit cynical or too harsh, but consider the reality of pressure and giving up your right to yourself as found among the Seven Giants. In John chapter 6, it provides an account in which a distinction can be made between a decision and a disciple. In this account, there had arisen a dispute with the Jews over who Jesus was, God or just a man. He tells the Jews that eating His flesh (the Bread of Life) and drinking His blood is synonymous with finding life in Him:

Whoever eats my flesh and drinks my blood remains in me, and I in them. Just as the living Father sent me and I live because of the Father, so the one who feeds on me will live because of me. This is the bread that came down from heaven. Your ancestors ate manna and died, but whoever feeds on this bread will live forever (John 6:56-58).

Losing Disciples

Jesus wasn't suggesting cannibalism, as some of these Jews asserted. He was saying that to become and remain His disciple, total submission and becoming one with Him was required. It's interesting to note that, unbeknownst to most people, at one point Jesus had 70 disciples, or 72 as some translations state (Luke 10:1), and not just the 12 primary ones. The confrontation with the Jews over the above declaration about His Body and Blood was so upsetting and offensive to them that "many of them walked with him no more" (John 6:66).

Offending the Flesh

Laying down our lives is most often offensive to our flesh. Our independent self nature rears its ugly head every time we're asked to do something that is contrary to our nature. Consequently, most of the time we have to act against ourselves. As with the 70 disciples reference, we also are often offended by others' behavior, particularly in the church, and because of this some "walk with Him no more." Their offense is geared toward the Lord as well as the people who offended them.

This is the primary reason our focus should never be on the church, a ministry (ours or anyone else's) or some Christian leader. Our focus must remain on Jesus Himself (Col. 1:3) and serve in the kingdom of God (Matt. 6:33) and not the church per se. Churches, ministries or sometimes a highly respected and adored minister will fail us, but Jesus won't!

If you serve the church as you're primary goal, you will likely become very disappointed, and if you haven't already left, it won't be long before you do. Church Hopping is in vogue. On the flip side, some people serve churches that have left traditional doctrines in favor of "cultural acceptance" or what's "politically correct," take your pick. They have decided that obedience to Christ first and the Word of God weren't worth the sacrifice.

Besides the pain, etc., mentioned here, becoming a disciple definitely has some temporal and eternal benefits. When the disciples reminded Jesus that they "had left all to follow Him," he replied:

"Truly I tell you," Jesus replied, *no one who has left home or brothers or sisters or mother or father or children or fields for me and the gospel will fail to receive a hundred times as much in this present age: homes, brothers, sisters, mothers, children and fields—along with persecutions—and in the age to come eternal life. But many who are first will be last, and the last first* (Mark 10-29-31 NIV).

Die Hard With a Vengeance

No, this has nothing to do with the Bruce Willis' series, although the tie-in is applicable to your life.

When it comes to living, Jesus said "dying" is the key:

(Luke 9:23 Amp). *²³ And He said to all, If any person wills to come after Me, let him deny himself [ᵃ disown himself, ᵇ forget, lose sight of himself and his own interests, ᶜ refuse and give up himself] and take up his cross daily and follow Me [ᵈ cleave steadfastly to Me, conform wholly to My example in living and, if need be, in dying also]*

²⁴ I assure you, most solemnly I tell you, Unless a grain of wheat falls into the earth and dies, it remains [just one grain; it never becomes more but lives] by itself alone. But if it dies, it produces many others and yields a rich harvest. ²⁵ Anyone who loves his life loses it, but anyone who hates his life in this world will keep it to life eternal. [Whoever has no love for, no concern for, no regard for his life here on earth, but despises it, preserves his life forever and ever.] ²⁶ If anyone serves Me, he must continue to follow Me [ᵇ to cleave steadfastly to Me, conform wholly to My example in living and, if need be, in dying] and wherever I am, there will My servant be also. If anyone serves Me, the Father will honor him (John 12:24-26 Amp).

The Upside Down Kingdom

The kingdom of God is in one sense upside down. To die to self is to live; to be first is to be the least of all; to be honored requires putting yourself in a lower position in your heart. This isn't popular in places where success, health and wealth are the foremost aspect of the gospel. The ego prefers being left intact, unbothered by the cost of discipleship. Yet, these verses teach that we all must give up ourselves to experience LIFE.

In many Christian circles, verses become the most important part rather than getting to know Jesus firsthand. We can ignore the PERSON of Jesus while jamming our heads full of knowledge. Like the Pharisees we can miss the forest for the trees!

You pore over the scriptures for you imagine that you will find eternal life in them. And all the time they give their testimony to me! But you are not willing to come to me to have real life! Men's approval or disapproval means nothing to me, but I can tell that you have none of the love of God in your hearts (John 5:39 JB Phillips NT)

I'm still amazed that in most churches today the cross is still not preached as a means of power. We go there to have our sins forgiven, but the self-life, which died there also (Rom. 6:6, 11) is ignored, as far as our application of the cross is concerned. And though it's not a sideline part of the Bible, this essential tool to living well and for a better reason is easily placed on the backburner if you're simply trying to build a bigger church while making everyone happy.

This isn't cushy. As a matter of fact, it can be downright painful when you decide that the will of God is more important than feeling good. The truth of the matter is that as you apply this truth to your life, joy will come "on the other side of the cross."

Like Sand in the Hourglass…

Or so that famous soap opera begins. Life is so short. Paul called it "a vapor." Seems when one hits 50, time speeds up, and the next thing you know, you're looking at 70, you have grandkids, and you're either fixed for retirement, or you're looking for more coupons. Next thing you know, the undertaker–or if you're a believer in Jesus –the uppertaker—will come calling, and we must give an account of our lives. Hebrews 9:27 says it's appointed for us to die once, and after this comes the judgment:

27 And just as it is appointed for [all] men once to die, and after that the [certain] judgment (Hebrews 9:27 Amp).

This verse doesn't tell us *when* this judgment is, although we are certain it happens after the bodies of every person dead and living will be called up from where they are to account for deeds done in the body:

10 *because we must all stand before Christ to be judged. Each of us will receive what we should get—good or bad—for the things we did in the earthly body (2 Cor. 5:10 New Century)*

Jesus assures us that one day everyone will hear His voice to receive one of two types of resurrections, some to eternal life and others to eternal damnation:

*Do not be astonished at this, for the hour is coming when all who are in the graves shall hear his voice, **29** And they shall come out: those who have done good things, to the resurrection of life, and those who have done evil deeds, to the resurrection of judgment (John 5:28-29 Aramaic Bible in Plain English).*

This should rattle anyone's cage. To think we have to give an account to the Son of God should get our attention. He knows everything we've ever done, why we did it (our motivation), for whom we did it, and under what circumstances, so then we have no excuse when we stand before the one who sees right through us.

This all seems like bad news unless we consider a few very important caveats. For one, the Christian has already been judged for his **sins** when Christ died on the cross on him. This is because God the Father judged our sins and took His wrath out on them by accepting the sacrifice of His Son in our place. Romans 8:1 tells our there is now no condemnation for those who are IN Christ Jesus. So, the believer's sins will not be judged, only his works:

11 *For no one can lay any foundation other than the one already laid, which is Jesus Christ. **12** If anyone builds on this foundation using gold, silver, costly stones, wood, hay or straw, **13** their work will be shown for what it is, because the Day will bring it* to light. It will be revealed with fire, and the fire will test the quality of each person's work. **14**If what has been built survives, the builder will receive a reward. **15**If it is burned up, the builder will suffer loss but yet will be saved—even though only as one escaping through the flames (1 Cor. 3:11-15).

On the other hand, people who have put their stock in their own goodness, morality, principles, or anything other than accepting the sacrifice of Jesus on the cross, will face the judgment of God for their own works, which Scripture says for any of us is "filthy rags" (Isa. 64:6).

Two books, Two Judgments

Quite simply, there are two books that matter in God's eternal library: *The Book of Life*, where every person's name, who has been redeemed, saved, forgiven and made righteous by believing in Christ, is written, and *the books*, where all the works of the unredeemed are kept. Deeds done by these folks are counted as an affront to the righteousness of Christ, which they rejected in place of their own self-righteousness and works, according to God's Word:

11 *Then I saw a great white throne and the One Who was seated upon it, from Whose presence and from the sight of Whose face earth and sky fled away, and no place was found for them.*

12 *I [also] saw the dead, great and small; they stood before the throne,* **and books were opened. Then another book was opened, which is [the Book] of Life.** *And the dead were judged (sentenced) by what they had done [[b]their whole way of feeling and acting, their aims and endeavors] in accordance with what was recorded in the books.*

13 *And the sea delivered up the dead who were in it, death and Hades ([c]the state of death or disembodied existence) surrendered the dead in them, and all were tried and their cases determined by what they had done [according to their motives, aims, and works].*

14 *Then death and Hades ([d]the state of death or disembodied existence) were thrown into the lake of fire. This is the second death, the lake of fire.*

15 *And if anyone's [name] was not found recorded in the Book of Life, he was hurled into the lake of fire* (Rev. 20:11-15).

The Self-Centered Lose Their Lives!

Let's take a look at the passage used previously regarding Christians who are interested in protecting their self-life:

Anyone who loves his life loses it, but anyone who hates his life in this world will keep it to life eternal. [Whoever has no love for, no concern for, no regard for his life here on earth, but despises it, preserves his life forever and ever.] [26] *If anyone serves Me, he must continue to follow Me [to cleave steadfastly to Me, conform wholly to My example in living and, if need be, in dying] and wherever I am, there will My servant be also. If anyone serves Me, the Father will honor* him (John 12:24-26 Amp).

This passage says, quite simply, that if you protect your self-life and refuse to give it up for Christ, you will lose everything in which you failed to give yourself over to Jesus for His glory and service. This is a scary thought, yes? But think of the many Christians you know who live for themselves, their comfort, and who are focused on preserving their energies, money and time for themselves. At the judgment seat of Christ, they lose everything that God doesn't determine is gold, silver and precious stones to Him. Saved? Yes. Rewards little or none (1 Cor. 3:11-15).

I've written this out of love for everyone who sits week after week under pastors' sermons that tickle their ears without calling them to a true death to self in service to their king. You may attend the most popular church in town, but if you miss what I've written here, it's tragic!

Understanding and receiving God's unconditional love could have a huge impact on the chemistry in the brain that has become unstable.

Jesus loves us with this unconditional love, but He made Himself clear on the subject of service. Like sand in the hourglass, our time here on earth is slowly slipping away. We all need to make some choices about how we live. Choosing to "Dine with Mephibosheth" (the next chapter) is a wonderful choice about God's provision.

CHAPTER 16

Dining with Mephibosheth

For anyone dealing with all the things that go with depression and a mind that filled with anxiety, anger, exhaustion and mental disturbance, take consolation. We're all in the same boat. We're just a bunch of humans living life on a planet filled with difficulty and brokenness that will someday be redeemed. I like that idea of this whole earth being renovated into a glorious state without sin, hate, war, crime and the like. God promises us that this is going to happen (see Revelation 21:1).

Until then God has given us ways to deal with these difficulties, particularly by understanding the principles in His Word for living with illumination and power from His Holy Spirit. Once we realize that all of us are needy, broken and can't conquer these things with the strength God provides, we are like Mephibosheth, who was lame in both feet.

Who? Mephibosheth.

Looking at 2 Sam. 9:1-13 you'll find that Mephibosheth was Jonathan's son and King Saul's grandson. Jonathan, Saul's son, was David's best friend with whom he had a Godly soul tie.

Mephibosheth was lame in both feet from being dropped as a 5-year-old child, as his family fled one of the intra-tribal wars in Israel. As a result, he was crippled in his feet and had to be carried his entire life (no wheelchairs back then). Because of this shame was his prevailing emotion, which was caused by his humiliation.

As you may recall from biblical history, Saul, who was filled with jealousy and rage toward David because of his prowess as a skilled military leader, beginning with his defeat of Goliath, tried to kill David on many occasions. Jonathan loved David and tried to hide him from Saul, risking his own life in the process.

Back to Mephibosheth. After Saul was killed in battle, David desired to show kindness and compassion to his former enemy's family by extending blessing and not cursing to them (as king he could have had them all killed). Not comprehending this love, all of them feared for their lives, including Mephibotheth, who was invited to the King David's palace to forever sit at David's table and eat with him.

Shame-Based Living

Mephibosheth's response to King David was typical of our often shame-based living, as we have seen. "And [the cripple] bowed himself and said, *'What is your servant, that you should look upon such a* **dead dog** *as I am?'"* (2 Sam. 9:8). We can be living like a "dead dog" instead of reigning with King Jesus on a daily basis!

For if because of one man's trespass (lapse, offense) death reigned through that one, much more surely will those who receive [God's] overflowing grace (unmerited favor) and the free gift of righteousness [putting them into right standing with Himself] reign as kings in life through the one Man Jesus Christ" (the Messiah, the Anointed One) (Rom. 5:17 Amp).

Do You Feel Like a Dead Dog?

Mephibosheth, whose name means "destroying shame," is a beautiful example of how Father God wants to remove our shame and bring us with full benefits to eat at His table. Until this happens, we may be reluctant to receive all God has for us. The truth of the matter is, without Jesus, we are all lame in both feet, poor, blind and naked:

For you say, I am rich; I have prospered **and** *grown wealthy,* **and** *I am in need of nothing;* **and** *you do not realize* **and** *understand that you are* **wretched**, *pitiable,* **poor, blind, and** *naked* (Revelation 3:17).

This scripture wasn't written to people who didn't know God, even though it's been used as an evangelical tool. It was written to Christians who had forgotten their former state and who had become proud of their religiosity, wealth and who felt no real need for intimacy with Jesus.

What a rebuke to all who find solace in their "success"! Like King David, Jesus' response was to say He was knocking at the doors of their hearts to come and dine with Him! The passage isn't speaking so much about food but intimacy and fellowship with the Son of God.

Behold, I stand at the door and knock; if anyone hears and listens to and heeds My voice and opens the door, I will come in to him and will eat with him, and he [will eat] with Me (Revelation 3:20).

The House of Abandonment

I was plagued with this mess my whole life until God showed me via a dream that even though He had redeemed me and called me His son, I was living in the "house of abandonment"! You see the stronghold is predicated on abandonment, which isn't necessarily physical abandonment (it could be) but emotional abandonment through neglect or a perception that we have been neglected or abandoned. In the house of abandonment are the rooms of guilt (false or true), shame, fear, anger, judgment, a critical spirit, rejection and the list goes on.

Psychologists call abandonment the "primal wound," which simply means it's the first sense of feeling alone and left to fend for ourselves. Abandonment opens wide the door to the shame-fear-control stronghold.

Unfortunately, most go on living with this thing the rest of their lives, thinking that God isn't really interested in their difficulties and that they are "fatally flawed" with no one to help. They may even feel abandoned by God Himself and living like a "dead dog" instead of "sitting in heavenly places" (Eph. 2:1-2) with the One who loves them so much that He paid it all so they come draw near to Him and their true Father.

Do you have an endless refrain that 'plays' in your thoughts? Are you continually thinking thoughts like, I am different, I am defective, I am embarrassed, I am guilty, I am inadequate? If so, shame has become a part of your identity? But the presence of shame is only the beginning. Shame is often allied with fear.

Ask yourself, "Is fear included in my frequent mental refrain? Am I afraid of being exposed, or abandoned, or rejected? Do fears like these dominate my thinking so that they have become my continual companions, deeply embedded within my personality as "normally abnormal" parts of my identity?"

Would You Like to Sit Next to Mephibosheth?

The Great King Jesus has spread a massive buffet. He's invited all those who will come:

"Now He told a parable to those who were invited, [when] He noticed how they were selecting the places of honor, saying to them, ⁸ When you are invited by anyone to a marriage feast, do not recline on the chief seat [in the place of honor], lest a more distinguished person than you has been invited by him, ⁹ And he who invited both of you will come to you and say, Let this man have the place [you have taken]. Then, with humiliation and a guilty sense of impropriety, you will begin to take the lowest place. ¹⁰ But when you are invited, go and recline in the lowest place, so that when your host comes in, he may say to you, Friend, go up higher! Then you will be honored in the presence of all who sit [at table] with you.¹¹ For everyone who exalts himself will be humbled (ranked below others who are honored or rewarded), and he who humbles himself (keeps a modest opinion of himself and behaves accordingly) will be exalted (elevated in rank). ¹² Jesus also said to the man who had invited Him, When you give a dinner or a supper, do not invite your friends or your brothers or your relatives or your wealthy neighbors, lest perhaps they also invite you in return, and so you are paid back. ¹³ But when you give a banquet or a reception, invite the poor, the disabled, the lame, and the blind. ¹⁴ Then you will be blessed (happy, fortunate, and to be envied), because they have no way of repaying you, and you will be recompensed at the resurrection of the just (upright). 1⁵ When one of those who reclined [at the table] with Him heard this, he said to Him, Blessed (happy, fortunate, and to be envied) is he who shall eat bread in the kingdom of God! (Luke 14:7-15, Amp).

Jesus like King David has invited all of us like Mephibosheth to join Him at the table. Will you allow shame or pride to keep you from the greatest banquet of all? You don't have to.

Then [the angel] said to me, Write this down: Blessed (happy, to be envied) are those who are summoned (invited, called) to **the marriage supper of the Lamb.** *And he said to me [further],* **The**se *are* **the** *true words* (**the** *genuine and exact declarations*) **of** *God* (Rev. 19:9).

If you've already accepted the invitation to the Marriage Supper of the Lamb, are you enjoying the daily joy of knowing He loves you and has removed your shame through His death on the cross and the shedding of His precious Blood? You can!

Are You Angry at God?

If you had been Mephibosheth, would you be angry at God? I mean, after all, an accident branded him for life. He was pitiful and had no future except to be taken care of by his family. How would you like the name "Destroying Shame"?

Everyone is mad at God to some extent, even those in denial. When something goes wrong, I mean really wrong that cuts at the depths of our souls, what do we say? "Why God?" "Why did you allow this horrible thing to happen to me"?

The answer is our waywardness from the start, thinking we know how to handle life, and yet it is a foolish way:

The foolishness of man subverts his way [ruins his affairs]; then his heart is resentful and frets against the Lord (Proverbs 19:3 AMP).

Lots of people–and many Christians–are angry at God, and very often it's because of the verse above–we are foolish in understanding life, His Ways and the way the Word of God works. Even after we become Christian believers, we have to unlearn how not to flow in diametric opposition to the Bible and God's spoken Word to us. As long as this tendency remains, our foolishness subverts our way and ruins our affairs. And guess who gets blamed? other people, obstacles, situations and ultimately God.

Toxic Faith

A lot has been written about toxic faith, but I can confirm that through terrible church experiences, awful theology and becoming offended, we can surely experience this. The problem is we blame people, organizations but include God who isn't "religion." He is simply God. Religion, or should I say religions, reflect poorly on Who God is. Man's perception of Who God is so distorted because of culture, tradition and prejudice that people rarely get to see His glorious nature.

If we experience negativity early enough, we paint a picture in our minds that is so far from the truth that it's pathetic. I honestly believe few have a true picture of Who God is, leaving us with denominational portraits, distorted views through mega-egomaniac evangelists, preachers and others who would provide us with a sad picture of who our God is.

When I write of "toxic faith," it isn't just a metaphor. It is a spiritual happening that happens inside people, making them feel hate, rebellion and retaliation for all God really is. It is so difficult that it puts us in denial because we can't imagine what we're feeling could be real, but it is.

In my book, Deeper Water for Thirsty Souls, I wrote about the **Religious Spirit**.

The Religious Spirit

Of all the demons that fill the demonic realm, none is worse that the religious spirit. This thing has opposed true spirituality from the beginning of time, and the sad thing is, it's so coy and deceptive than most of us Christians don't realize it's gotten hold of us! We all recognize that the Pharisees, with a few exceptions, were "blind guides," who totally opposed the Holy Spirit through Christ, and who ultimately killed Jesus for telling them the truth (see John 8).

However, many Christians (and some people who just name the name), having been deceived by this spirit through their denominational instruction and the doctrines of men, oppose the real power of God the Holy Spirit in their churches every time they get together, "holding to a form of godliness but denying its power" (2 Tim. 3:5). Americans, excepting a minority, are sickly religious!

Is it any wonder why people quit church, rarely finding any real power to save and heal them? One of my good buddies, now deceased, said, "I'd rather be in a bar where everybody knows your name" (instead the Cheers' bar) if I couldn't find an alive in the Holy Spirit church!" Before I move on, I want to make it clear that the Bible declares that true religion is not showy, puffed up or done with impure motives:

External religious worship [religion as it is expressed in outward acts] that is pure and unblemished in the sight of God the Father is this: to visit and help and care for the orphans and widows in their affliction and need, and to keep oneself unspotted and uncontaminated from the world (James 1:27).

You may think I'm being too harsh about this, but your Lord and mine had no patience with the religious façade of His day. Yes, he most often answered the Pharisees and Sadducees' religious questions through which they were more interested in tricking Jesus than looking for real truth, but ultimately, He exposed their hypocrisy, calling them "snakes" and "sons of hell." Interestingly, He said the curse of their forefathers, who killed the prophets, had reached its fulfillment in them (Matthew 23)!

Jude summed up the religious spirit by citing three examples (Jude 11): the way of Cain (bloodless religion and good works save); the way of Balaam, a double-minded prophet for profit, who used his power to seduce the Children of Israel to cohabitate with pagans; and last, Korah, who's rebellion against Moses, is the precipice upon which all religious rebellion is built—no honor, submission and respect for true godly authority.

What sorrow awaits them! For they follow in the footsteps of Cain, who killed his brother. Like Balaam, they deceive people for money. And like Korah, they perish in their rebellion (Jude 11) TLB.

All these were motivated by the religious spirit. And, yes, you will find the spirits of Jezebel and antichrist at work every time this hellish thing shows up. What amazes me most are the well-known scholarly, God-fearing men and women, whose erroneous teaching about the Holy Spirit, can sometimes border on blasphemy. These people, sincere but wrong in what they believe, have been deceived by the religious spirit to think that God's power somehow—through no particular biblical reason –or even common sense—ceased after the first hundred years of the church!

Referred to as "Cessationists," they, on the other hand, know and teach that the devil is alive and well on planet earth and is going to show up incarnate one day, but the church, powerless, except for prayer and good Bible preaching, will win or have to be raptured. Huh? Somebody help me with this, but the apostles and early church were totally dependent on the manifested power of the Holy Spirit to do great and miraculous things! (See the Book of Acts)

Incidentally, if you have friends who believe that somehow the power of God just passed away, I recommend the book, *Surprised by the Power of the Spirit*, by Jack Deere, a former Dallas Theological Seminary professor, who once believed the Cessationists' tripe himself. He does a wonderfully biblical, experiential and historical account of the works of the Holy Spirit. People, we may not always see what we want to see or experience, but this in no way prohibits the "right now" Jesus power of the Holy Spirit!

Freedom in Christ

Life should be filled with the joy of the Father so that we have the strength and faith to worship, walk and work with the Holy Spirit, (Nehemiah 8:10). We need to enjoy life, people, ministry, our families, food and even our own jokes. We need to never let life get stale. We need to practice the key of a godly lifestyle by embracing change as the Holy Spirit leads so we can continually walk in the freedom that Christ has bought for us as children of God. This is the liberty that Jesus has demonstrated for us and has provided for us in His kingdom. When God decides to bring change into the earth we need to lift our hands and say "Lord use me I am ready and willing'" In John 5:19 Jesus said, "The Son can do nothing of Himself but what he sees the Father do, for whatever He does, the Son also does in like manner." We need to make good choices. We can go up the worldly road (the end is spiritual death), the religious road (legalism) or the Agape Road, where we are healed to receive and give God's love.

Most of the difficulties anyone has go back to father and mother. The Scripture is clear that if we honor them, it will go well for us. However, in most cases, American fathers and those across the pond, have little understanding of what is takes to be a spiritual father. One writer and spiritually gifted brother said, "Most people's problems could have been cut dramatically by having a good father. In the next chapter we'll look at how to find your true Father, and by doing this you could do wonders for your brain difficulties!

CHAPTER 17

Finding Your True Father

For many years now there has been a search for fathers. People usually want to connect with their father down deep in their spirits, even if they had a bad father. The desire for reconciliation, and maybe even restoration, is extremely intense in some of us. The theme of fatherhood runs throughout Hollywood movies and books of every description. Unfortunately, most examples of fathers are not good with rare exceptions.

One of the more popular ones in recent years was that of the evil Darth Vader, formerly Anakin Skywalker, who ruled the galaxy alongside the Satanic-like Emperor Palpatine, and his son Luke, whose initial reaction to Vader's declaration that "I am your father" was something akin to finding out your father was Hitler, Pol Pot or Ted Bundy! "Noooooooooooooooo!" The rest of the story was several fights to the death between these two before Luke knew there was "still good" in Vader, whom he eventually "saved," only to have him die in his arms when the Death Star blew up. (Okay, I'm a Star Wars nut).

God the Father, who created all in His Son Jesus, wants very badly to intimately connect with every son or daughter He created for his pleasure (Rev. 4:11). Despite accusations that He is to blame for many of the world's ills, this wonderful Person truly loves each person on planet earth and desires their greatest blessings and for them to experience real love and peace. His heart longs to know you and for you to know Him, but things have gotten in the way.

God is self-revealing. Moses first found out in the Old Testament in Exodus 34:6-7 when he asked God to show Him his glory:

18 *Then Moses said, "Now show me your glory."*

19 *And the Lord said, "I will cause all my goodness to pass in front of you, and I will proclaim my name, the Lord, in your presence. I will have mercy on whom I will have mercy, and I will have compassion on whom I will have compassion.* **20** *But,"* *he said, "you cannot see my face, for no one may see me and live."* **21** *Then the Lord said, "There is a place near me where you may stand on a rock.* **22** *When my glory passes by, I will put you in a cleft in the rock and cover you with my hand until I have passed by.* **23** *Then I will remove my hand and you will see my back; but my face must not be seen."*

God said:

I am:

Compassionate

Slow to anger

Merciful

Forgiving

Faithful to my covenant.

So even in the Old Testament where God has been accused of being mean and punishing all who disobeyed, you can see His very nature of that of Christ in the New Testament.

Jesus the Way AND the Revelation

Theologically speaking, Evangelicals customarily quote John 14:6 as Jesus saying He's the only way to heaven: "I am the way, the truth and the life, and no one comes to the Father except by me." Although this is a true statement, the context is that of Jesus answering not only the *way* to the father but of Phillip's query that Jesus "*show* us the father."

Jesus' heart desire for all people was and is to reveal His Father to them and to glorify Him in every situation. In John 17, the high priestly prayer of Christ, He is found asking the Father to make us one with them, to join the Holy Trinity in such an enveloping presence that people may know us by their love that shines through us.

It's interesting that Christians usually relate to different persons of the Godhead: Some are more focused on God the Father in some churches, although real intimacy with the Father may be sorely lacking. Other Christians relate more to Jesus as Savior and Lord, while Pentecostals and Charismatics may relate more intimately to the Holy Spirit. The truth is, like the crude example of the three-legged stool, if one leg is missing, the stool is unbalanced! Our Lord wants all His people to have intimate fellowship with all three members of the Godhead!

In God's dispensational economy, He has revealed Himself to humankind in various ways with more emphasis on one Person of the Trinity than the other. Until the time of Jesus, God revealed Himself as Jehovah God, primarily through leaders such as Moses, Daniel and other prophets, and the Kings such as David and Solomon. Then Jesus came to reveal the Father and do His works, and to leave us the sweet Holy Spirit to take His place. Since Pentecost the Holy Spirit's power and presence have been available to every Christian who would receive and be blessed with the Comforter and His gifts.

It's also interesting that in church history, after several hundred years of being lost in formality and rituals, God began to restore us once again to the richness of the Trinity by giving us Luther (teaching justification), the Wesleys (teaching sanctification) and from there to the 1920s Azusa Street outpouring of the Holy Spirit's power and love until now, sometimes known as "the Latter Rain." In our day we are beginning to see a greater emphasis once again on the Fatherhood of God.

Unfortunately, this understanding and revelation was lost to many people who were poorly fathered by their earthly dads. So, God began to teach us what was wrong – what was blocking this intimacy with the Father.

God has been faithful for many years to begin unraveling the mystery of fatherhood. One well-known TV preacher had this to say about fatherhood: "A good father would solve 90 percent of the problems incurred by most people."

He wasn't kidding, as backed up by the latest statistics about what poor fathering does. Or on the other hand, what positive father can bring about in the heart of a child.

Can you envision not only the impact of human fatherlessness on generation after generation, but also the perception foisted upon our Heavenly Father, whose goodness and light are obscured by our darkened spiritual eyes?

"He who curses his father or his mother, his lamp will go out in time of darkness" (Proverbs 20:20).

But it's God's desire that our eyes be enlightened to know the hope of His calling and our the rich inheritance we have in Him:

"By having the eyes of your heart flooded with light, so that you can know and understand the hope to which He has called you, and how rich is His glorious inheritance in the saints (His set-apart ones)" (Ephesians 1:18 AMP).

Cursing Parents?

To curse, as in the 20/20 scripture above (interesting that God named the ability to see clearly by giving us that numbered verse, isn't it?), means to take lightly; to treat as worthless; to treat contemptuously; to curse. Under the Mosaic Law this brought a death penalty (Ex. 21:17; Lev 20:9; Deut. 27:16).

This was indeed severe, but today, rather than experience physical harm or death (praise the Lord!), we've cursed ourselves with sicknesses, a shortened life, embattled relationships, job loss, devastated finances, etc. The sad thing is this happens to good people, people who shouldn't be experiencing such things, but dishonoring parents brings hardship and trials that are inexplicable.

This is not to say some of these things are just part of living and life, but in many cases they are the result of dishonor and judgments made against parents. One Christian author says dishonoring parents is the number one reason for most difficulties in life! I think you agree that's a mouthful!

In the New Testament we find the same commandment as in the above Old Testament references with two promises – that you may live long and prosper.

"Children, obey your parents in the Lord [as His representatives], for this is just and right. ² Honor (esteem and value as precious) your father and your mother—this is the first commandment with a promise—³ That all may be well with you and that you may live long on the earth" (Eph. 6:1-3 Amp).

How We See God

In every way we have judged our parents, to that degree, our view of God is distorted. In other words, we see through a bad pair of spectacles. This is not to say all of them are honorable, but judging is something we can choose not to do through God's power and grace.

The eye is the lamp of the body. So if your eye is sound, your entire body will be full of light. But if your eye is unsound, your whole body will be full of darkness. If then the very light in you [your ⁻ᴱconscience] is darkened, how dense is that darkness! (Matt. 6:23-24 Amp).

I once worked for an eye bank. Eye banks specialize in extracting a donor's cornea and providing it to surgeons for transplantation in a patient's eye who is experiencing very poor sight or even blindness. A cornea is often referred to as "the window of the eye" because it allows light to enter the eye to be ultimately refracted by the retina that sends signals to the brain so we can see. From an ophthalmological point of view, you can see how necessary it is for the cornea to receive proper light to enact the process described here. A bad cornea equals a distorted view of life or no view at all!

In essence, our view of God is reflected by how we have honored or dishonored our parents. Again, some people have had horrendous parents, who don't deserve honor. However, law is law. As we forgive and give up bitterness and judgments, our view of Father God changes.

God's Bad Rap

God very often is seen as angry, vindictive and longing to judge the people of the earth with severity. That's a very poor picture of who He is. To the contrary, the Father of Lights is a wonderful, loving Father who loves freely and abundantly. As we have emphasized here, Moses once asked God to "show me your glory" (Ex. 34:6). God passed by Moses and described Himself – or His glory – as the following:

"The LORD, the LORD, the compassionate and gracious God, slow to anger, abounding in love and faithfulness..." God the Father is compassionate, gracious, slow to get angry, abounding in love and faithfulness. This doesn't sound like the God most people envision, but it is who He truly is.

Salvation is First Light

When we first come to believe in Jesus, the light of the Holy Spirit is given to us, showing us in greater measure WHO Jesus is. As we advance in our maturity in both knowledge and experience, even greater light should illuminate our being, bringing us closer and closer to God the Father UNLESS we've made those parental judgments! If we're cursed in the respect mentioned earlier, our eyes are dimmed, and our image of The Father is obscured.

A Summation of Father's Love by Dr. Henry Wright

Be in Health®

4178 Crest Highway

Thomaston, GA 30286 706 646 2074

Father God Loves You

The Father's Love teaching from the For My Life program covers one of the most important truths you will ever hear. It serves as the foundation for all physical and psychological healing to begin.

It is so important for your relationships and your health to understand that you are loved by a perfect Father in heaven! He's not mad at you or criticizing your every move. He is working to draw you to Him and desires to heal your heart.

The I am Changed webcast featured on our website contains a portion of that teaching, but the highlighted points are below.

Knowing Father God's Love for You is Foundational

A lot of times, the focus is on our relationship with Jesus but we are unable to be in relationship with the Father like we should. It can be easier to relate to Jesus because of who He was and what He did. It's possible the reason we have difficulty relating to God the Father is because of the mistakes of our earthly fathers. And if we did not have good experiences with our earthly fathers, the name "father" may be tainted even when we think of Father God. We may consider our earthly fathers and the heavenly Father to be similar - but that's not the case. Our earthly fathers have not always represented Father God to us the way they should have.

It's time to release your heavenly Father from the stigma of the failures associated with your earthly father. Prepare to let go of the fear that says He doesn't smile; He hates sin so He hates you, and you're nothing. These are all lies. Jesus said if you've seen Me you've seen the Father. Jesus only said the things He heard His Father saying and He only did the things He saw His Father doing. So the character and nature of the Father and the Lord Jesus are quite similar.

Healing Begins with Reconciliation

Over the 30 years of ministering to people, Be in Health has observed that up to 80% of all diseases and syndromes are the result of separation from the Godhead, ourselves, and others.

The Godhead is no longer a mystery. Jesus came to show us the Father. The living Word became flesh - Jesus Christ.

Being reconciled to the Father, the Word, and the Holy Spirit is critical to your journey. Not being reconciled to all three members of the Godhead especially affects diseases coming from fear.

Being reconciled to yourself is also very important. Many people don't like themselves. Autoimmune diseases and tumors come from being separated from yourself.

Being reconciled with others can even go back to your childhood.

If 80% of diseases come from separation on these three levels, then healing begins with being reconciled on all three of these levels. This is also the beginning of all disease prevention.

Hearing You are Loved and Acceptable is Crucial to Receiving the Father's Love

In every culture and nation where Be in Health has taught, we find that 95% of audience members do not remember hearing their earthly father say "I love you."

It is important to hear these words!

In two of the three times that the Bible records the Father's words to His Son Jesus, He said, "... this is My beloved Son, in Whom I am well pleased." That's your Father!

Have you yearned for the day you can hear this from a father?

Receiving the Father's love is where healing begins! By seeking to establish a proper relationship with the Godhead, yourself and others you can be on your way to healing and disease prevention.

Enjoy receiving His love and hearing these words from your Father in heaven: "I love you."

Dr. Henry Wright

What to do

Ask God to show you all the ways in which you have judged your parents, especially your father.

Repent for making these judgments. You may find this extremely difficult, but do it, anyway.

Forgive your parents/father, and release them from any "debt" they owe you. You want to wipe the slate clean.

Ask Jesus to take you to His Father, revealing all He truly is to you – your real father!

If you're a guy who's failed at being a good father to your children, repent of this and begin to ask God to show you how to be the father you need to be.

Your earthly father isn't your true father (somebody said "thank God!"), but we can experience a greater depth of understanding and appreciating our Heavenly Father by dealing with that earthly one. Believe me, I've seen this happen countless times, and I'm sorry, but you don't get to be the exception –LOL! Healing may take a long time, but it's worth it. Find out as you read "My Story."

CHAPTER 18

My Story

You may be wondering what this author went through and why he would write such a book for people suffering from bipolar disorder. I could write a book on this... Hmmm... I just did! Actually, at one point in my life I think I would have been labeled "bipolar disorder" by a psychiatrist. I know at another point I was certainly very double-minded and what some would term "spiritually schizophrenic." This is double-mindedness on steroids. James says, "A doubleminded man (literally two souls) is unstable in all his ways (Jas. 1:5). The soul is divided into two parts in which good and evil may take up residence. In my first deliverance session around 1981, the couple praying told me they had never seen such a phenomenon—light and dark angels were fighting over me! Certainly, my brain chemistry felt like scrambled eggs! I had no idea how I got that way until I began to study and apply inner healing and transformation of my mind.

During those days, I thought I was becoming the Apostle Paul and the next day something akin to a "kook"—at least it felt like that in my brain, which on most days was highly oppressed as far back as I can recall. I certainly was into highs and lows most days. However, I was functional as a kid and into my adulthood and carried out what I needed to do fairly well and got a B.A. and M.A. in communication, and over the course of many years during my career, I held really good jobs. I wasn't ever monetarily wealthy, but I never went without because of God's blessing on my life.

Growing Up

But let me go back to the beginning to give you're a clearer perspective on where I'm coming from. I was raised well in a Christian family that was often more "religious" than Christian. By that I mean the family went to church and served God. However, in all fairness, our family wasn't spiritual in the sense of having a deep relationship with Jesus and through whom the Holy Spirit could flow. That generally starts with a spiritual father, a man who loves God and allows that love to flow through him to his kids. He is to be the "head." However, my mother wore the spiritual pants, and my dad, a good man, but who was always pretty passive, provided very little input into my life concerning right and wrong or direction. Not to be unkind, I don't remember much of anything he ever told me, and I really don't remember his ever hugging me and saying how much he loved me. With a 9th grade education, he was a "workaholic," whose self-esteem was wrapped to his job.

My mother was high school educated, a very sweet woman, who was loved by most everyone. She taught Sunday school for 35 years and loved God as much as she knew how to. Our family was essentially quite normal, although many families, like ours, may experience dysfunctionality because a father cannot/doesn't become the spiritual leader of his home. This one thing, as I wrote in chapter five was make a major difference in the family's life.

My life growing up in my neighborhood was enviable. I had great friends, just a wonderful time in "the Safe City," Chickasaw, Alabama. Even today at high school reunions my friends and classmates who grew up together almost unanimously agree we couldn't have had a better time – anywhere!

No Love Story

Personally, growing up, I never felt loved nor did I necessarily feel I could love others through no fault of anyone. I felt like I was "blocked out" of real emotions, although I was always a "nice guy," and deeply desired intimacy. In school I was consistently a popular kid, who was a lot of fun to be with, they tell me. But to make this clear to you, I need to go back to what I remember about what happened and what God has revealed to me about myself through His Spirit, His Word and prophetic people. Like most people, I was in denial most of my life and was pushing hard to be "spiritual" after I asked the Lord to save me at age 27. Truth is, I continued to strive like crazy until I was into my 60s. By age 27 I was full of anger and rage for a number of reasons—mostly from the things I've written about in this book because I had violated God's Word myself and more often than not, I wasn't even aware of it!

Molested at 4

All my life, until about 10 years ago when what I thought was confirmed through a dream God gave to one of my Christian prophetic brothers (he described to me the whole molestation at 4), I believed I had been molested around four years old by several boys in the public park next to our home in Birmingham. I remember they told me it was an "initiation" into their club. It seemed to me from that day forward something was wrong with me, and certainly molestation damages the spirit and soul of anyone touched by it, defiling them in ways that are indescribable, but I need to tell more to make this picture more complete.

"Darth Vader"

Moving forward, I was saved in 1975, but in 1980 I was baptized in the Holy Spirit. After that God began to clean up the inside of me. I began to have to learn about all kinds of spiritual things that up to that time had somehow eluded me—like inner healing and deliverance from demons. I will spare you a great deal of this, but allow me to recount one episode.

By1982 the demonic oppression was so bad that I had reached a point of screaming out at times for help from the Lord! One particularly frightening episode occurred two nights before I got married. I awakened to find a spirit that looked like old Star Wars' Darth Vader standing at the foot of my bed. It was very tall (6' 5" or so), majestic looking, with a long veil that covered its face, which was silky black like its robe that covered its feet. I sat straight up and said, "I rebuke you in the name of Jesus!" It left immediately. However, I'm convinced this same spirit returned about two weeks later, as my wife and I were praying before going to sleep. I "felt" its footsteps coming down the hall to the bedroom, and I asked my wife if she sensed the same thing, to which she replied yes. We got up and battled that thing for at least 45 minutes with prayer and quoting the Word of God.

What preceded this spirit's visitation that night was a prophetic word given my wife and me that day, as we prayed for a student at the college where I taught. Seemed she had lupus, and we were praying for healing, but in the middle of our prayer, she interrupted us with, "God says there's a spirit over your house, and it's gonna be revealed tonight!"

Until recently, I never knew what I/we had encountered. I am certain now it was a spirit of freemasonry. My grandparents were the heads of the Eastern Star in Alabama, and because of this, I was cursed. I don't have time to go into this in any depth, so be sure to read the chapters that deal with curses in this book (mostly chapters 4 & 5). Additionally, my wife's father was the "worshipful master" in the masons in her hometown. This compounded the problem. Until you understand what this stuff is and how much evil is involved it, you cannot appreciate how much harm their oaths and unchristian beliefs affect their ancestry. In the past year, I found out this thing was a masonic spirit through some friends of mine, who had prayed against a masonic temple! Right after they had done this, their house sitter, a very spiritual young lady, saw in the spirit, what she said looked like "something like Darth Vader." Case closed. I can tell you that spirit tormented me most of my life!

In utero (prenatal wounding)

As I wrote in chapter 5, entry wounds can begin in the womb, and such was my case. Let me summarize this by saying, unequivocally, that I felt rejected all my life until a few years ago. I had this feeling over many years that I was an "alien"—like I didn't belong here on planet earth. Although my parents loved me after I was born, I knew somehow I wasn't a "planned" child. My older brother confirmed this one day when I asked him pointblank: "Was I planned?" He chuckled and said, "No, but you were a great mistake!" As I wrote earlier, in spite of parents' best intentions or lack of them, a child can feel rejected from the womb, and unless healing occurs for this, some feelings of rejection may remain a lifelong companion. Two things can occur out of the kind of rejection: 1) a slumbering spirit in which the person never seems to wake up to the things of God but often feels "asleep" in their spirit; 2) a captive spirit in which evil spirits gather around the person's soul to torment for rebelling against life. I had both.

Three Strikes, but I Was Not Out!

All of us face many difficulties, hurts and tragedies in life that can retard our growth mentally, spiritually, emotionally and even physically because of the mind-body connection or psychosomatic reality. My major strikes–prenatal rejection, molestation and the curses from freemasonry–were hell wrapped in a very uncomfortable package, and except for God's amazing intervention and faithful friends and Godly brothers and sisters, I wouldn't be writing this. One counselor, who read "my story" many years ago told me, without hesitation, "You should be dead by now!"

The Revelations

I've had many prophetic dreams and similitudes. A similitude is seeing something from God in your spirit. It is not a vision but a picture or word that describes what you or someone else needs or is experiencing. Both these were instrumental in my healing. First, I was sitting in an activation seminar that we do for people being brought into the ministry of Resorting the Foundations, an international ministry that brings healing to thousands across the globe (www.RestoringTheFoundations.org). The heads of the national ministry of RTF were ministering to a woman who was troubled with her past. All of a sudden the Holy Spirit opened the spirit realm for me to "see" very early into my past—the hospital where I was born! I could actually smell the hospital, see the walls, and the environment in which I lay in my crib. I was enraged! I felt completely alone—no family, no nurses, just me. Then I saw Jesus in the room, but I was really angry at Him as well, and I cried to Him not to come near me! Apparently, the trauma in the womb had so aggravated me that I had no desire to be born! I was mad at God for what had happened. This was the beginning of my rage and anger that I carried most of my life.

The second revelation came in 2015, and this was a dream in which I was fighting someone – me! The dream made perfect sense because I was enraged because I had to fight someone I knew would kill me! I was mad about life but primarily because I could never find the "love of my life" I had been searching for more than 50 years! Somehow this whole thing had avoided me. When I fought this very angry person, I began to lose, as I expected. Suddenly, a man, a friend, appeared, and said, "Enough of this!" He miraculously pounced on the other person with his foot and crushed his head to the ground (Rom. 16:20). When I looked down, I saw a face that looked like a bloody pancake! I knew this person was dead, but somehow was resurrected later in the dream, which meant I had to deal with him again. As I processed the dream, Father God's love entered in and showed me how to defeat the remaining difficulties.

"No One Cares for My Life"

Sometime later, a friend of mine and I were ministering to a man who had been molested early in his life. The molestations were suppressed along with certain demonic terror he had experienced. As he read Psalm 142 aloud, which all those who receive RTF Issue Focused Ministry (IFM) do, I **heard in my spirit** the words from a portion of the Psalm, verse 4:

"I look for someone to come and help me,

but no one gives me a passing thought!

No one will help me;

No One Cares a Bit What Happens to Me."

I started weeping because I knew that not only was I deeply empathizing with this man, I was sensing in my own spirit what had happened to me in abandonment. I had known this by the former revelation (hospital experience as an infant and in my brain), but I had never gotten that in my spirit. I knew very well that I had prenatal wounding because of abandonment. By hearing those words in my spirit, I knew the enemy had subtly perpetuated the lie all my life that "there was no one there for me—no one cared for my life." Can you see how Satan wants us to believe that not even God cares for us at times?

This Psalm and Psalm 143 are both highly descriptive of how Satan works against us to "bring our spirit to a place of despair"—and as David writes in 143 like it has died! We must remember that we are spiritual beings who have a soul through which we communicate.

As I have written here, much of brain chemistry difficulties are anchored in fear and anxiety, the opposite of agape love. Traumas are huge in people's lives, as abandonment, rejection, self-rejection, angers, and as a result, misperceptions of life become rampant. Strongholds follow on the heels of such things, rendering us feeling that nothing can help with the situation. Despair becomes an every day occurrence, and sometimes depression can last for days and even weeks. Hope seems beyond hope. But as I reiterated, Jesus Christ is our HOPE:

Paul, an apostle of Jesus Christ by the commandment of God our Savior, and **LORD Jesus Christ, which is our hope**" (1 Timothy 1:1).

To whom God would make known what is the riches of the glory of this mystery among the Gentiles; which is **Christ in you, the Hope of Glory** (Colossians 1:27).

I can say, quite honestly, this road has been very hard–some of it was my own stupid fault, but much of it wasn't–it was just what life handed me. As the old saying goes, you can take lemons and make lemonade, or you can eat sour lemons! Let me end this manual by giving you a summary of recommendations I have for overcoming bipolar disorder.

Conclusion

We've looked at a lot of difficulties facing not only those who are suffering with bipolar disorder or other mental difficulties but who simply have experienced trouble by living on this planet. We can choose to remain with these problems, or begin to take steps toward healing. There is no magic bullet. You may experience a "download from heaven" that could radically change a lot in you, or you may have to walk it out step by step. Many in the Bible were instantly healed of various diseases, while others may have taken years to apply God's truth to set them free. My prayer is that you find your true Father in heaven so you can realize the real love He has for you so that you may find stability, health and wholeness. Allow me now to make suggestions about how you may expedite your own healing or that of another.

First and foremost, make sure you have believed on the Lord Jesus Christ as your Savior and Lord. Without this knowledge and understanding, you will not have the foundation for what follows. If you have never prayed to receive Jesus (John 1:12), do so now. Say, "Father in heaven, I acknowledge than I am a sinner who is saved by faith alone in you and your Son Jesus, and that it is only because of your grace that I am forgiven. I repent of every known sin in my life. I ask for your forgiveness for these sins and accept your forgiveness. I also forgive every person who has done me wrong in my life. Thank you, Lord. Amen.

Realize that your bipolar disorder may likely have begun with very early wounding, such as abandonment, and subsequent rejection in your spirit or soul. In other words, you have conscious or unconscious deep-rooted fear that is causing your torment and ultimately an attempt to control your own life. You may need a faithful spiritual Christian who understands these things to help you with this. Also, realize the possibility that you may indeed have brain injury that may need physical healing.

Know that we have the God who has never been defeated, and who can heal you instantaneously, or who may allow you to walk out your healing step by step.

Understand that you have several weapons at your disposal including the Word of God, memorization of Scripture, biblical meditation, prayer and transformation of your mind by replacing ungodly beliefs with Godly ones.

You should check into your lineage to determine if there is generational sin (iniquity) that could be contributing to your problem. In this case, you likely have curses on your mind that are causing your to think and behave "abnormally."

It is particularly important with regard to the previous admonition that you could very well have ancestors who were involved in freemasonry, witchcraft, Druidic or New Age beliefs that are currently affecting you spiritually, mentally or even physically. In this situation, these generational curses can be broken by the power of Jesus Christ's Blood and death on the cross that paid for the legal debt owed by your ancestry.

Know that you may be double-minded, hovering between really wanting Jesus and at the same time pursuing, if not a sinful lifestyle, at the least a mindset that is focused on wanting sin more than true righteousness.

"Religion" could well be one of your greatest enemies, as you may have focused more on rules and regulations than on the true grace of God. Learning to focus on Jesus and not religious efforts may set you free to experience a very new real life.

Be certain to forgive your ancestry or others you need to forgive who have hurt you or done you harm by depriving you of happiness, peace or monetary gains. Repent for wanting revenge or retaliation against these people. Let God avenge you (Rom. 12:9).

Remember that the most important thing in life is to love God with your whole heart, your soul, your mind and your strength.

Never give up the pursuit of freedom – God wants you free!

Joseph Beckham February 2016

CPSIA information can be obtained
at www.ICGtesting.com
Printed in the USA
BVOW08s0800041217
501906BV00001B/231/P

9 781365 045684